IMAGES
of America

ALLEGHENY CEMETERY

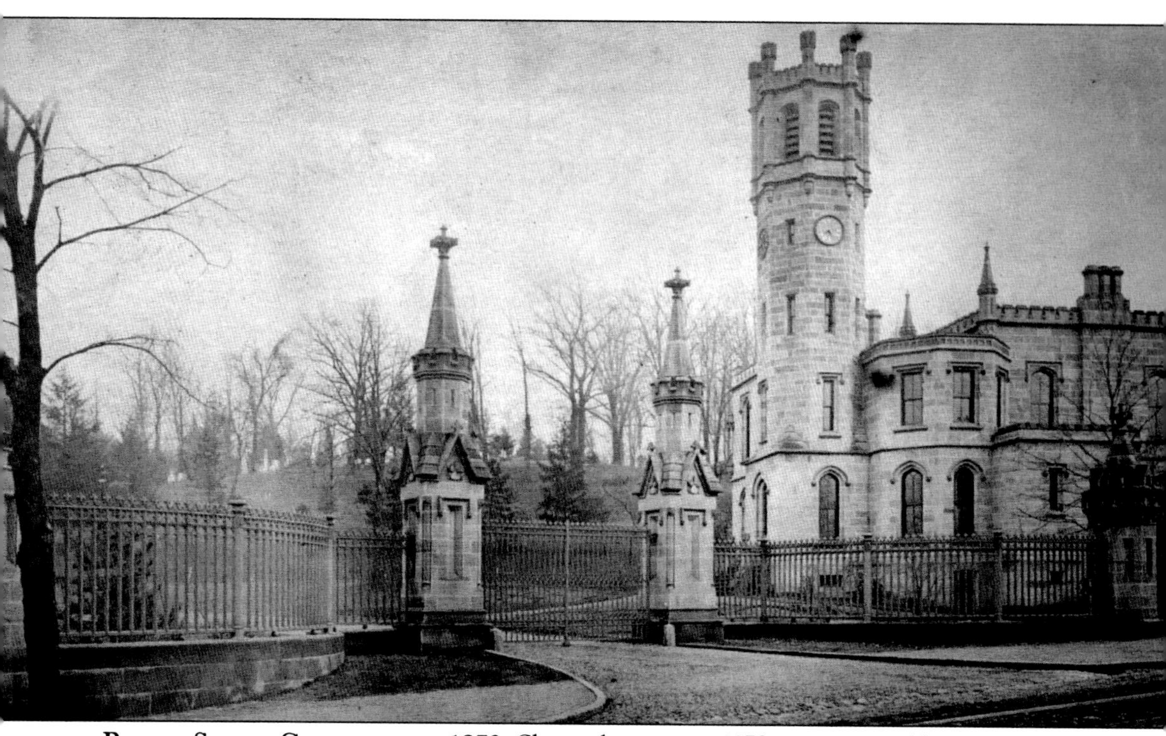

Butler Street Gatehouse, c. 1873. Shown here in an 1873 cemetery publication, the Butler Street Gatehouse appears much as it does today. Added only three years before this photograph was taken, the portion of the building featuring the clock tower was a secondary addition to the first section of the gatehouse, which was built when the cemetery originally opened. In 1848, the stone gate screen and gate keepers lodge (Porter's House) were developed in the Early Gothic Revival style. In 1868–1870, the complex was enlarged to include a two-story stone building with a chapel, administration offices, and the clock tower. The latter addition was designed by Henry Moser of the firm Barr & Moser in the style of 19th century Romantic Picturesque architecture. While built at varying times, these structures flow seamlessly and stand as a testament to both the aesthetic quality and durability of the craftsmanship. (AC.)

On the Cover: Memorial Day 1918. Pittsburgh's Memorial Day tradition began as early as 1872. Surviving Union veterans, as members of the Grand Army of the Republic, organized and led the original processions down Butler Street and into the cemetery, where a memorial service with full military honors was held in Section 33, where the Soldiers Memorial now stands. (AC.)

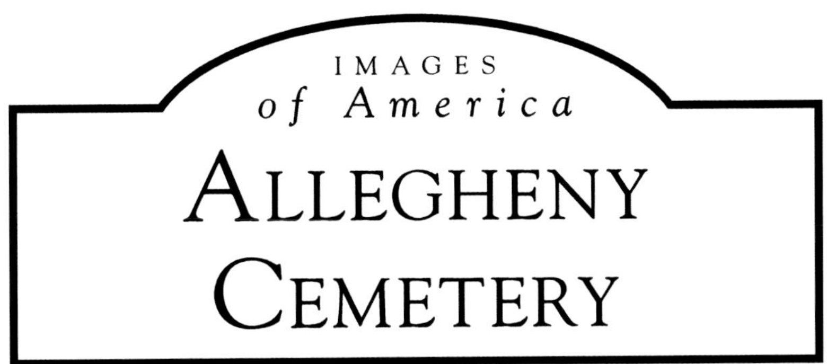

Lisa Speranza and Nancy Foley

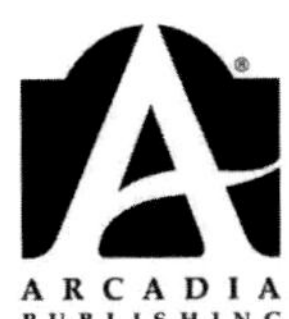

Copyright © 2016 by Lisa Speranza and Nancy Foley
ISBN 978-1-4671-1738-8

Published by Arcadia Publishing
Charleston, South Carolina

Printed in the United States of America

Library of Congress Control Number: 2016932608

For all general information, please contact Arcadia Publishing:
Telephone 843-853-2070
Fax 843-853-0044
E-mail sales@arcadiapublishing.com
For customer service and orders:
Toll-Free 1-888-313-2665

Visit us on the Internet at www.arcadiapublishing.com

The authors humbly dedicate this book in loving memory of every person at rest in Allegheny Cemetery. To quote George Thornton Fleming's 1919 introduction to his Life and Letters of Alexander Hays, *"Above the dust of the beloved dead, who passed to immortality this way, we bare our head and reverently tread, and tenderly our heartfelt homage pay."*

Contents

ACKNOWLEDGMENTS

The authors wish to acknowledge the love and support of their families and friends. Thank you to Nancy's husband and constant companion, Stephen Foley, who is the light of her life and inspiration in all things. A heartfelt thanks to Nancy's mother, Deborah Craigo, and aunt Barbara Held, who have both served Allegheny Cemetery loyally and who keep the Tiso and Held family histories alive and well. Lisa wishes to express her most sincere and humble appreciation for her family's endless hours of listening to stories about people they never met. She is incredibly grateful for her treasured daughter Becca and her love and support through countless hours of research. Lisa also wishes to thank her mother, Catherine, for constantly reiterating who was in the family plot until it finally clicked (well, mostly). Lastly, Lisa wishes to thank Grampy for his patience and enthusiasm and assures him he may now enjoy the stories he has so anxiously awaited.

A very special thanks to cemetery treasurer James M. Edwards, longtime director of Allegheny Cemetery and ardent supporter of all things historic, whose friendship, encouragement, and detailed research we have found invaluable. Allegheny Cemetery superintendent Roger Galbraith deserves our heartfelt thanks for his tireless service to the cemetery and helpfulness to the authors in too many capacities to be listed here.

The authors wish to recognize, with deep admiration, the efforts of the board of directors of Allegheny Cemetery, its chairman, Torrence M. Hunt Jr.; president, David J. Michener; and the management and staff of each department for their dedicated work as stewards and guardians of this priceless national treasure. Harmar D. Denny IV deserves our sincere thanks for his leadership as president and chairman of the board of the Allegheny Cemetery Historical Association.

Several people have endeared themselves to the authors during this process with their kind support and willingness to share precious family photographs and oral histories that greatly enhanced this work. For their assistance and the immediacy of their friendship, the authors humbly thank Frank and Kathy Eaton and Emanuel Ecker V. Nancy Janda and J. Dustin Williams provided wonderful images from the Hunt Institute for Botanical Documentation at Carnegie Mellon University.

The authors also acknowledge, with appreciation, the community and those who purchase this book, as it is only by sharing these stories that each person within lives on in the memory of generations yet to come.

Image sources have been credited as follows: Allegheny Cemetery (AC), Nancy Foley (NF), Lisa Speranza (LS), the Library of Congress (LOC), and Archive Service Center (ASC).

INTRODUCTION

On the western slope of the Allegheny Mountains, about three miles northeast of where its namesake river meets the Monongahela to form the great Ohio, nestled right in the heart of the urban neighborhoods of Lawrenceville, Bloomfield, Garfield, and Stanton Heights, lies a spectacular historic landscape, hiding in plain sight.

There are lakelets here, winding country paths, forested hillsides that climb beyond vision, expanses of lush green lawns adorned with flower beds and ornamental grasses, secluded ravines flanked by steep ridges offering stunning views of downtown, and, on clear winter days, the Allegheny River. In sylvan splendor it stands alone. Trees—several thousand of them, many rare or exotic to the region—populate this urban oasis. Their ancient roots, as thick as trunks themselves, penetrate deep into the earth to intercept and absorb rainfall, control groundwater, and offer natural flood protection during storms. There are cool caves of shale where foxes escape the summer heat, leave tiny paw-print paths in winter's snow, and curious cubs emerge each spring. On summer mornings, the canopy reverberates with the sound of unseen songbirds, their melodies composed before the dawn of man. A purposeful harmony with nature suits Allegheny's identity as a rural cemetery—a curiously modern concept arising during the Romantic period of the mid- to late 19th century.

Initial interest in dedicating a parcel of land outside the city began in 1834 when sanitary and ethical concerns arose in response to overcrowded graveyards connected to churches. For Dr. James Ramsey Speer, Stephen Colwell, and noted architect John Chislett (all members of the Third Presbyterian Church, whose yard was a prime example of this issue), the establishment of a rural cemetery was deemed not only fundamentally necessary, but also culturally meaningful. The cemetery's charter members were of fine old Pittsburgh families who settled here during the Colonial era and were invested personally in the growth of the city and its environs. As these men already had a hand in establishing and expanding what was quickly becoming a bustling metropolis, they felt it proper that a "City of the Dead" ought, likewise, to be planned. After touring Mount Auburn in Boston and later Laurel Hill in Philadelphia, Dr. Speer had firsthand examples of the benefits of a nonprofit, nondenominational rural cemetery, which he incorporated wholly into the establishment of Allegheny Cemetery in Pittsburgh, making it the sixth incorporated cemetery in America and the first of this kind west of the Alleghenies.

In an age when some Shawnee and Lenape Indians still called this county home, the village of Lawrenceville was a veritable Eden of green pastures dotted with sleepy cabins, cottages, and country estates. In 1844, Allegheny Cemetery's founders purchased the first 50 acres from the farm of George A. Bayard, descendant of a family of pioneers who were awarded vast depreciation land grants following service in the Revolutionary War. Other neighbors with large landholdings would offer parcels for sale as well, including many who served on the original board of corporators, and by the turn of the 20th century, the cemetery had grown to encompass nearly 300 acres of pristine green space.

From its inception, Allegheny was pragmatically set apart for eternity. The board quickly adopted a threefold mission to provide "Security, Perpetuity and Adornment" and important early developments display their dedication to this doctrine. An unyielding stone wall over seven feet tall encircles the park. Solid cast-iron gates and castle-like complexes with imposing towers command the scene of each entrance as a physical representation of the cemetery's role as sentinel, keeping watch day and night, ever respecting, ever guarding its honored dead. The message was and is this—may all who enter know they tread on sacred soil. In this aspect, and in many others, Allegheny remains unchanged by the hand of time. Her gateways still serve as a demarcation point between the city and the serene, chaos and peace. On the inside, however, a vastly important treasury of regional history has been slowly accumulated and preserved. In the course of 170 years, Allegheny Cemetery has been filled with incredible examples of memorial statuary, prized historic architecture, genealogical records, archives, family heirlooms, correspondence, and a museum-quality collection of fine art in nearly every medium.

As local industry boomed, immigrants from around the world traveled to Pittsburgh in search of the American Dream, expanding the cultural identity of the region and its history. The story of Allegheny Cemetery is really the story of Pittsburgh and, in a broader sense, America. Land that was once untamed became masterfully designed for civic benefit. Natural resources were harnessed, and great wealth amassed. The rugged frontier outpost made of mostly French, English, and Scots-Irish pioneers grew into a colorful port city with ethnic ties to Poland, Hungary, Austria, Germany, Italy, and every corner of the world. Today, over 130,000 citizens representing every possible religious background are interred in Allegheny Cemetery. Some of them were major players on a global stage, building empires of steel, coal, and oil and establishing family names that are recognized today as American royalty. A far greater number of them toiled in furnaces illuminated by molten metal, rising for work seven days a week to a sunless sky, blackened with the perpetual smoke so characteristic of a city once described as "hell with the lid off." All of them contributed to the great might of the nation, forged in fire, right here in Pittsburgh. When the sun set on their time on earth, when the whistle called them to end their mortal shift, each in his turn has come "home" to rest in Allegheny Cemetery.

It was our hope, with this publication, to share with readers the proud legacy of Pittsburgh that is preserved in Allegheny Cemetery. There is far too much in Allegheny's rich heritage to be contained within this text and much has been written on it throughout the ages. Due to necessary limitations in time and scope, this work should not be considered complete in capturing all the depth and breadth of Allegheny's cultural value. There are people at rest within these walls whose stories still resonate in popular culture around the world but who are mentioned only briefly in this volume. There are others whose names have been scarcely heard since their passing but are now resurrected. For formatting purposes only, stories and people have been organized by chapters according to their most prevailing aspect. Many of them, however, cannot be limited to one category and several, if not all, could easily span two or three of them. Our attempt was never to limit anyone mentioned in this work to only one facet of who they were. Rather, the restriction of brevity inherent to the nature of this book serves a dual purpose, namely, that we intend the reader to be intrigued by these faces, places, and stories. Ultimately, our goal is to inspire our audience to lean in even closer, to seek and find more detail on their own, to spend some time in the cemetery if they are able, and to revisit and retell these stories to friends and family members, perpetuating our collective memory of what it means to be a Pittsburgher to each new generation. Without further delay, we invite you, dear reader, to join us on a journey through time as we peer into a looking glass filled with images of a bygone age and, perhaps, discover a little more about ourselves in the reflection.

One

In the Beginning

These are the men who conceived of the dream that would become Allegheny Cemetery and gave of themselves in every capacity to see it through to fruition. They would travel to other cities to observe their cemeteries and return with reports of lavish English-style gardens where cities of the dead were as resplendent with beauty as those for the living. They would search the countrysides of Pittsburgh for 10 long years before finding and acquiring the perfect piece of earth to preserve for all time. They would draft their own unique charter to guard against infringement of civilization or "modern" development and to set the grounds apart perpetually for the eternal rest of the dead. They would open their personal checkbooks to provide the funds necessary for purchasing large and valuable tracts of land, incorporating the organization, developing the property, securing it with walls and skilled personnel, and acquiring the necessary equipment for proper burial and preparation of the grounds to suit its sacred purpose. They would meet regularly, overseeing each developmental and operational detail, offering their varied and extensive business acumen without ever receiving compensation in any form. The task ahead of them was magnanimous in scope and would demand decades of dedicated service. As the minutes from an 1891 meeting state, "Nothing but the hand of death itself could strip their charitable compassion for others," and "after fulfilling so well life's destiny, and leaving the fragrance of their integrity, benevolence and good will to men, they sleep peacefully in the beautiful spot to which they had given so much of their living care and thought."

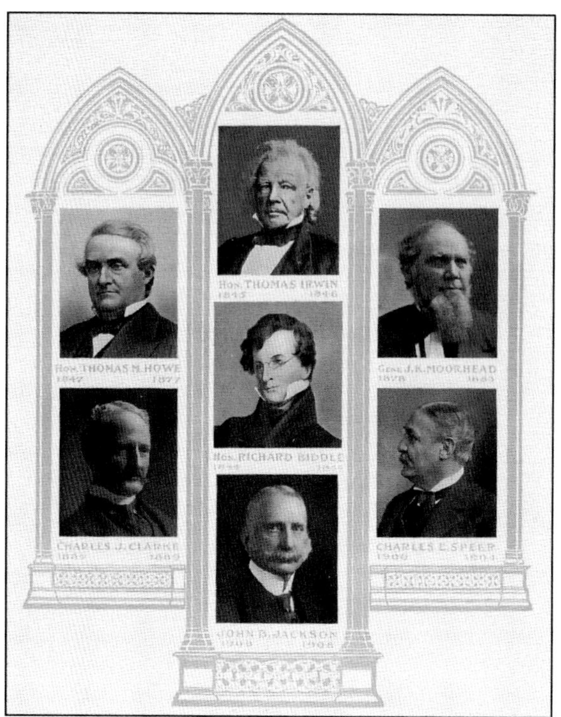

FIRST PRESIDENTS. Here are the men who guided Allegheny through its formative decades and who invested personal time, expertise, and funds to see that it was successful. The cemetery's board remains uncompensated, and several current members are direct descendants of its founders, with long traditions of family service to the organization. (AC.)

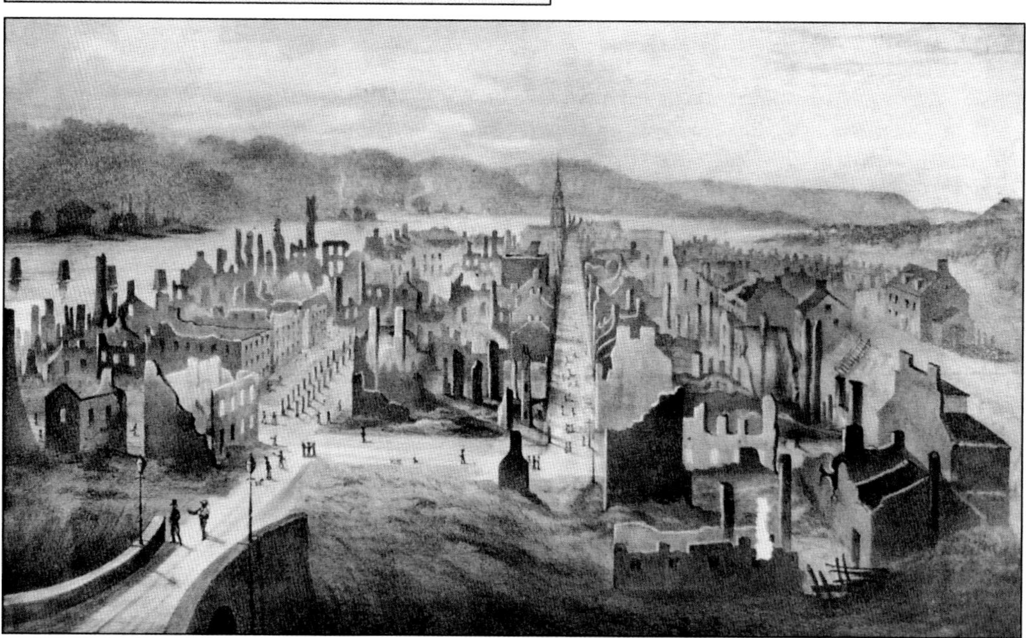

A UNIQUE CHARTER. The cemetery's first president, revered lawyer Hon. Richard Biddle (Section 1, Lot 7), drafted Allegheny Cemetery's charter. As the cemetery's report of 1910 explains, "The Charter of Allegheny Cemetery is not limited in time, nor does it contain any clause reserving the right to revoke the privileges granted. If it be asked why this is so, it may be answered, that the field of its operation is as extensive as the ravages of death, and that the time when they will cease will be the end of time itself." The original document was lost from Biddle's downtown law office in the great fire of 1845, the devastation of which is portrayed here. (AC.)

MARGARETTA BAYARD BRIGGS (D. APRIL 14, 1845; SECTION 2, LOT 142). Beyond having the distinguished honor of being Allegheny Cemetery's first burial, little is known about Margaretta Bayard Briggs from the historical record. Her father, Col. George A. Bayard, owned the original farm property on which the cemetery would later be situated. He sold this property to the cemetery around 1844. Shortly thereafter, his daughter Margaret died and is now buried under a small but beautifully weathered Rococo monument, not far from where her farmhouse once stood. (NF.)

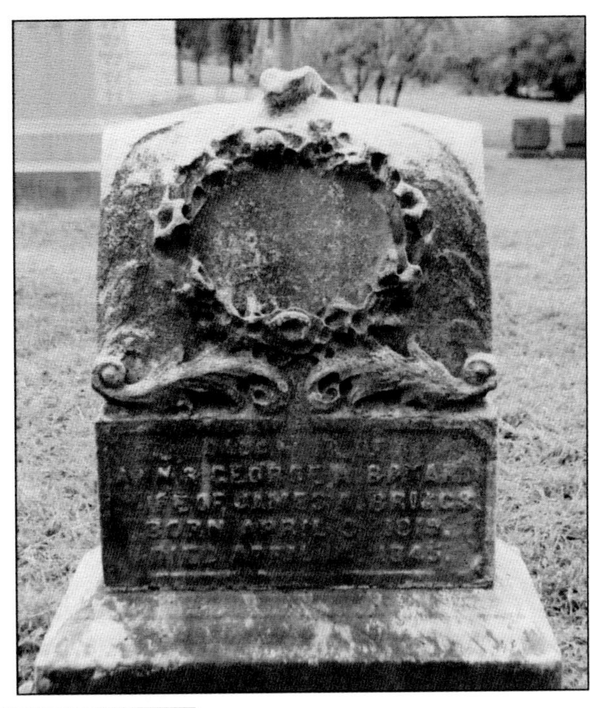

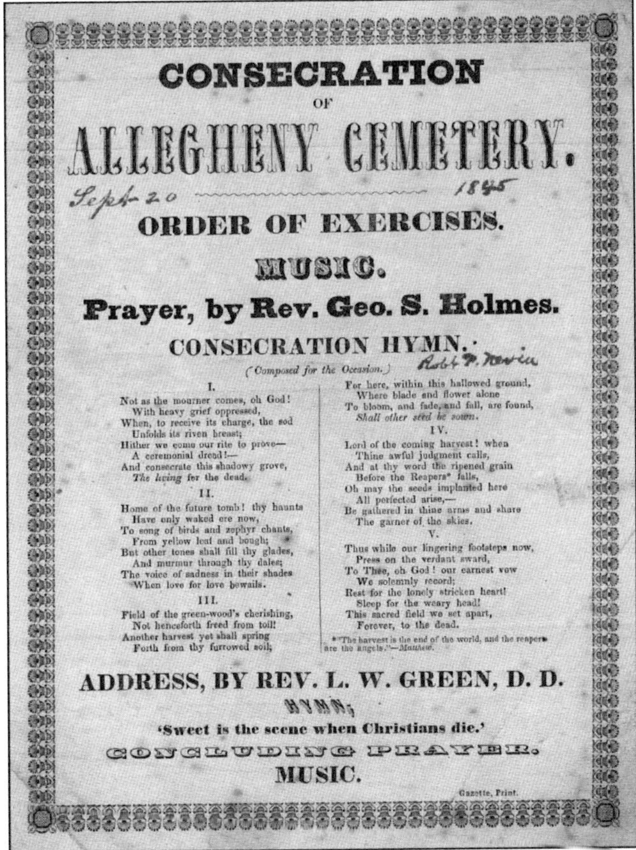

CONSECRATION

OF

ALLEGHENY CEMETERY.

Sept 20 1845

ORDER OF EXERCISES.

MUSIC.

Prayer, by Rev. Geo. S. Holmes.

CONSECRATION HYMN.

(Composed for the Occasion.) Robt P. Nevin

I.

Not as the mourner comes, oh God!
With heavy grief oppressed,
When, to receive its charge, the sod
Unfolds its riven breast;
Hither we come our rite to prove—
A ceremonial dread!—
And consecrate this shadowy grove,
The living for the dead.

II.

Home of the future tomb! thy haunts
Have only waked ere now,
To song of birds and zephyr chants,
From yellow leaf and bough;
But other tones shall fill thy glades,
And murmur through thy dales;
The voice of sadness in their shades
When love for love bewails.

III.

Field of the green-wood's cherishing,
Not henceforth freed from toil!
Another harvest yet shall spring
Forth from thy furrowed soil;
For here, within this hallowed ground,
Where blade and flower alone
To bloom, and fade, and fall, are found,
Shall other seed be sown.

IV.

Lord of the coming harvest! when
Thine awful judgment calls,
And at thy word the ripened grain
Before the Reapers* falls,
Oh may the seeds implanted here
All perfected arise,—
Be gathered in thine arms and share
The garner of the skies.

V.

Thus while our lingering footsteps now,
Press on the verdant sward,
To Thee, oh God! our earnest vow
We solemnly record;
Rest for the lonely stricken heart!
Sleep for the weary head!
This sacred field we set apart,
Forever, to the dead.

*"The harvest is the end of the world, and the reapers are the angels."—*Matthew.*

ADDRESS, BY REV. L. W. GREEN, D. D.

HYMN;

'Sweet is the scene when Christians die.'

CONCLUDING PRAYER.

MUSIC.

Gazette, Print.

CONSECRATION OF GROUNDS. While the cemetery as a nonprofit entity was incorporated with the state on April 24, 1844, the consecration of its grounds for the dignified burial of the dead was not until September 20, 1845. Original founders gathered amid a large crowd that included local dignitaries and citizens alike. The reverend, George S. Holmes, was of a prominent Pittsburgh family and was himself interred at Allegheny not 10 years later. (AC.)

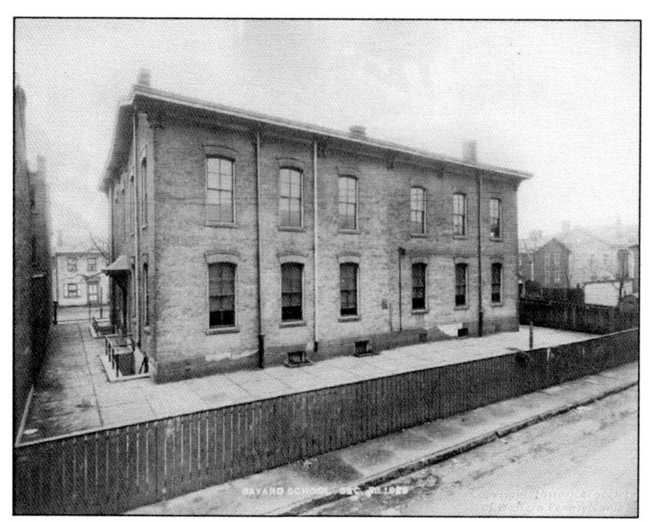

George A. Bayard (1792–1864; Section 2, Lot 142). Allegheny Cemetery's first parcels of property were purchased from Bayard's farm, where he lived in a cabin of rough-hewn logs, near the current Civil War National Cemetery. Another structure on this property was described as a large, handsome stone manse with an octagonal reception hall. At one time, the Fifth Ward was called Bayardstown. Lawrenceville's Bayard School, shown here in 1929, was named in the family's honor. (Pittsburgh Public Schools Photographs.)

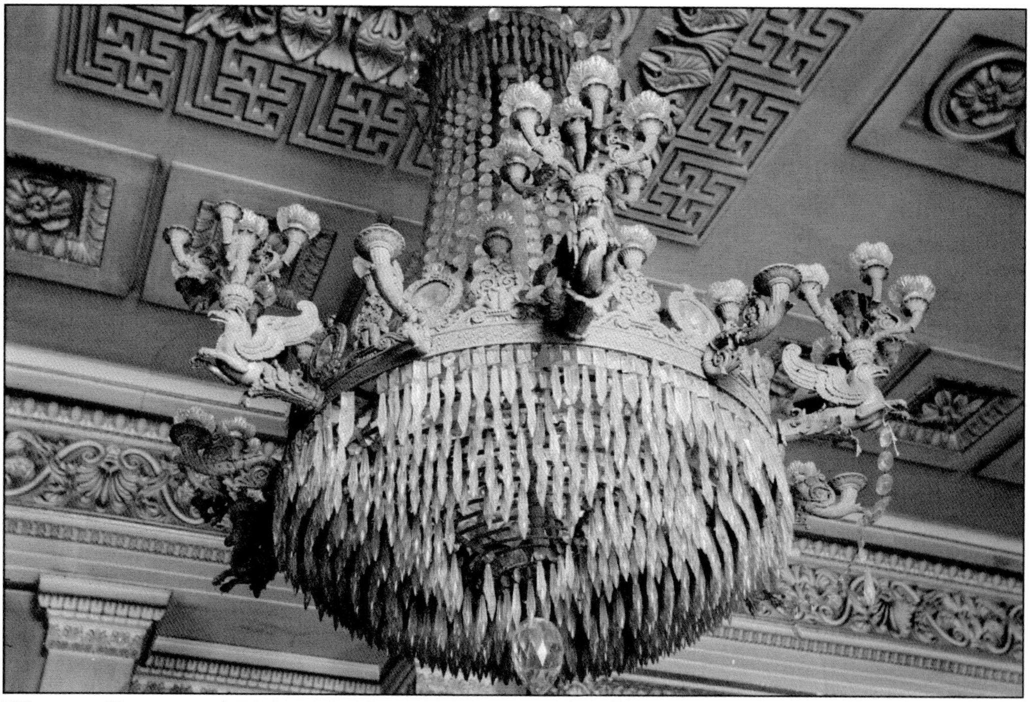

William Croghan (1794–1850; Section 2, Lot 99). The son of a Kentucky patriot, Croghan personally befriended Lewis and Clark, Pres. James Monroe, Gen. Andrew Jackson, Aaron Burr, and James Audobon. In 1821, he married Pittsburgh's Mary O'Hara. In 1827, Mary died, followed a year later by their infant son. Raising his only daughter, Mary, alone, Croghan moved to Pittsburgh in an opulent house he built for them (their grand chandelier is shown here). Upon the news that Mary eloped with British captain Edward Schenley at the age of 15, Croghan suffered several severe strokes that ultimately cost him his life. In 1850, he died alone, with Mary having never returned home. (LOC.)

William Barclay Foster (1779–1855; Section 21, Lot 30). Foster moved to Pittsburgh alone as a teen when it was a pioneer outpost. He established himself as a wealthy landowner and sold 30 acres to the US government for use in establishing the Allegheny Arsenal. Shortly after, in 1816, Foster established the town of Lawrenceville (shown here) and chose this neighborhood to raise his family, including son Stephen Collins Foster. The town was named after James Lawrence, a naval commander during the War of 1812, whose dying command "Don't Give up the Ship!" is now famous. (AC.)

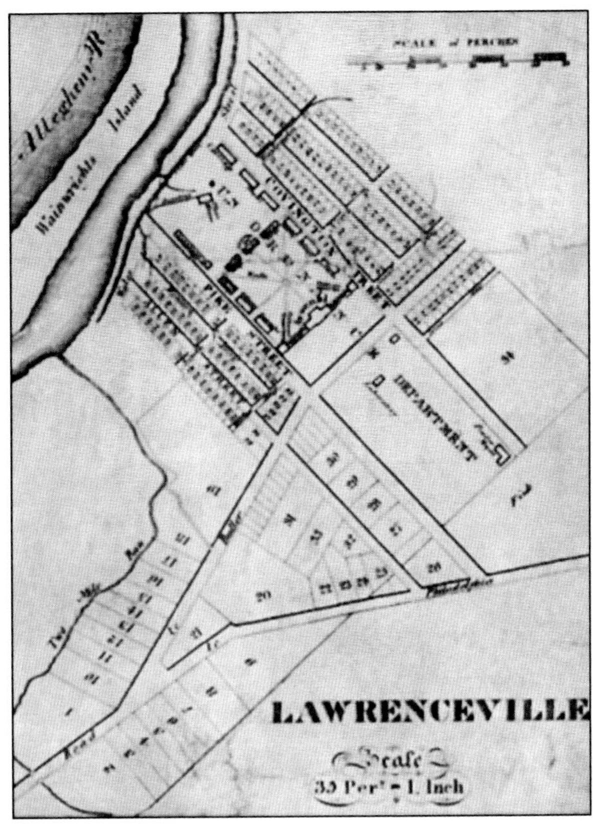

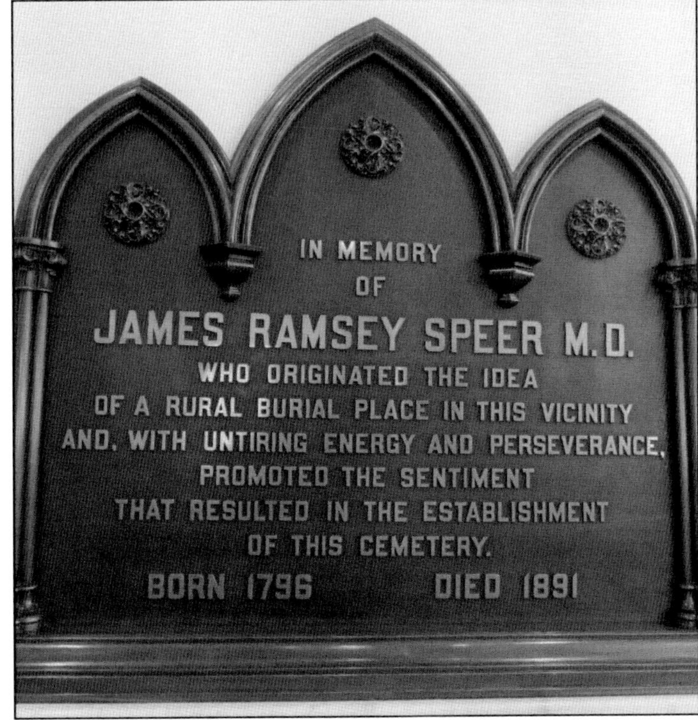

Dr. James Ramsey Speer (1796–1891; Section 2, Lot 89). This tablet, stationed prominently just inside the administration office, honors Speer. Board minutes state, "Impressed by the westward course of Asiatic cholera in 1832 and afterwards, as Chairman of a committee of physicians, Dr. Speer made the subject of crowded church yards in the large cities of the world, and the contagion arising therefrom, his special study." (AC.)

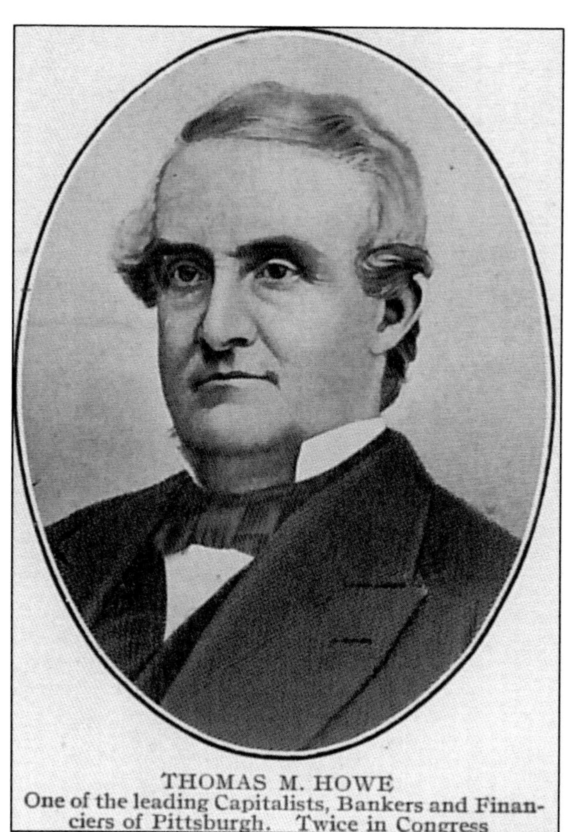

THOMAS M. HOWE
One of the leading Capitalists, Bankers and Financiers of Pittsburgh. Twice in Congress

Thomas Marshall Howe (1808–1877; Section 20, Lot 1). Howe was the cemetery's second president, serving from 1847 to 1877. His innumerable business ventures in copper, steel, banking, and railroad interests generated millions. Howe's public esteem was equally as elevated, being described as dignified but gentle and courteous, encouraging to all, and devoted to improving Pittsburgh. Twice he was elected to Congress, and when the Civil War came, he served as adjutant general on the staff of Governor Curtin. Board minutes note his death as "a loss for which no language can give adequate expression." (AC.)

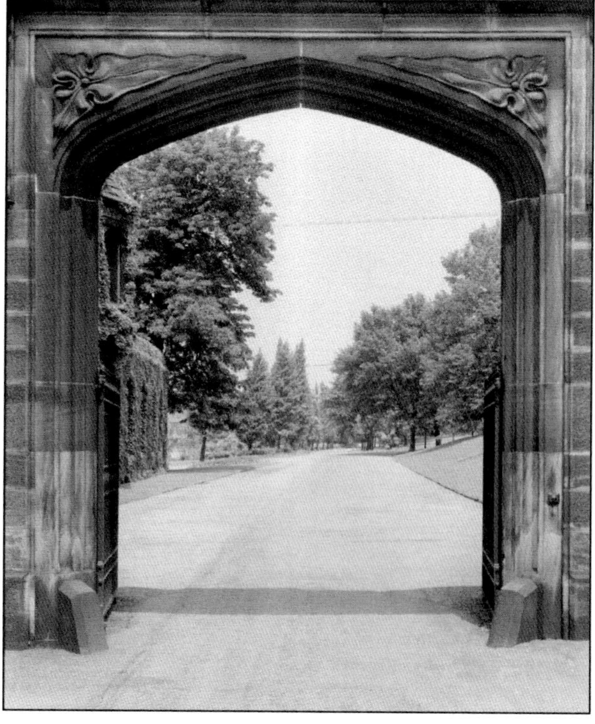

Removals to Allegheny. Once Pittsburghers were given the option between compact churchyards and the green expanse of Allegheny, which stood in stark contrast, they chose to have loved ones removed from their original resting place and reinterred here. This has been the case for several prominent persons, and these so called "removals" would often accompany the purchase of family plots large enough for several generations to be buried together. Spaces available for purchase were often advertised in newspapers, and it was quite fashionable at the time to preplan one's burial. (AC.)

Two

Maintaining a Rural Cemetery

Almost as soon as its charter was accepted, Allegheny's founders set about the task of developing and making real their novel vision of a rural cemetery, a concept distinctly Romantic in its ideals. The goal was to preserve as much of the rustic landscape as possible and incorporate dignified burial into the natural beauty already present. Romantics believed that time spent in nature was cleansing to the soul, and the curving pathways at Allegheny were meant to mimic the catharsis of a long meandering walk through pastoral countryside. Artistic expression was encouraged and individuality celebrated among Romantic intellectuals. At Allegheny, each section is as varied as the next and each monument a reflection of the individual taste of the family. As a rural cemetery, Allegheny was designed to offer aesthetic awe, spiritual peace, and a reconnection with nature and that which is eternal. Allegheny's importance extends far beyond its core function—it is also the city's first park, preceding Mary Schenley's 1889 dedication of her property in Oakland by 45 years. In order to accommodate its dual identity as a place of dignified repose for the dead, as well as inspiration for the living, a team of experts in burial, architecture, horticulture, and landscape design were recruited from around the country and the globe. Fifteen miles of roadway were graded, offering access to each far-reaching corner of the park. Miles of trenches were dug to install water lines for use by guests. Sewer systems were developed for water control. A quarry was established on-site with native stone used to construct artful buildings and structures. Security measures were taken to guard against trespassing and vandalism and to preserve the peace. Ornamental entrances and offices were built to preserve documents, meet with families, and conduct business. Laborers were employed en masse, the roster tipping past 100 men at one time. Ornamental flower beds were planted and soaring obelisks raised. All of this and much more was accomplished tirelessly, and the culmination of these efforts has created the Allegheny Cemetery that people enjoy and treasure to this day.

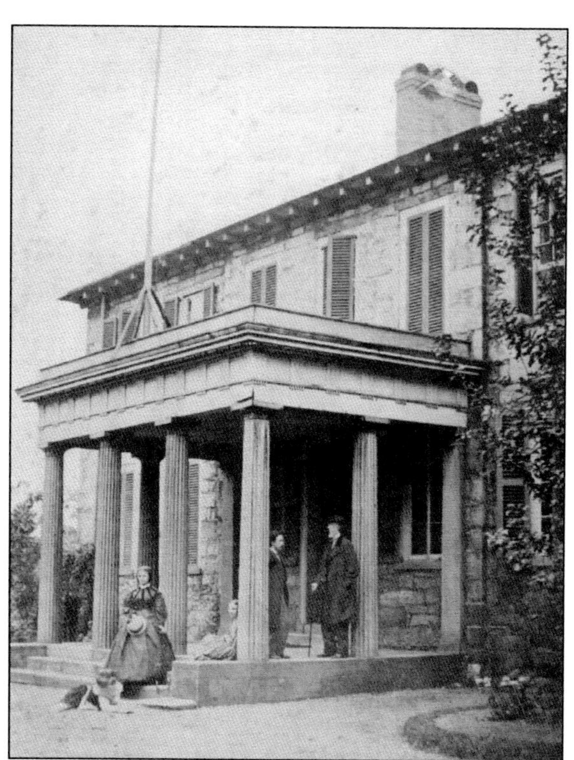

JOHN CHISLETT SR. (1800–1869; SECTION 20, LOT 19). John Chislett was a renaissance man; a painter, sculptor, and—most significantly—an architect. A few of his works remain, including the Butler Street Gatehouse. Chislett was the first superintendent of Allegheny Cemetery, beginning in 1844 until his 1867 resignation. The declining years of his life left him literally blind to the beauty he created around him, and he now rests among the quiet hills of the cemetery he helped design. Found in the cemetery's archives, pictured with a cane, this is the only photograph of him known to exist. (AC.)

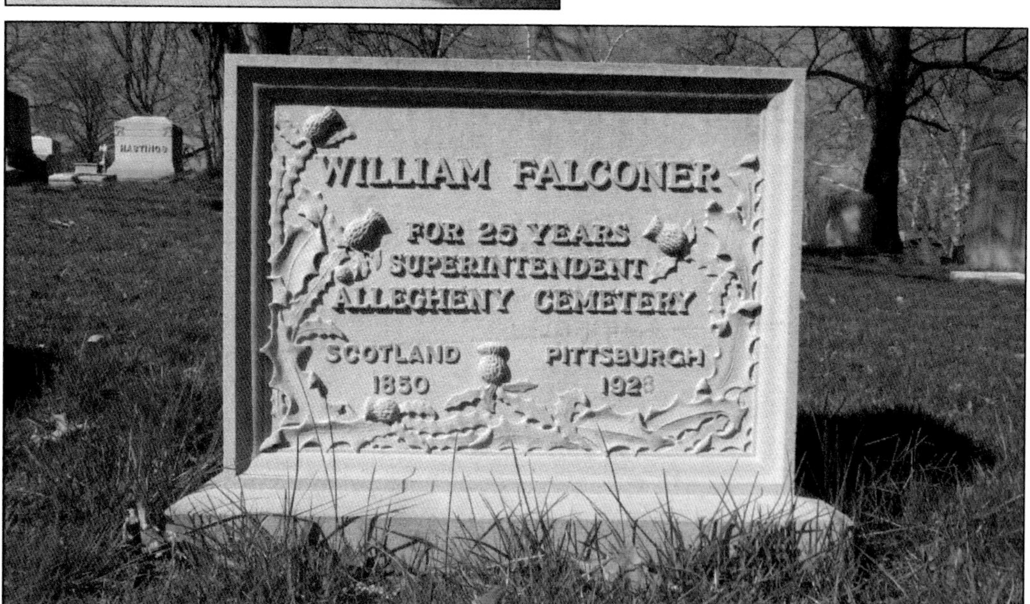

WILLIAM FALCONER (1850–1928; SECTION 28, LOT 230). Born in Scotland, Falconer was a celebrated horticulturist who studied at the Royal Botanic Gardens at Kew. Allegheny Cemetery hired him as superintendent after his work for Schenley Park, and from 1903 until his death in 1928, he resided in the former Schoenberger mansion on the property. Falconer focused on refined ornamental plantings and elegant landscape design. His efforts to retain the cemetery's original framework earned him recognition by the Association of American Cemetery Superintendents and were considered to be the crowning jewel of his accomplishments. (NF.)

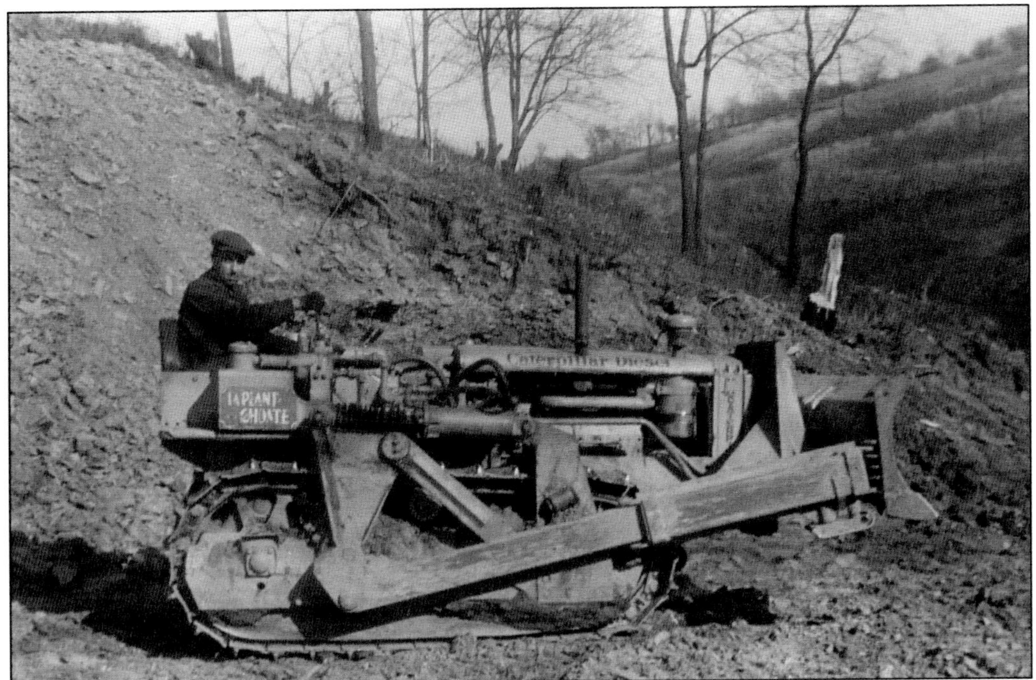

Developing the Land. Allegheny Cemetery's varied topography requires special attention to care and maintenance. The amount of skilled surveying, planning, and manpower needed to carve out roadways and new sections for burial was, and is, significant. Originally, the cemetery relied on mules and horses for pulling equipment and, of course, transportation. Over time, innovations in mechanics and technology would aid greatly in landscape design and development efforts. Seen here sometime in the 1930s or 1940s, a laborer is driving a bulldozer to do the job. (AC.)

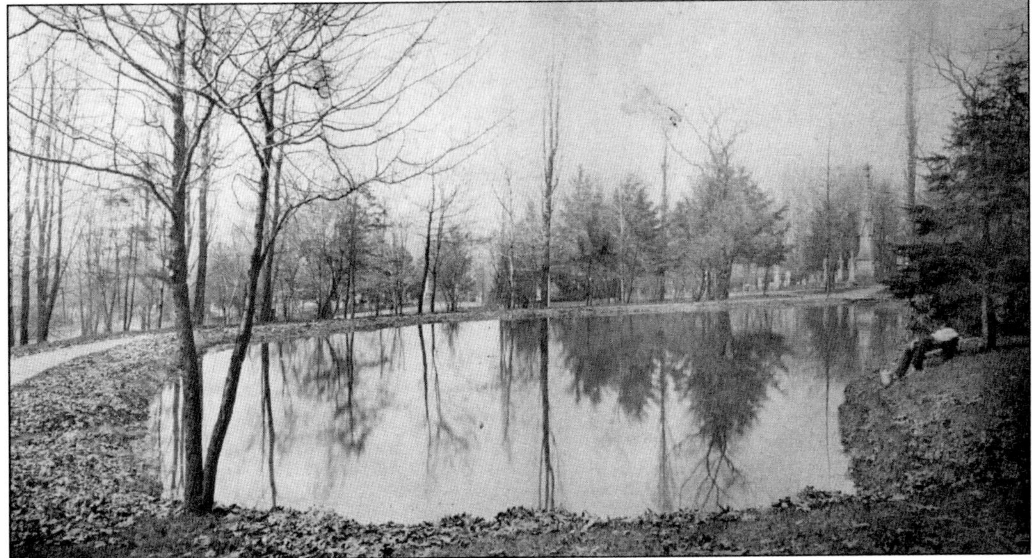

Twin Ponds (Section 14). Legend has it that Allegheny's twin ponds were formed during the Civil War, when God looked down on the fallen and wept great tears. In 1861, the cemetery's landscape architects channeled natural spring water to shape and form these sylvan lakes (shown here in 1873), of which there were once five total, as well as a waterfall. (AC.)

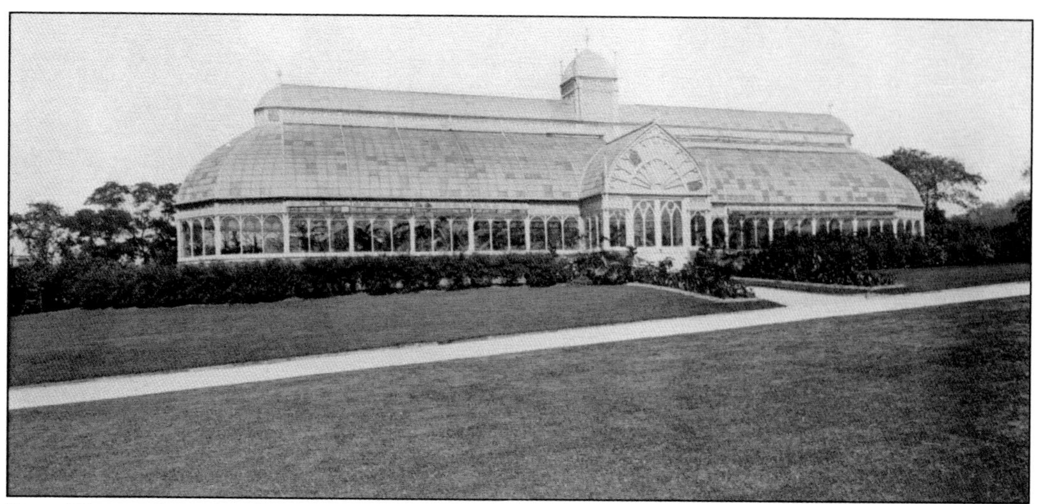

Palm House (1893). The Palm House Conservatory was built in 1893 by the architectural firm Lord & Burnham. At the same time, the firm was designing Pittsburgh's grand and famous Phipps Conservatory and Botanical Gardens. The delicate and ornate Palm House lasted only 50 short years, and dilapidation necessitated its removal by the end of the 1940s. (AC.)

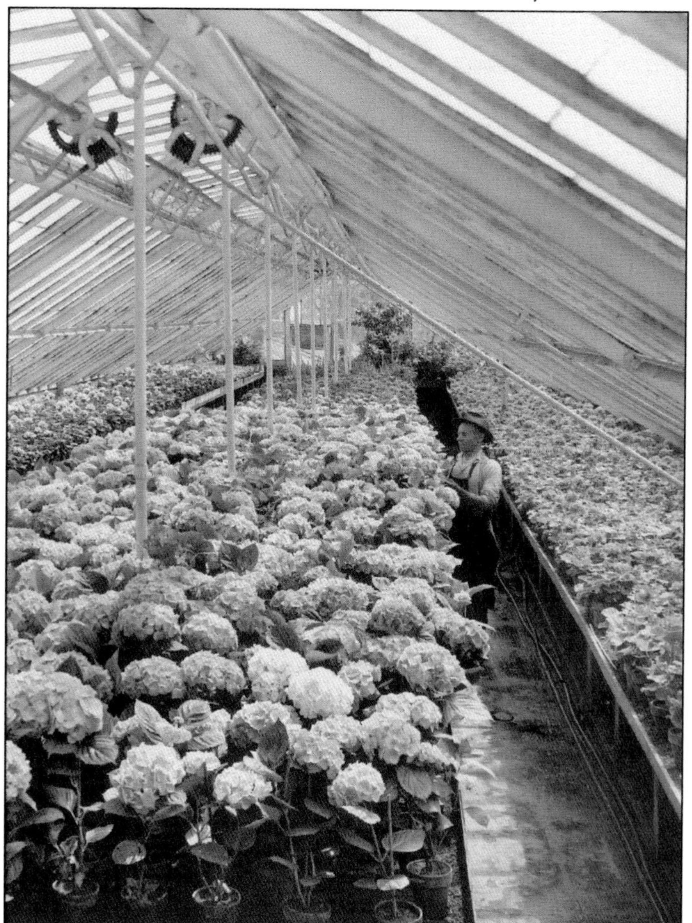

The Greenhouse. This structure still stands, and at one time propagated over one million plants annually for ornamental beautification of Allegheny's garden-park landscape. Palm and ivy were the Victorian standard in floral decor, though over time, the cemetery's florals became more colorful and varied. Seen here in the early 1950s, a gardener tends to hydrangea in preparation for the summer season. (AC.)

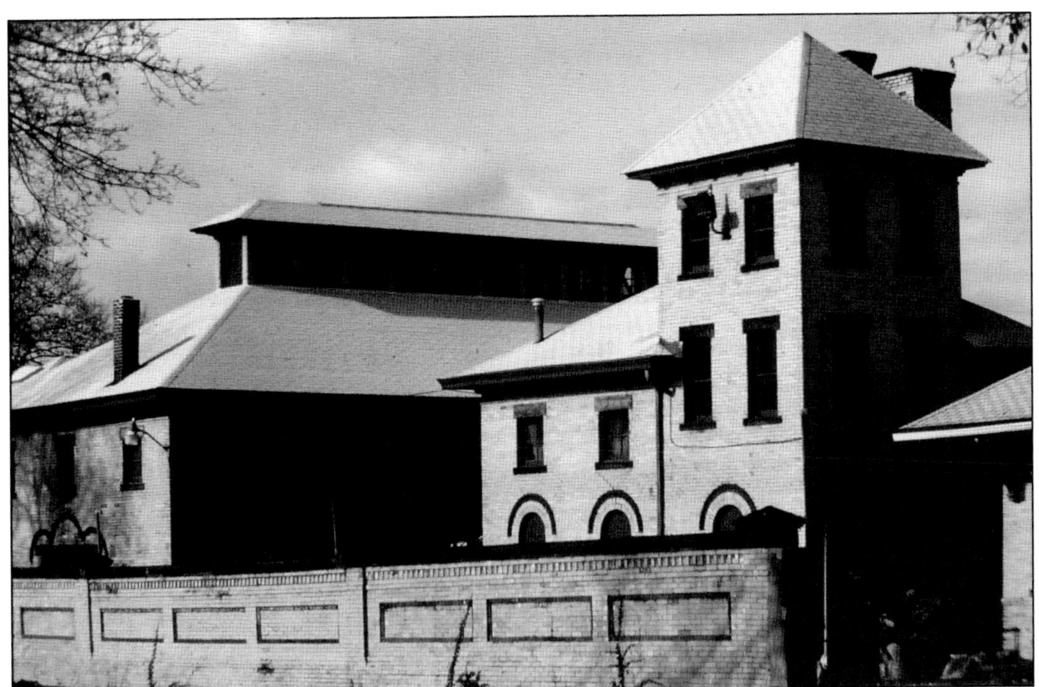

Maintenance Complex. This historic structure was a crucial improvement to Allegheny's operations at the turn of the 20th century. Originally housing a fleet of horses and mules, and complete with hayloft, today the complex is used as command central for the entire department. Superintendents' offices are here, as well as a machine shop, equipment and vehicle hangar, and repository for seasonal signage and the innumerable tools necessary to care for Allegheny's unique property. This complex has survived fires, flash floods, and the 2002 macroburst. (AC.)

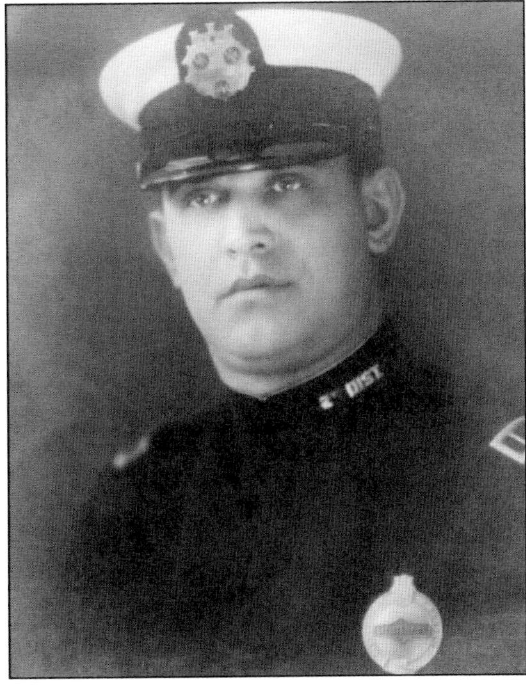

The Night Watch. Allegheny Cemetery employed armed night watchmen in the early to mid-20th century to conduct regular patrols and make citizen arrests. John Held, seen here, was a retired lieutenant with the City of Pittsburgh police and brought a lifetime of experience to the job. In the 1940s and 1950s, he lived with his wife, Agnes, in the Penn Avenue complex that served as the cemetery's own police station and remains today as headquarters of the Security Department. John and Agnes Held are entombed in the Temple of Memories, 121 B4. (Deborah Craigo.)

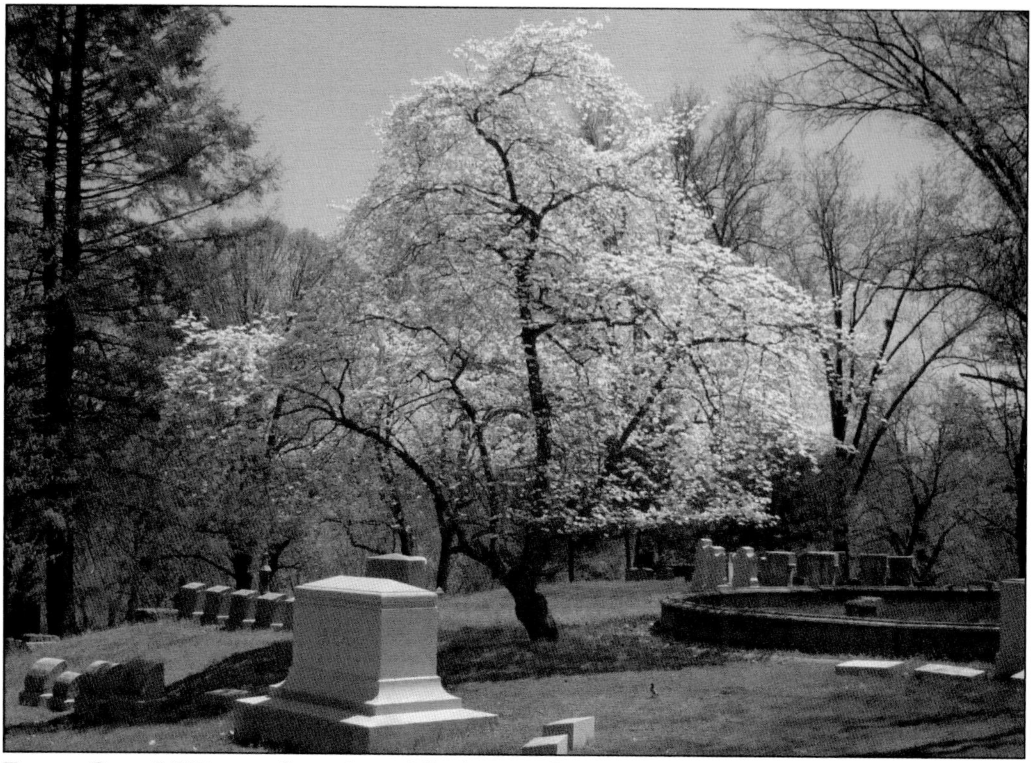

Flora. Over 3,500 trees flourish at Allegheny, offering both aesthetic and ecological value. Seen here, a beautifully pruned dogwood adds a touch of refinery to suit more Victorian tastes. Allegheny's conserved green space is treasured by nature lovers and those wishing to escape the sights and sounds of the city for a relaxing evening stroll, particularly by the fountain in late fall when two rows of iconic Asian ginkgo trees transform into a vivid gold. (NF.)

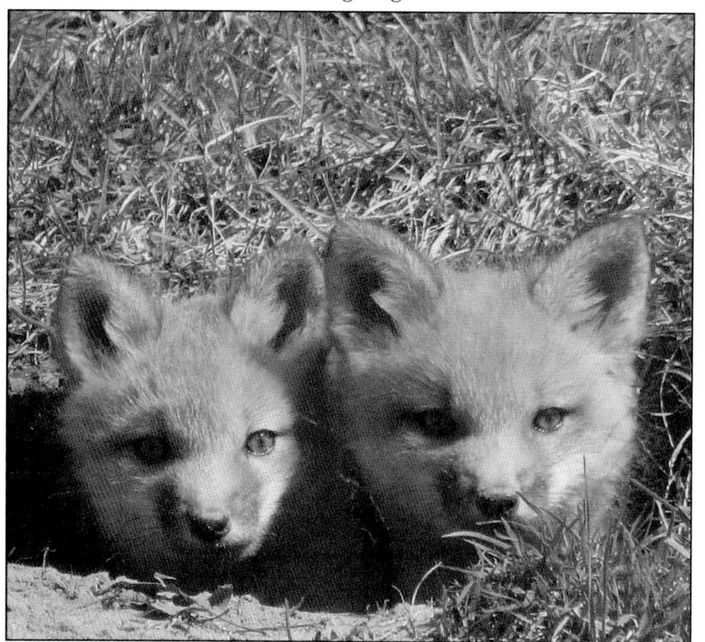

Fauna. Allegheny Cemetery's landscaping and maintenance efforts also support the vitality of its thriving ecosystem. Two fox cubs, called kits, peek their heads out of homes made in Allegheny's rolling hills and forests. Each spring, abundant wildlife can be seen enjoying this vibrant green space. Photography enthusiasts enjoy catching a glimpse of blue heron, pileated woodpeckers, red-tailed hawks, deer, turtles, and more. (Stephen Foley.)

Three

Art and Architecture

Allegheny Cemetery is known as much for the individuals who lie within as it is for its stunning array of art and architecture. While it is true that beauty is in the eye of the beholder, one cannot help but marvel at the myriad of monuments, tributes, legacies, and sculptures within these walls. Setting aside for a moment the very visceral nature of the collective experiences held within, it is easy to appreciate the aesthetic that serves to complement these lives. Graceful pillars, weathered sandstone, faded photographs, and sweeping symbolism all serve to enwrap the senses and hold them if only for a moment. From the striking scope of the cemetery gatehouses to a few words that speak volumes, this chapter includes just some of the touchstones that have captured visitors' souls. Some are visible still today, and some have been lost to the ravages of time; however, within all is an ethereal beauty that speaks of not just an individual, but an era. Through varying styles, compositions, expressions, and mediums, these structures are sometimes the only connection with the individuals for whom they were created. There is something beautiful in that—the smallest monument can evoke as much of a personal connection as the grand gatehouse towers. Though varied in structure, they speak as a tribute to lives lived, loved, and lost and the pieces of those still held within the living.

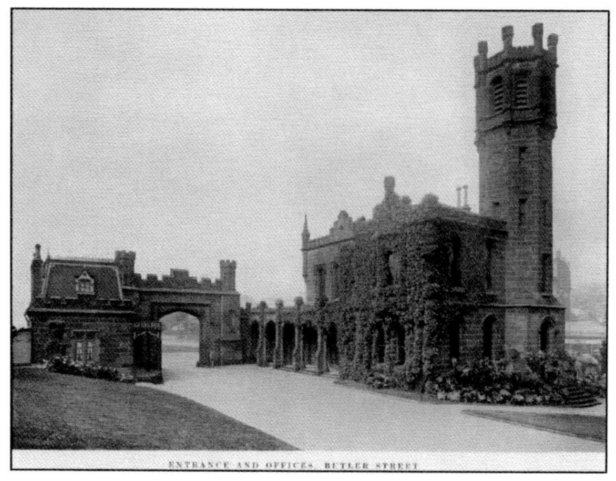

BUTLER STREET GATEHOUSE. Designed by John Chislett, Allegheny Cemetery's Butler Street Gatehouse is listed in the National Register of Historic Places. Developed in 1848, the stone gate and porter's house are early Gothic Revival. From 1868 to 1870, the complex was enlarged, including a two-story stone chapel, administration offices, and Henry Moser's 19th-century Romantic Picturesque clock tower. This Seth V. Albee image is from the cemetery's own 1873 publication. The gatehouse remains generally unchanged well over a century after its construction. (AC.)

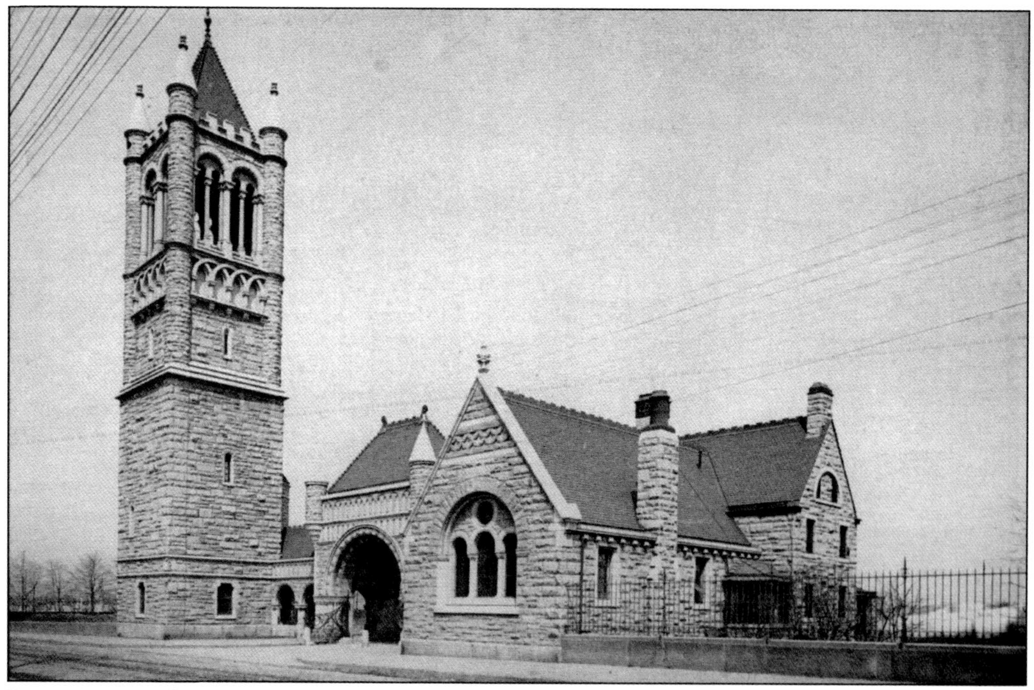

PENN AVENUE GATEHOUSE. The Penn Avenue Gatehouse was designed by architects Macomb & Dull and built from 1887 to 1889. The 135-foot graceful tower rises above the grounds and was meant to be a permanent ornament in the greater Pittsburgh skyline. The gatehouse contains a small chapel with mosaics by Philadelphia tile manufacturers Sharpless & Watts. In 1947, consultants advised the gatehouse be demolished. Fortunately, it remains as one of the cemetery's distinguished features. Restoration work in 1984 was done by hand, cleaning the masonry and red roof tiling, and the structure appears today much as it did in the 19th century. (AC.)

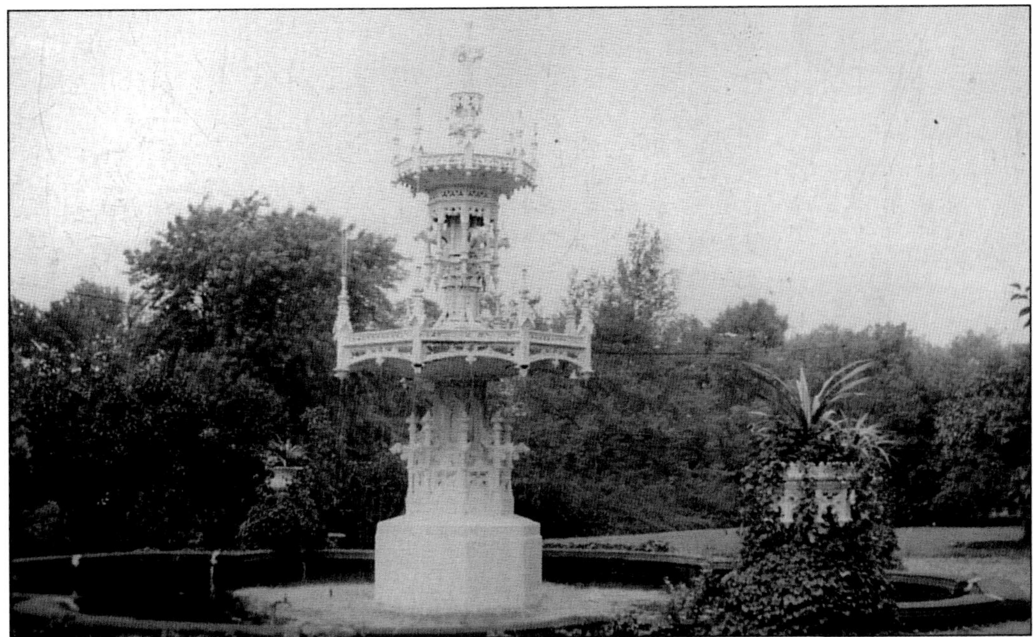

ORIGINAL FOUNTAIN. At a cost of $4,294 in 1874, an intricately decorated solid cast-iron fountain was installed with a quatrefoil sandstone pool spanning 33 feet in diameter. This impressive water feature was one of the cemetery's earliest attempts at beautification for the enjoyment of the public, bringing Pittsburgh even more in stride with public spaces in the Victorian age. (AC.)

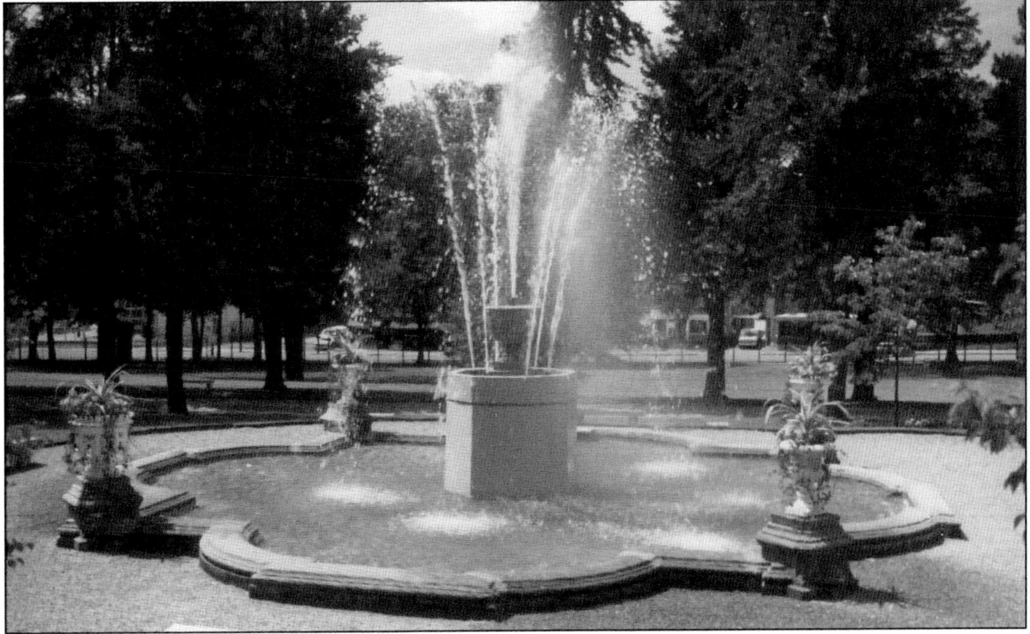

PRESENT-DAY FOUNTAIN, 1982. One of the first major projects of the Allegheny Cemetery Historical Association was to preserve what could be saved from the original Victorian fountain and incorporate it into a functional successor for present generations to enjoy. Plans included relocating the structure and rerouting waterlines to return it to working order. Today's fountain includes the original sandstone pool and two of four original cast-iron floral urns. (AC.)

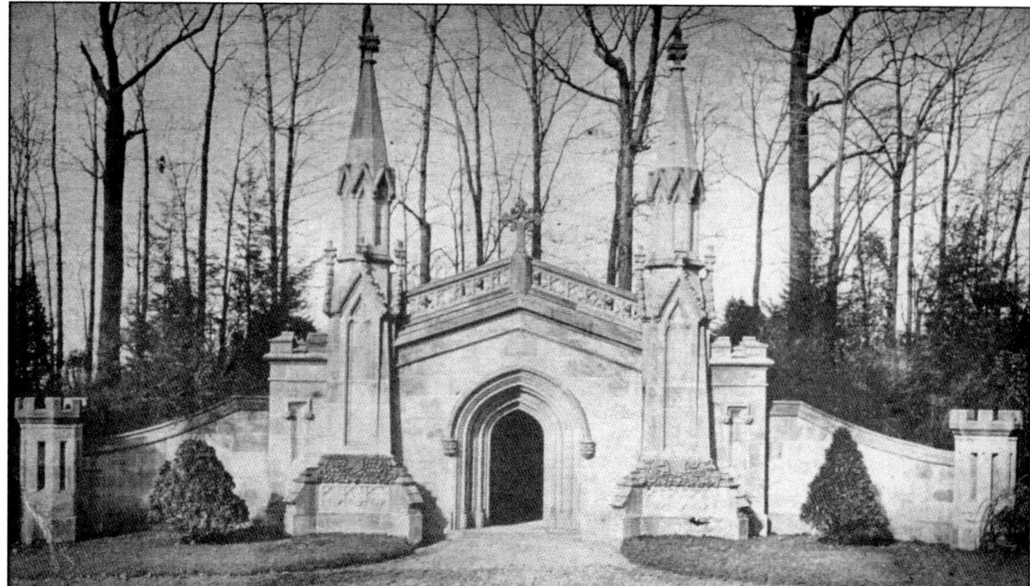

RECEIVING VAULTS. Allegheny Cemetery's original receiving vault was designed by John Chislett and constructed around 1857. It appears here in an 1873 photograph commissioned from Seth V. Albee, taken from the report "Allegheny Cemetery: Historical Account of Incidents and Events Connected with Its Establishment." The initial vault was in the middle of the cemetery and was 55 feet in length and 35 feet wide. Built less than a decade after Pittsburgh's Great Fire, it was designed to accommodate any mass emergency the city might have, with provisions for enlargements as necessary or to provide temporary entombment when winter's frozen earth would not allow immediate burial. A secondary vault was added in 1905, replacing the original, which still stands today just inside the Butler Street entrance. (AC.)

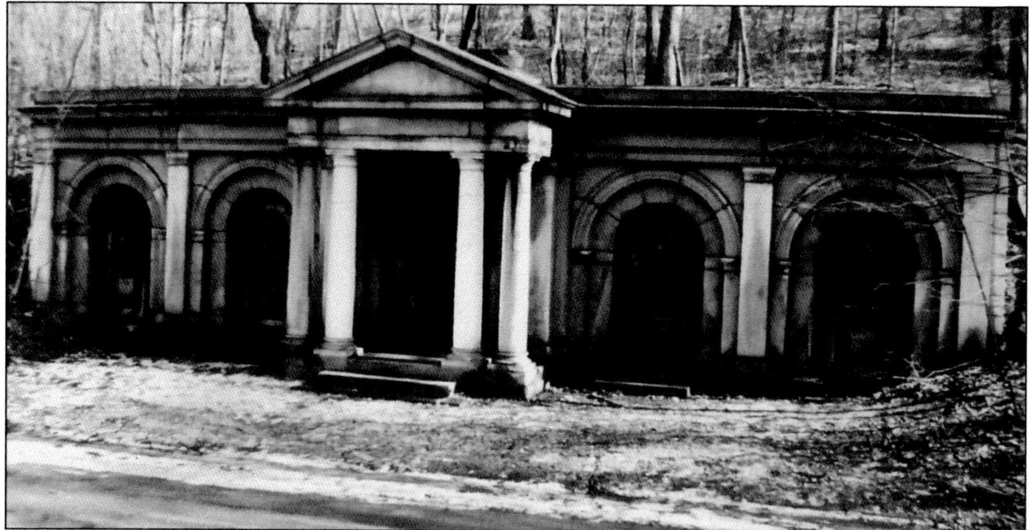

COLUMBARIUM. A grand columbarium once stood in Section 6. An 1892 account in "Factory and Industrial Management" notes that the columbarium was "built upon the hillside and contains 100 niches for urns. The material used is granite, and the style is that of ancient Greece. There are five wide doors and two vaults. The door opening into the Columbarium is a fine specimen of bronze." (AC.)

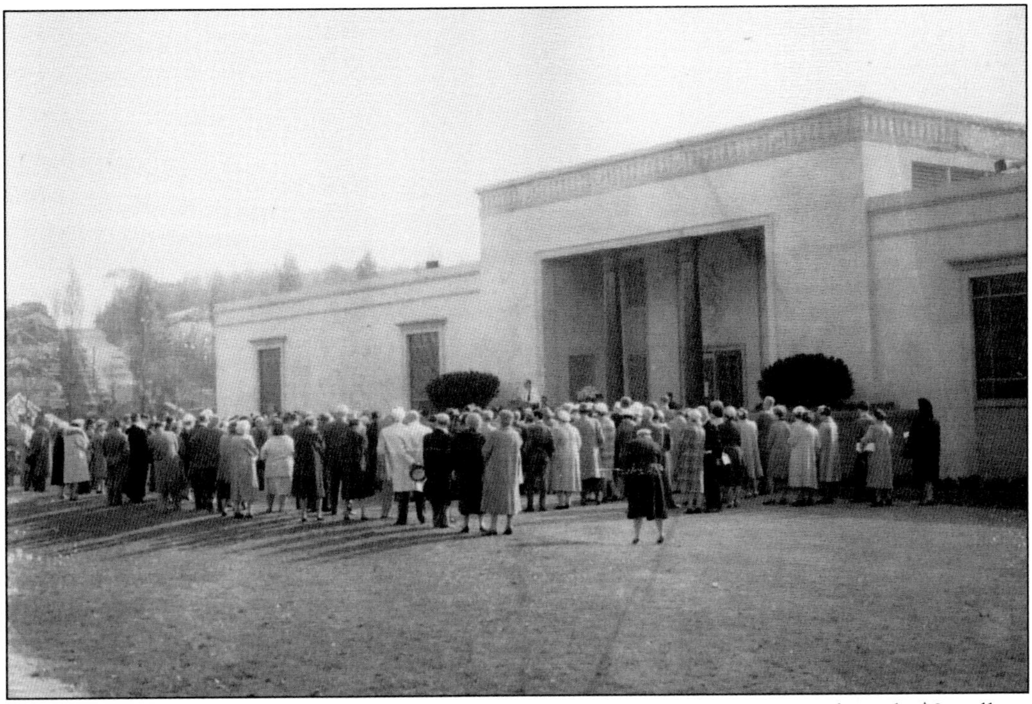

Temple of Memories. This aptly named public mausoleum came at a cost of nearly $3 million in 1961 with the cemetery's board aiming "to create an atmosphere of refinement and beauty in harmony with the great stained glass windows and other works of art in the mausoleum." Twenty-two varieties of Italian marble line hallways where 10 custom motifs in stained glass filter light into secluded alcoves. A 17th-century Flemish tapestry is displayed in the Raymond F. Moreland Memorial Chapel and galleries along the main floor showcase a collection of fine art donated by Pittsburgh's oldest families. (AC.)

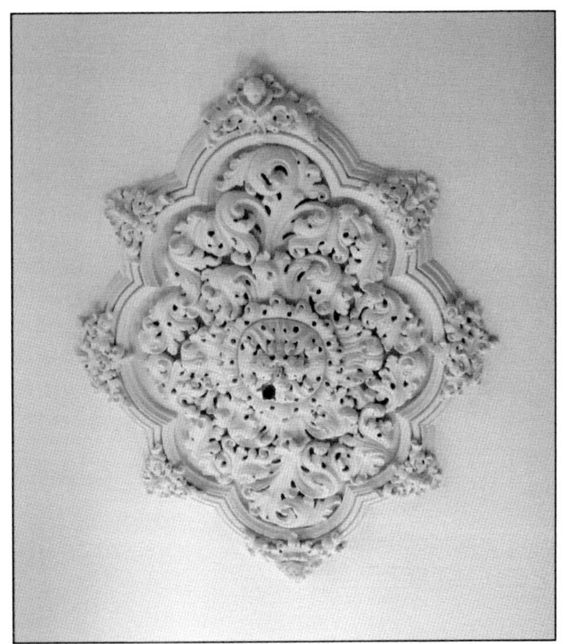

Board of Trade Rooms. These rooms on the second floor of the 1870 administration office are exquisite examples of Gothic Revival in Victorian age interior design, complete with 15-foot ceilings, walnut flooring, and marble fireplaces. Ornate ceiling medallions set the tone for magnificent replica chandeliers originally lit by gaslight, hung low enough to illuminate tables that would have been covered in surveys, maps, and minutes, as these rooms originally hosted meetings of the cemetery's board and the office of the superintendent. This floor was completely restored in 2010 by the cemetery's expert craftsman, Tony Ruggiero. (NF.)

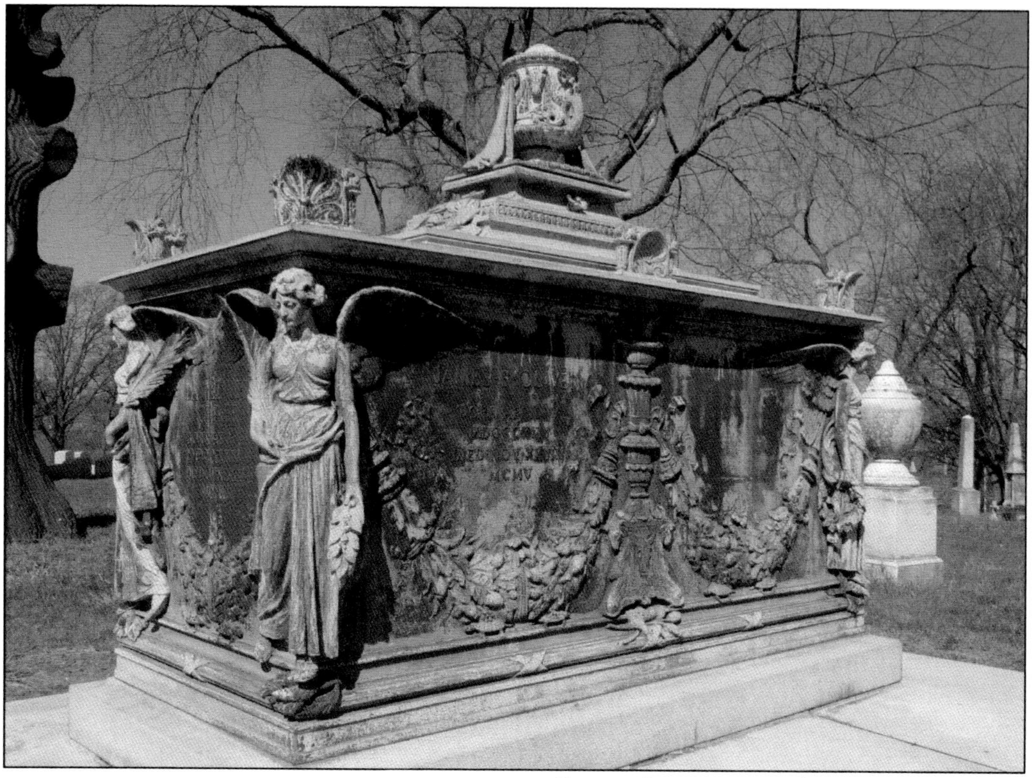

OLIVER SARCOPHAGUS (SECTION 14, LOT 75). Here lies James B. Oliver with his wife, Amelia, and son Daniel, who died at age 21. James served as president of the Oliver Iron and Steel Company, founded by his father, who lies entombed in a modestly designed family mausoleum in Section 20. James opted for this spectacular original work in bronze, which depicts angels, virtues, and boughs of plenty held up on the shells of turtles. (NF.)

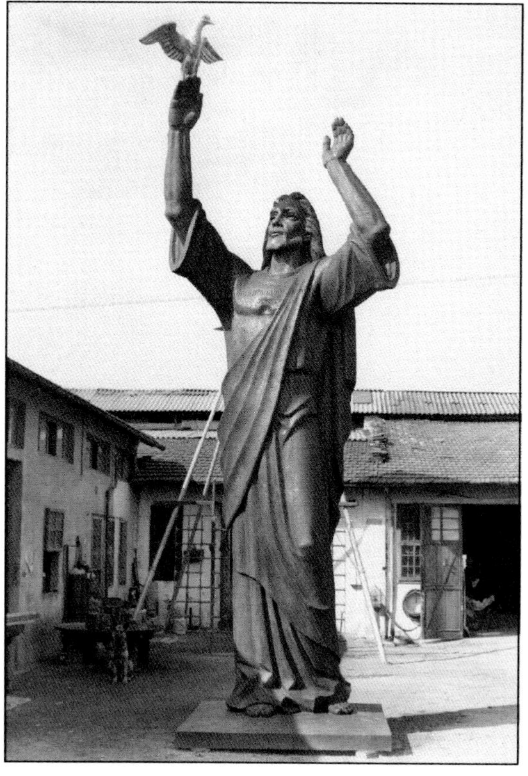

CHRISTUS STATUE. Allegheny Cemetery's *Christus* statue is shown being handcrafted by artisans in Carrara, Italy, including (then world-renowned) artist Ferenc Varga. The 21-foot-tall cast bronze statue was made with the same proportions as Michelangelo's *David* and placed on its pedestal in the summer of 1967. When commissioned, the board envisioned a monument to serve as a beacon of comfort for those grieving the loss of a loved one. With the dove being a symbol of peace, the statue represents both man's search for peace and a compassionate message to those in mourning, "peace be with you." (AC.)

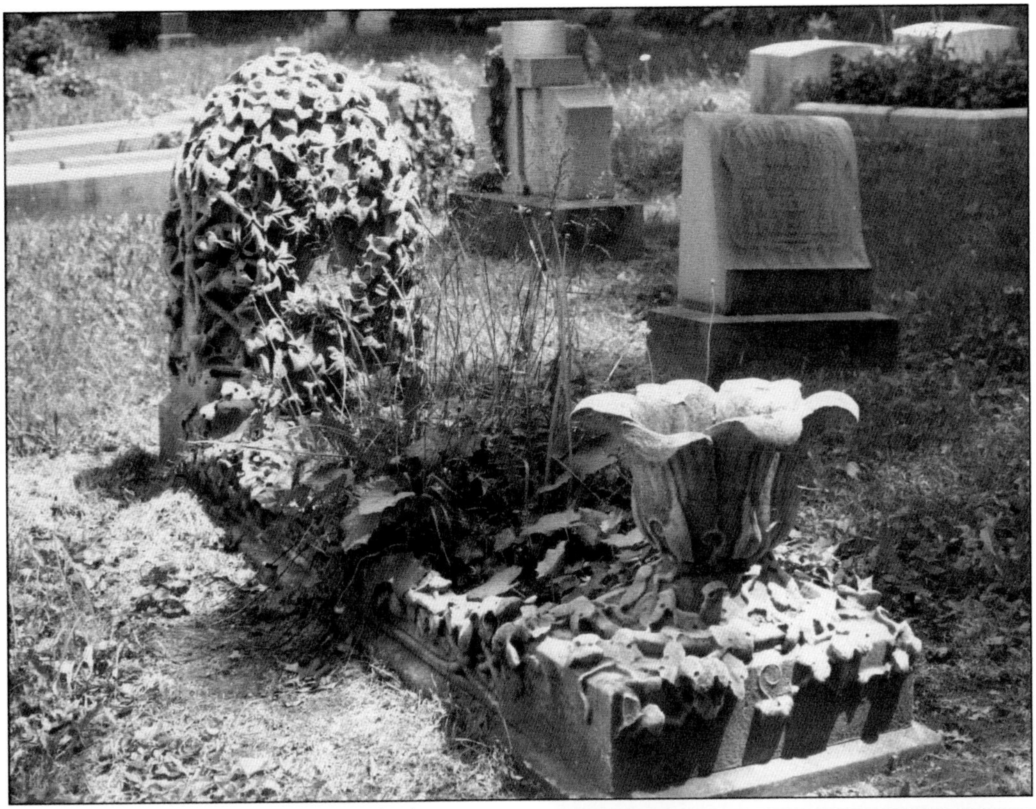

Lewis Tomb (Section 12, Lot 92). A traditional open tomb would allow space for floral or ivy plantings; however, A. Kirk Lewis had this 1850 work "planted" permanently with ivy, lily, and morning glory, complete with a large lily-shaped urn for fresh flowers to be placed at the foot. Flowers return again and again in memorial design and are symbolic of rebirth, renewal, resilience, and hope. In life, A. Kirk Lewis was a pioneer in the coal industry and built an incline from Mount Washington to the Monongahela River in order to transport coal downriver. (AC.)

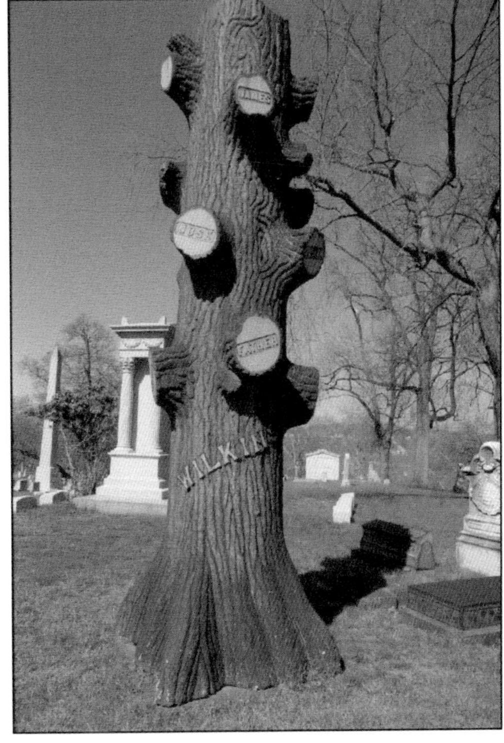

Wilkins Family Tree (Section 14, Lot 119). This memorial is a unique physical representation of the genealogical Wilkins family tree, with each cut limb symbolizing a branch of the Edward Wilkins family and a life that has come to an end. According to a handwritten letter in the cemetery's archives, John Pschirer, a German immigrant, sculpted this monument in 1888 at age 26. Pschirer carved the cross at St. Anna's Roman Catholic Church in Vienna, Austria, at age 17. (NF.)

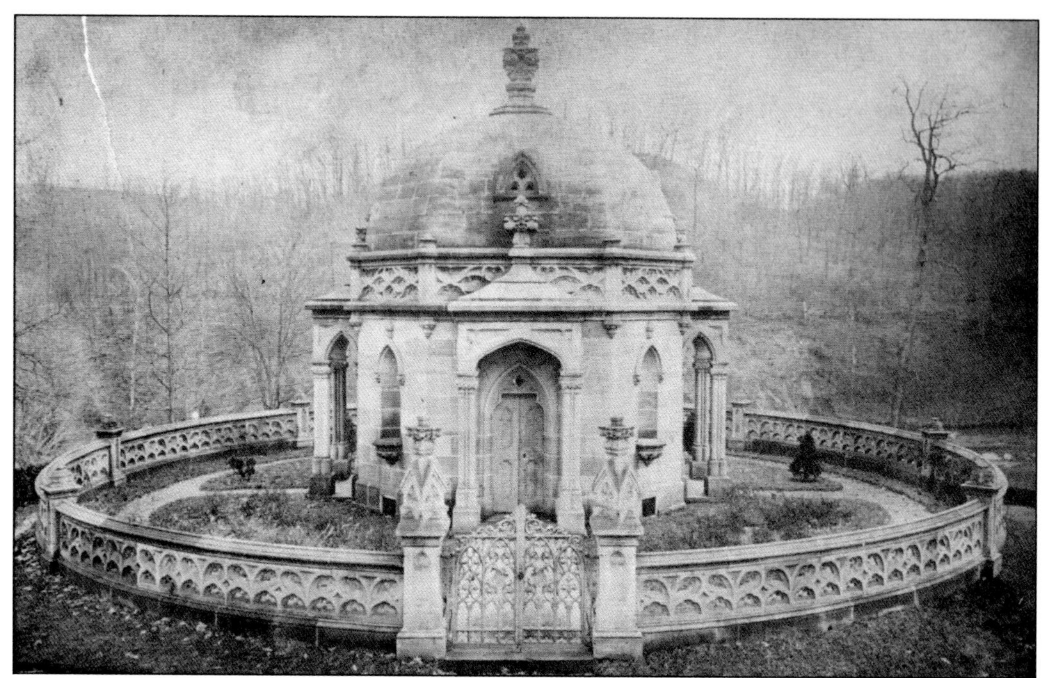

Moorhead Mausoleum. In 1862, architect Louis Morgenroth designed the graceful and Gothic Moorhead mausoleum, which is one of the most notable in the cemetery. While it currently rests in isolated splendor atop a gently sloping hillside, the original monument (pictured here in an 1873 cemetery publication) featured a large detailed stonework fence that encircled the mausoleum. It was originally built for James Kennedy Moorhead, who died several years after the construction was completed. He served as a corporator of the cemetery and is noted for his work on the Pennsylvania canals and the Monongahela Navigation Company. (AC.)

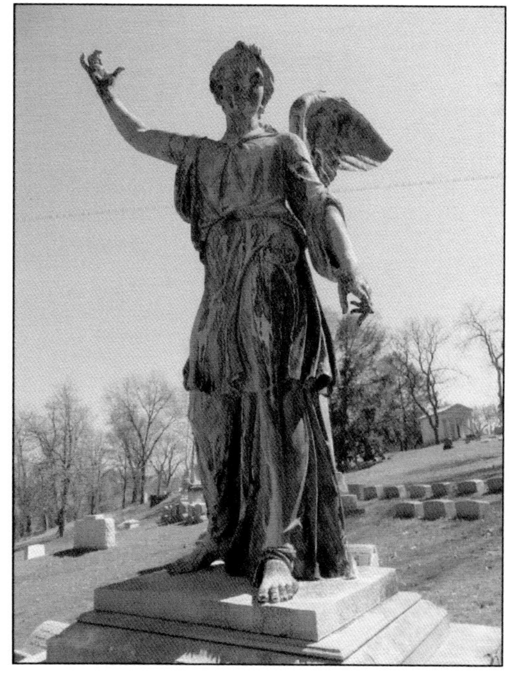

Hogg Angel. George Hogg was born in England in 1784 and came to the United States in 1804. He was known in Pittsburgh for having developed the Brownsville Glass Factory and later as founder of the Monongahela Navigation Company in 1836. Upon his death in 1851, the current monument, affectionately known as the Hogg Angel, was created by well-known sculptor Henry K. Brown. Situated on a sandstone pedestal, the exquisite Hogg Angel reaches one hand toward the heavens and one toward Earth, alerting the creator that a Christian soul rests here, among the tree-lined paths at Allegheny. (NF.)

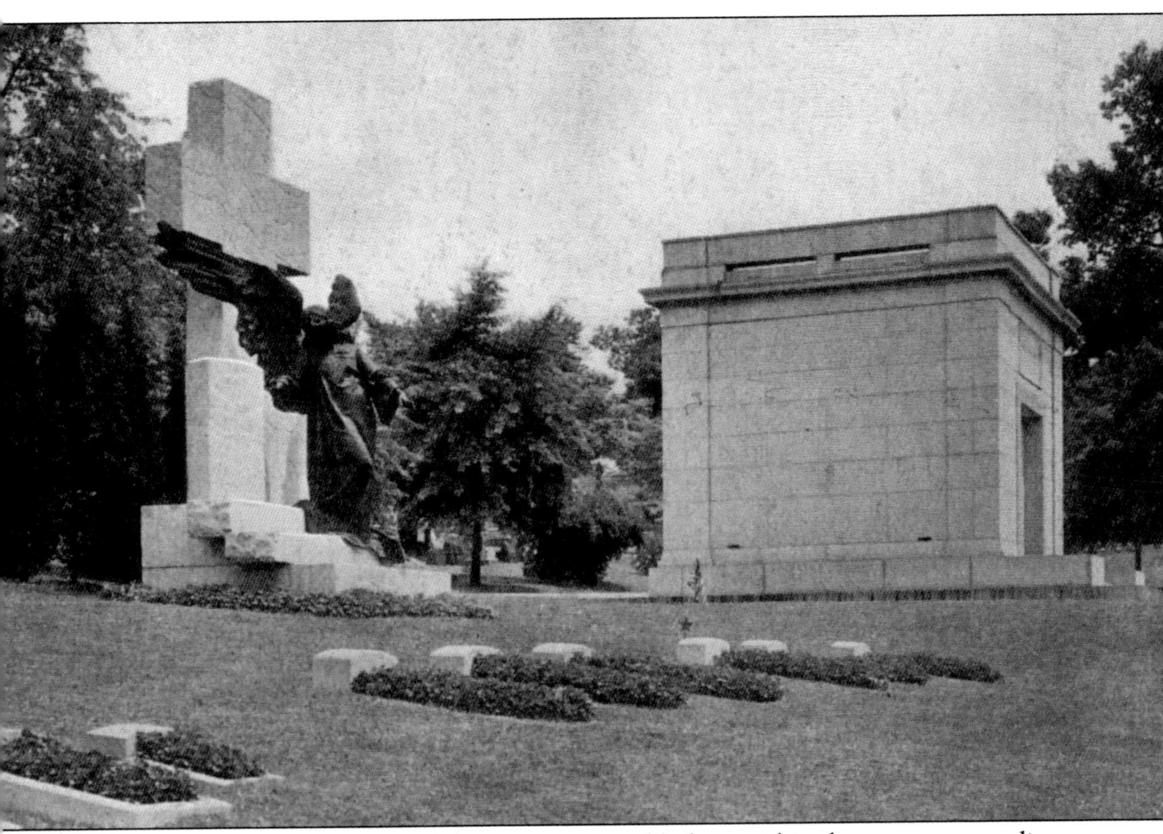

PORTER ANGEL. She is perhaps one of the most recognizable faces within the cemetery, standing watch over the family of Henry Kirke Porter, an American businessman and member of the US Congress, who died in 1921. Known as the Porter Angel, many are familiar with her serene countenance and gracefully outstretched wings. The patina of time has enveloped her like a cloak, and yet she is ever more graceful after all these years. The current Porter Angel likely dates to the 1920s. However, as early as 1906, a *Pittsburgh Daily Post* article shows a marble angel and sandstone cross at the family grave. Imported from Italy, it was reputed to be one of the most striking examples of marble carving in any cemetery in America. As it weathered, it was likely replaced with the stunning bronze monument that so many recognize today. The Porter Angel is shown here in a 1940s cemetery publication. (AC.)

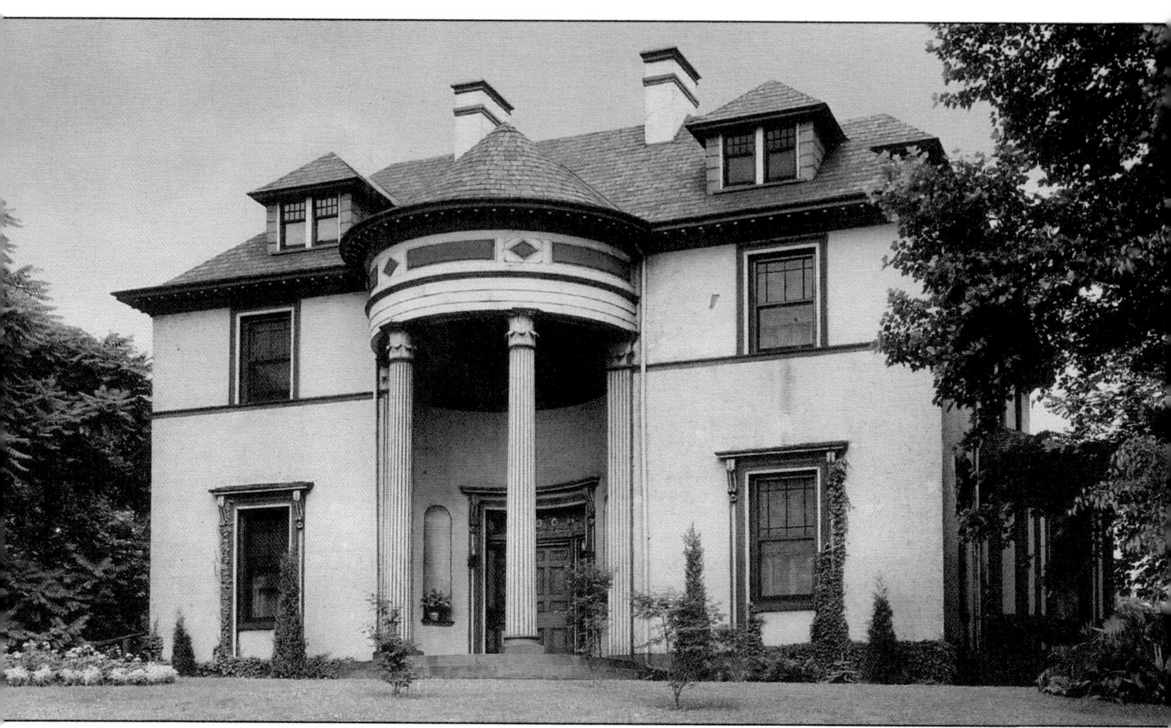

John (1810–1889) and Margaret (1809–1878) Shoenberger (Section 4, Lot 1). With an understated benevolence that defined their lives, the Shoenbergers resided in this opulent residence just outside the gates of Allegheny Cemetery. Their love for each other encapsulated their many other passions in life, including the arts, humanities, and numerous philanthropic efforts, which would leave the world a better place for them simply having been a part of it. John made his fortune in iron manufacturing, and Margaret was well-remembered for her numerous kindnesses. Upon her death in 1878, John left their home (pictured here) and eventually sold the estate to the Allegheny Cemetery, where it served as the superintendent's home for a number of years. His philanthropy continued after his death when he bequeathed a gift of nearly $10 million in today's value to establish St. Margaret Memorial Hospital in memory of his beloved wife. (AC.).

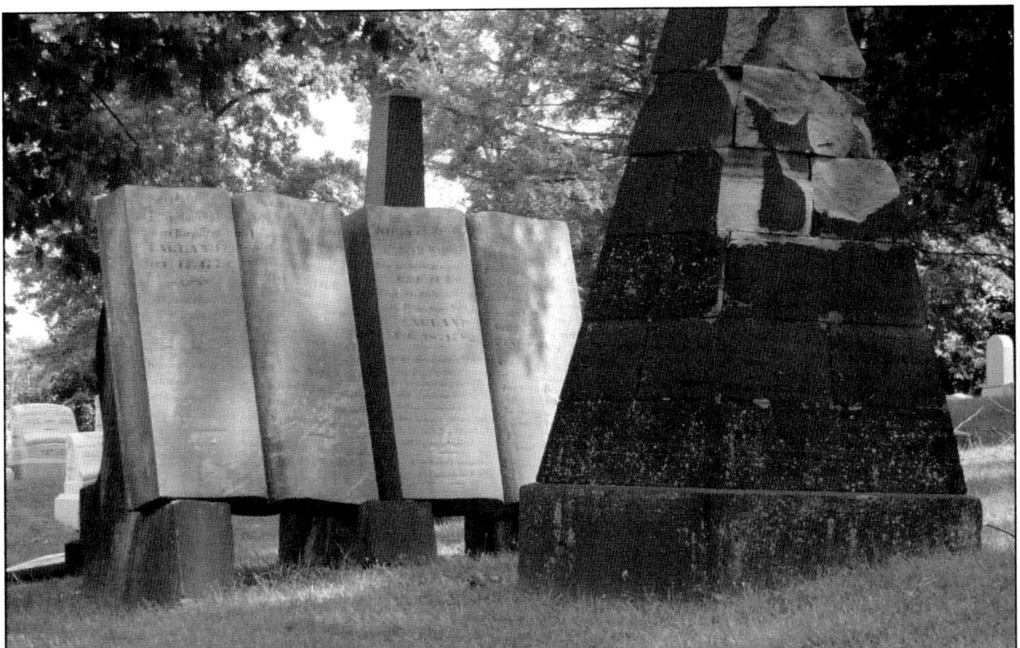

The Wainwright Pyramid (Section 7, Lot 14). In a copse of shady trees sits a dark pyramid and a large sandstone book, its words lost to time. This is the Wainwright Pyramid, belonging to brothers who were mid-19th-century brewers. The monument was once a replica of a family Bible where Joseph and Elizabeth Wainwright's birth and death dates were inscribed. The pyramid's soft stone has also suffered the ravages of time, now standing in silent testament to a bygone era. (AC.)

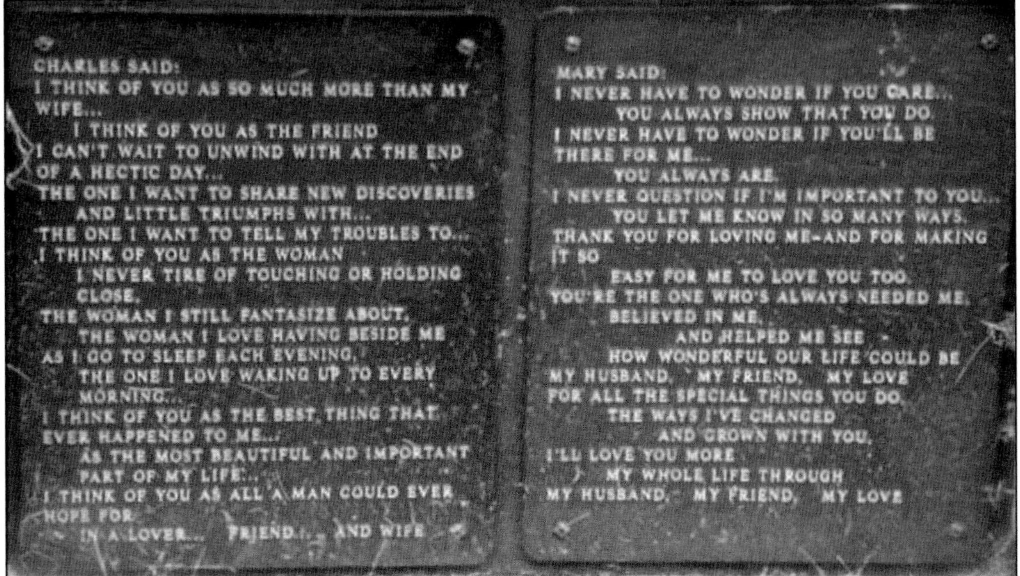

Charles and Mary Jackson (Section 26, Lot 384). The inscriptions on this tombstone were reportedly written before their deaths and then sealed in envelopes without ever having been read by each other. Their instructions were to place the words upon their final resting place when both were gone. Both simple and striking in its prose, their touching words serve as an eternal reminder of the love they shared for one another. (LS.)

William Bingham, Notary Public, No. 143 Smithfield Street, Pittsburgh, Pa,

No. 8457 Issued Oct. 4. 1870

United States of America.

STATE OF PENNSYLVANIA, County of Allegheny, CITY OF PITTSBURGH. } SS.

I, Ellen H. Pusey do swear that I was born in the City of Pittsburgh on or about the 5th day of December 1841; that I am a Native and LOYAL CITIZEN OF THE UNITED STATES, and about to travel abroad.

Ellen H. Pusey

Sworn to before me this Third day of October 1870

Wm Bingham
Notary Public.

I, William Bingham Jr do swear that I am acquainted with the above named Ellen H. Pusey and with the facts above stated by him, and that the same are true to the best of my knowledge and belief.

William Bingham Jr

Sworn to before me this Third day of October 1870

Wm Bingham
Notary Public.

Description of Ellen H. Pusey

Age, 29 years,	Mouth, Small
Stature, 5 ft. 3 inches (English.)	Chin, Round
Forehead, High	Hair, brown
Eyes, blue	Complexion, Fair
Nose, Medium	Face, Round

Ella Pusey (1841–1870; Section 23, Lot 38). She was 29 years old; small at five feet, three inches; and alone, but with the world ahead of her. However, six days after signing this passport application, she was dead. Pusey boarded the steamship *Cambria* in October 1870. Her passage was paid for by an uncle after the passing of her brother a few months prior. Nearing Ireland in the dark night, cold black water, and treacherous seas, the *Cambria* struck rocks just off the coast. Only one lifeboat survived. Clinging to it, a man—the only survivor—climbed aboard. There, he found he was not alone. The body of a woman—noted in historical records as "dressed in a black silk gown"—remained under a seat in the boat, where she had drowned. It is uncertain if the woman in black was Ella Pusey. This is a curious possibility, though, as she was mourning the recent loss of her brother and would likely have been dressed in black, as was Victorian standard. After the ship's sinking, a touching cenotaph was placed in the family's plot, honoring Ella's memory. At the base, the inscription read: "The sea shall give up its dead." (NF.)

Four

Titans of Industry

In the gilded age of industry that dominated the 19th century, Pittsburgh was the undisputed center of the world. In this "nursery of vast fortunes," shop boys and coal kids grew up to be millionaires. Unimaginable wealth was accumulated from extracting coal, iron, and oil, all of which were naturally abundant in this region, and shipping it around the country for use in developing every major city in the nation. Those iconic photographs by Lewis Hine showing construction workers lunching on massive steel beams stories high while building the Empire State Building? Those beams, along with more than half the iron and steel produced at the time, were from Pittsburgh. There were savvy investors in cotton, coffee, railroads, and banking interests who generated millions that grew into billions in today's values. Above the river flats, usually set upon hills or in fashionable areas like Shadyside's "Millionaire's Row," mansions and country estates were constructed with an attention to detail and opulence to rival the palaces of Europe. These are the stories of American "Kings of Capitalism," who, unlike their European counterparts, built their own fortunes from the ground up. The prosperity enjoyed by those who rose to the top in the last 200 years has been philanthropically invested back into the city, resulting in public parks, libraries, extravagantly decorated theaters and opera halls, ornate bridges, inclines that seemed to do the impossible, and buildings that are now signature features in Pittsburgh's skyline. Much of Pittsburgh's identity today still lies in its storied industrial past, and many natives come from families who either worked for businesses established by these men or who still enjoy a thriving art and cultural presence due to their foresight and public-minded giving. A prime example of this legacy of civic improvement is steel tycoon Andrew Carnegie, who chose a modest, closed tomb for his parents in Section 20, Lot 18, and opted instead to focus on the schools, libraries, concert halls, and public institutions to serve as their memorial.

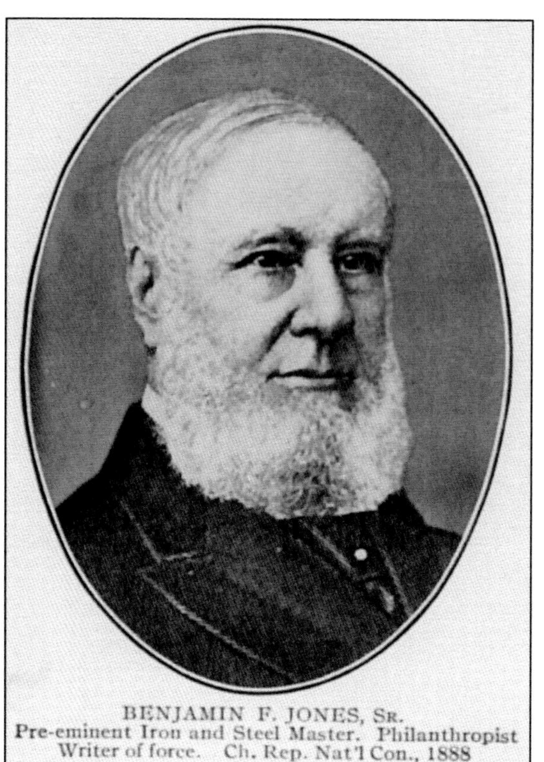

BENJAMIN F. JONES, SR.
Pre-eminent Iron and Steel Master. Philanthropist
Writer of force. Ch. Rep. Nat'l Con., 1888

BENJAMIN FRANKLIN JONES (1824–1903; SECTION 19, LOT 72). Partners with James H. Laughlin, B.F. Jones solidified his position as a leading industrialist on the brink of the Industrial Revolution. The renowned Jones & Laughlin Steel Company relied heavily on the transportation that Pittsburgh's rivers provided. Jones had his roots in the river barge industry and coupled this with his business acumen to develop a company that would be synonymous with the steel industry for generations to follow. Four members of the family have also served as corporators of Allegheny Cemetery throughout the years. (AC.).

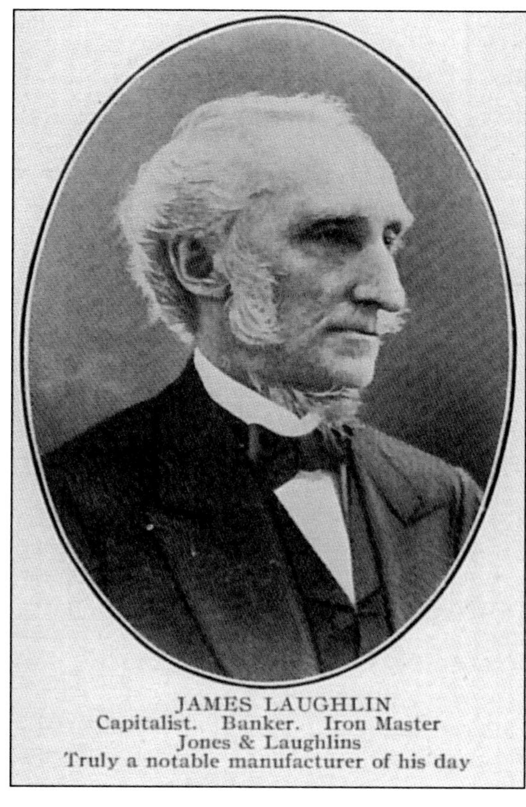

JAMES LAUGHLIN
Capitalist. Banker. Iron Master
Jones & Laughlins
Truly a notable manufacturer of his day

JAMES H. LAUGHLIN (1806–1882; SECTION 8.5, LOT 34/35/36/37). In 1854, Laughlin joined B.F. Jones in forming the Jones & Laughlin Steel Company (later J&L Steel). He was also one of the founding corporators of Allegheny Cemetery and had founding interests in the First National Bank of Pittsburgh, the Western Theological Seminary of Pittsburgh, and the Pennsylvania Female College (now Chatham University). From humble beginnings as an Irish immigrant, he rose to a role of prominence in Pittsburgh history. (AC.)

J.B. Ford (1811–1903; Section 1, Lot 32). John Baptiste Ford was born in a log cabin in Kentucky, the son of a soldier and a French immigrant. He rose to prominence in Pittsburgh as the founder (along with his sons) of Pittsburgh Plate Glass (PPG) in 1883. By 1897, the family sold their shares of PPG and opened the Ford Glass Company in Toledo, Ohio, which later became the Libbey Owens Ford Glass Company. Ford died at home in Tarentum, Pennsylvania, and is buried in a large angular Victorian Gothic mausoleum. (AC.)

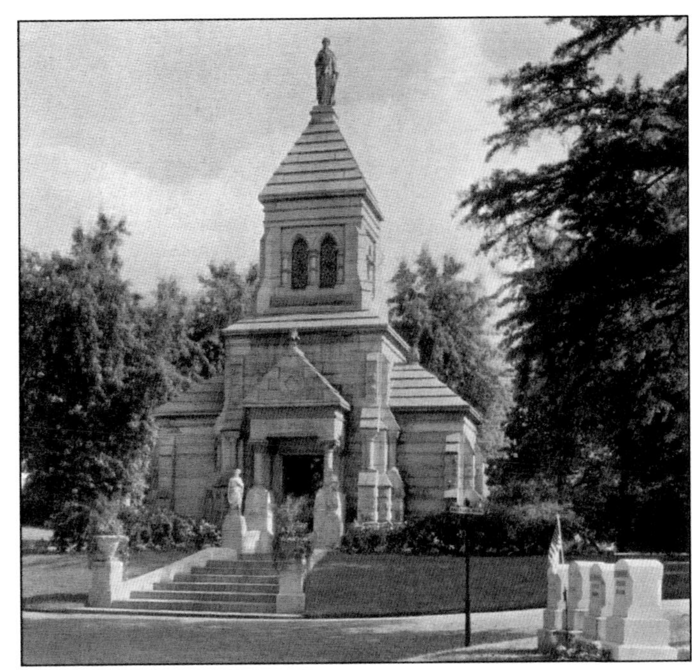

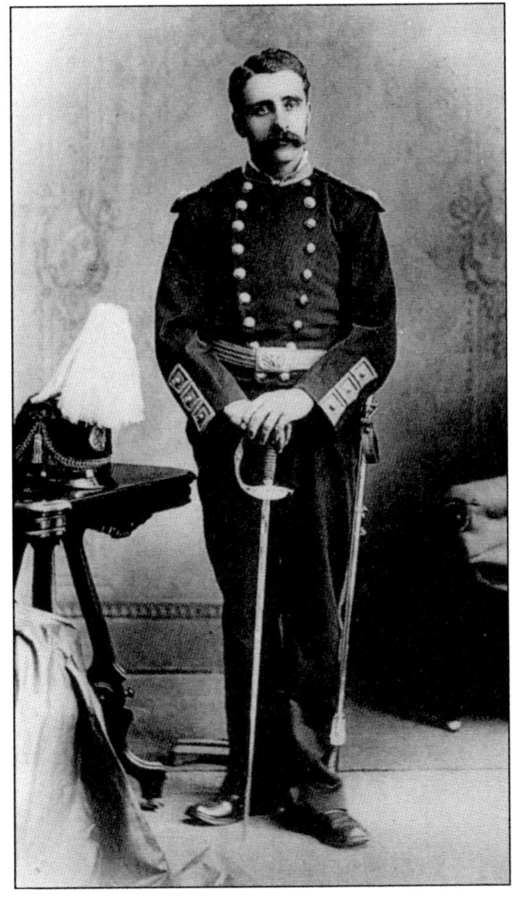

The Hunt Family (Section 28, Lot 3; Section 44, Lot 5). The Hunt family has a long tradition of service to Allegheny Cemetery, with several generations serving on its board. Pictured here, Captain Alfred E. Hunt studied metallurgy at the Massachusetts Institute of Technology and purchased Charles Martin Hall's patent for aluminum extraction, later founding the Pittsburgh Reduction Company. Captain Hunt contracted malaria while stationed in Puerto Rico during the Spanish American War and died upon his return. His son Roy A. Hunt served in his place as president of the company, which was renamed the Aluminum Company of America, or ALCOA. (Hunt Institute for Botanical Documentation)

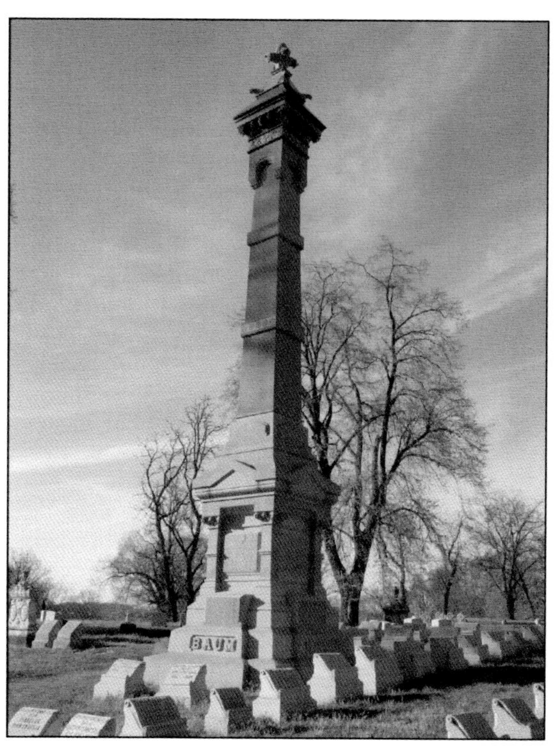

WILLIAM PENN BAUM (1800–1867; SECTION 16, LOT 126). At age 12, Baum arrived in Pittsburgh with family friend Charles Volz. He worked in Volz's office and, at night, obtained his schooling. Involved in both manufacturing and toy businesses, he served as director of the Merchants and Manufacturers National Bank. Best known as an ardent abolitionist, Baum was appointed to a committee protecting soldiers of the Civil War. He was a vestryman and founder of East End Calvary Church. Baum and his wife, Rebecca Roup Baum, had 12 children, 10 of whom survived to adulthood. (NF.)

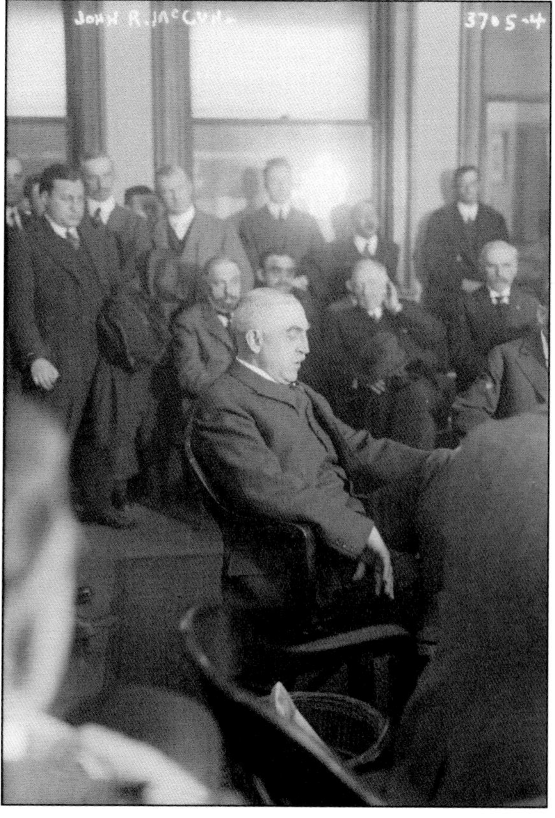

JOHN R. McCUNE (1826–1888; SECTION 12, LOT 21). McCune moved to Pittsburgh at age 15 and began his business career as an apprentice in a leather shop. He was made the first president of the Union Banking Company, later the Union National Bank, and sat on the board of many civic and philanthropic organizations. He was an influential citizen and highly respected for his keen intellect, Christian conviction, and humility of character. There is a fine mausoleum in Section 25 where McCune's son Charles rests. His will established the family's benevolent McCune Foundation. (AC.)

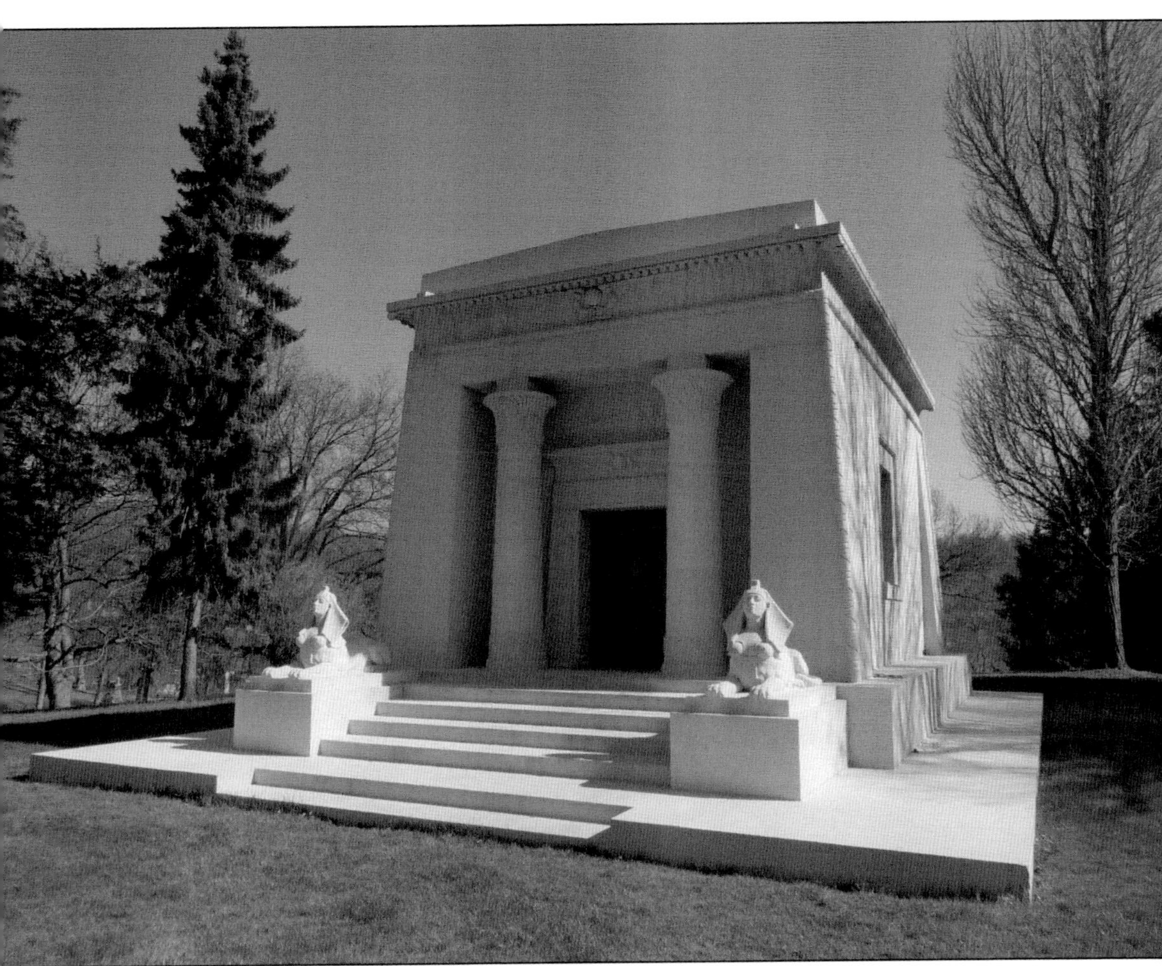

Emil Winter (1857–1941; Section 40, Lots 6 and 6.5). The Winter family mausoleum is the largest and most opulent in the cemetery. While all other private mausoleums at Allegheny were built with marble interiors, Emil Winter had his done in granite—at a significant cost increase. As one of the founders of the Pittsburgh Steel Company, Winter was a man of vast wealth. Living in New York City in his later years, he saw the Egyptian-style Woolworth family mausoleum in Woodlawn Cemetery in the Bronx and had a replica made for him in 1930 for his own lot back home in Allegheny Cemetery. In life, he and his wife, Mary, were ardent patrons of the arts, and after his death, public auctions revealed Winter's personal art collection to have been substantial. Among the pieces were paintings by Corot; etchings by Rembrandt, Durer, and Whistler; and Auguste Rodin's iconic bronze sculpture *The Thinker.* (NF.)

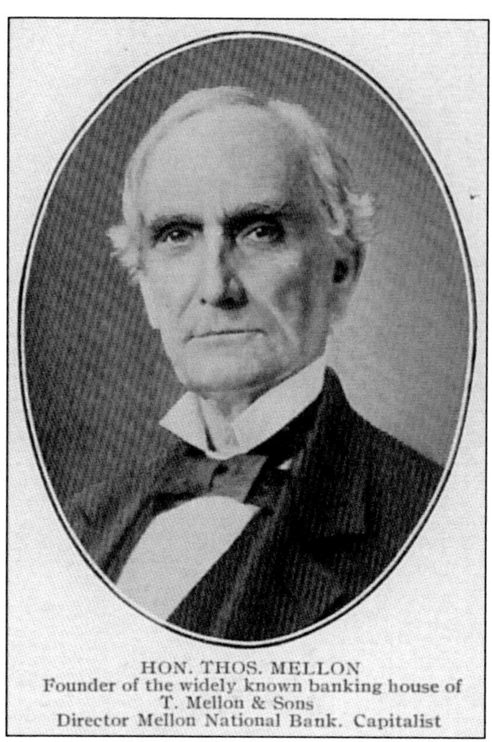

HON. THOS. MELLON
Founder of the widely known banking house of T. Mellon & Sons
Director Mellon National Bank. Capitalist

Thomas Alexander Mellon (1813–1908; Section 19, Lots 23 and 24). Here lies the founder of the eponymous banking house, today under the name Bank of New York Mellon. An immigrant from Northern Ireland, Mellon came to western Pennsylvania as a toddler with his family. In his autobiography, Mellon recalled seeing as a 10-year-old never before imagined opulence in the form of the Jacob Negley Mansion, and the effect on the boy was profound. He grew into a young man of incessant toil, studying law and marrying the daughter of the very same Negley whose estate inspired him as a child. A man of prudence in all business matters, he invested his profits from practicing law into real estate, which grew into a sum large enough for him to abandon the law and open a banking house, originally located on present-day Smithfield Street. This endeavor became the Mellon family legacy, which continues to this day. (Left, AC; below, LOC.)

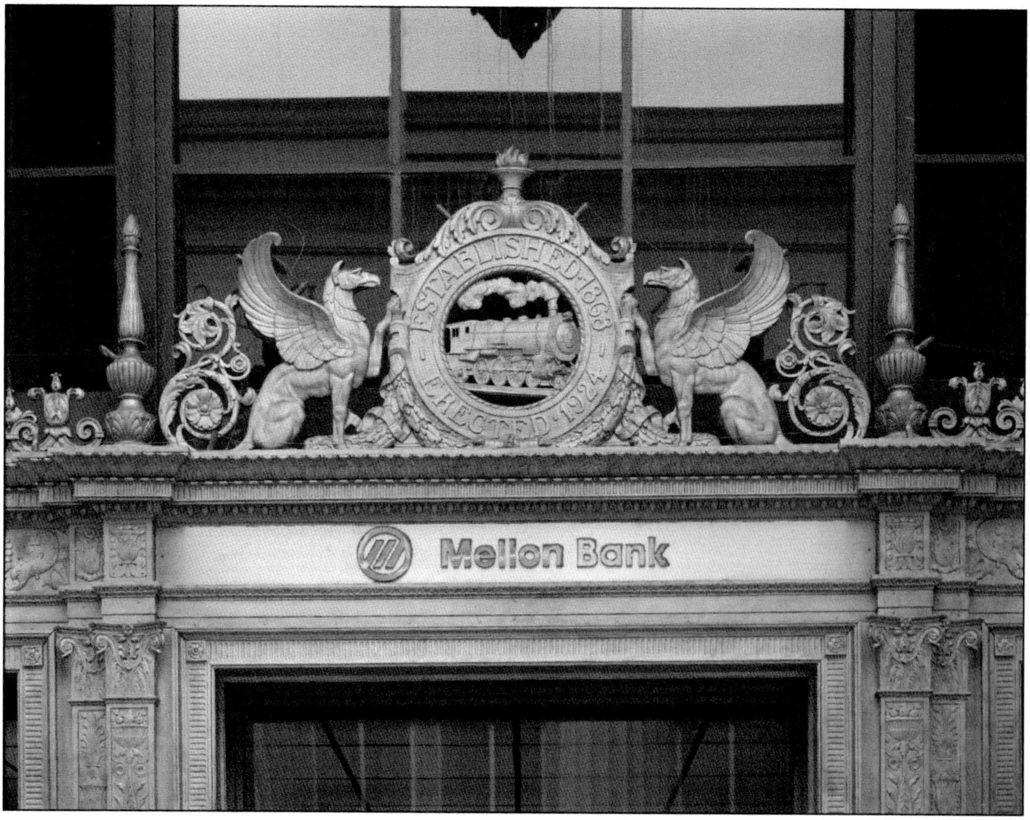

N. Holmes & Sons (Section 11, Lot 3). Nathaniel Holmes came from Northern Ireland to America and established what was one of the most financially sound and profitable private banking houses ever seen in this nation. N. Holmes & Sons was the first private bank west of the Alleghenies and was the choice of Pittsburgh's finest families and institutions, including Allegheny Cemetery, where Holmes served as a founding corporator, offering valuable financial guidance to insure the cemetery's viability in the coming ages. (AC.)

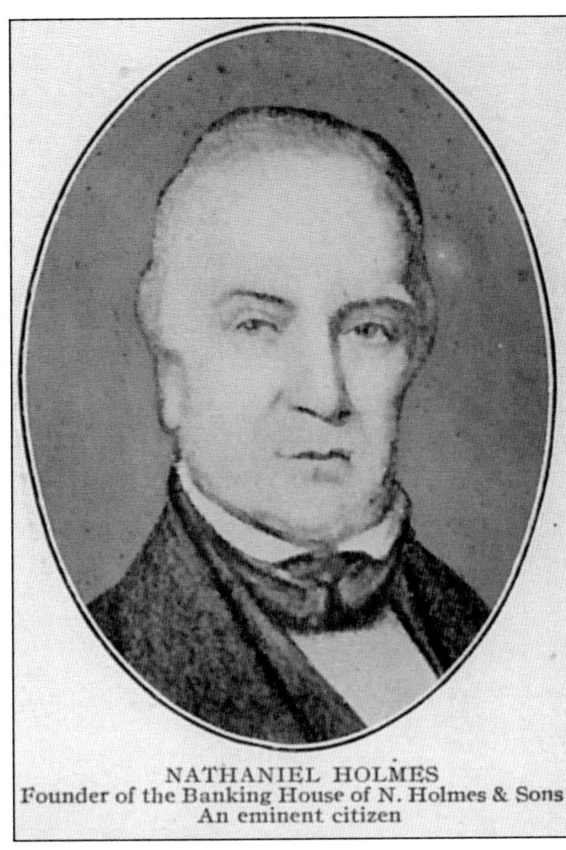
NATHANIEL HOLMES
Founder of the Banking House of N. Holmes & Sons
An eminent citizen

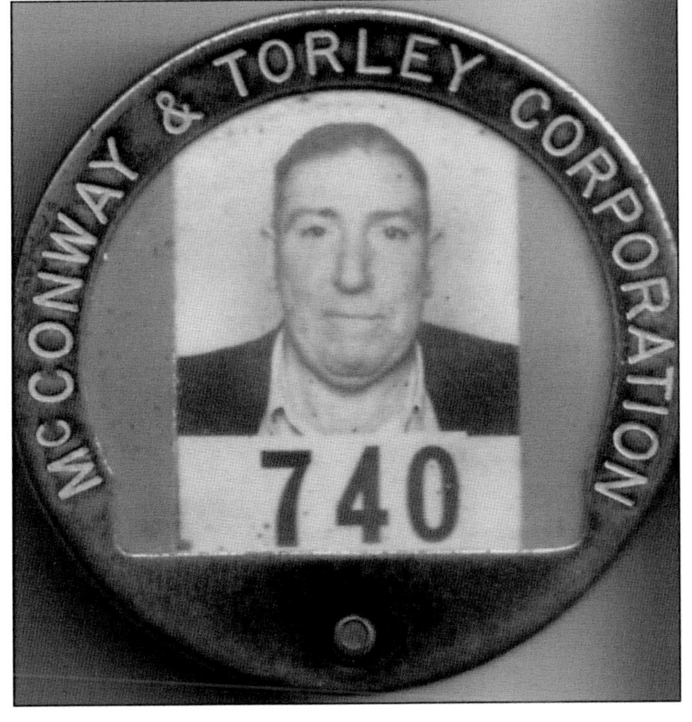

William McConway Sr. (Section 30, Lot 55) and John J. Torley (Section 31, Lot 853). During the mid-19th century, railroads were a dominant form of passenger and commercial transportation, which required a way of safely coupling cars as they traversed a bustling nation. In 1869, William McConway Sr. and John J. Torley partnered to form the McConway & Torley Corporation, which designed and manufactured the Pitt Passenger Coupler, an integral advancement in safety. Pictured here is the employee badge of Robert Henry Fadzen, one of the many workers who helped make these successes possible during the burgeoning industrial age. (LS.)

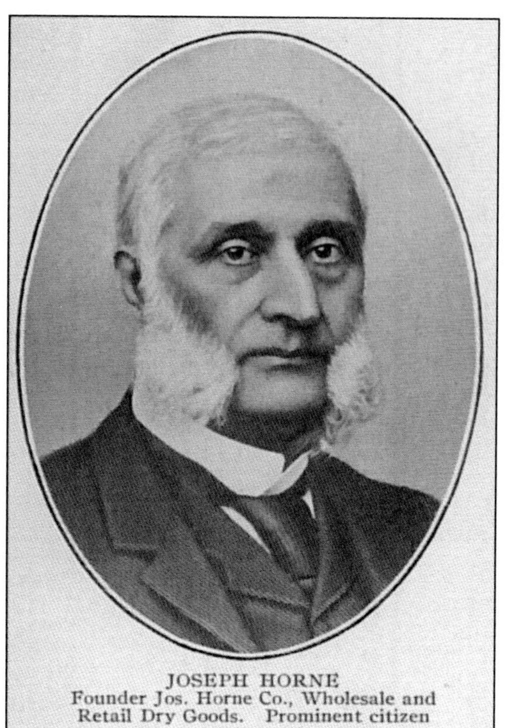

JOSEPH HORNE
Founder Jos. Horne Co., Wholesale and Retail Dry Goods. Prominent citizen

Joseph Horne (1826–1892; Section 13, Lot 66). Many Pittsburghers happily recall Joseph Horne Co., "The Best Place to Shop, After All," and some may have dined at the Tick Tock Café in the flagship department store on Penn Avenue and Stanwix Street. The company's double inverted French horn logo was a symbol of good taste on boxes and bags filled with treasures. Horne's locale near the Allegheny River resulted in utter devastation during the great flood of 1936, after which the company responded, "Let us be thankful: Our losses to the building and merchandise were tremendous, but they are nothing compared to that which we would have felt if a single one of our employees had lost his life. . . . Out of the flood of 1936 there will emerge a greater Horne's." The Joseph Horne Co. would later become Lazarus and then Macy's, each now living only in Pittsburgh's memory, though it is Horne's iconic six-story Christmas tree covered in dazzling electric lights that continues to dominate memories of holidays gone by and the golden age of the downtown shopping scene. (Left, AC; below, LOC.)

072226 PENN AVE. AND JOSEPH HORNE'S STORE, PITTSBURGH, PA.

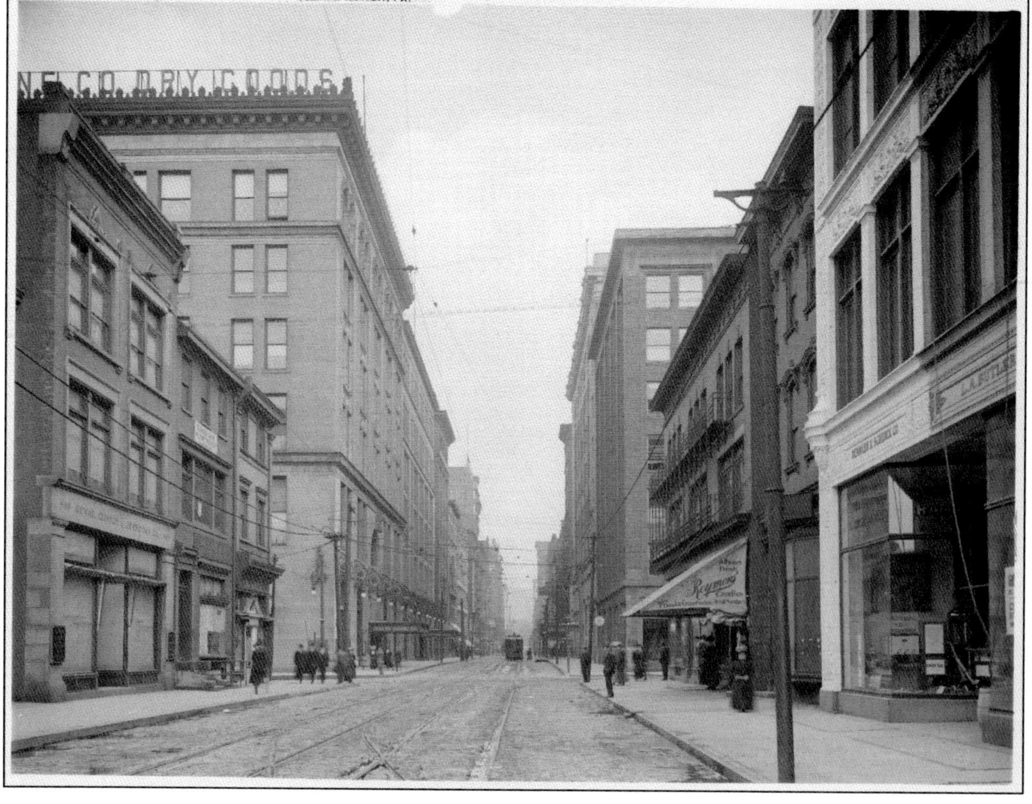

JOHN R. ARBUCKLE (D. MARCH 27, 1912; SECTION 16, LOT 179). Long before Folgers, Arbuckle's Ariosa blend was keeping America going full steam ahead. John Arbuckle was the first man to discover a way to roast coffee beans and then coat them with a sugar glaze to keep them fresh for shipment across the country where they would be ground for brewing. Prior to Arbuckle's blend, each person had to roast his own beans, which were often scorched. Arbuckle was soon the "King of Coffee"—his product was so popular in the Wild West, most cowboys did not know there was another brand. John and his brother Charles were savvy marketers as well, including a peppermint stick in each bag, coupons, and trading cards featuring exotic locations, animals, and world wonders. Upon John Arbuckle's retirement, Arbuckle's Coffee was sold to a much smaller outfit—Maxwell House. (AC.)

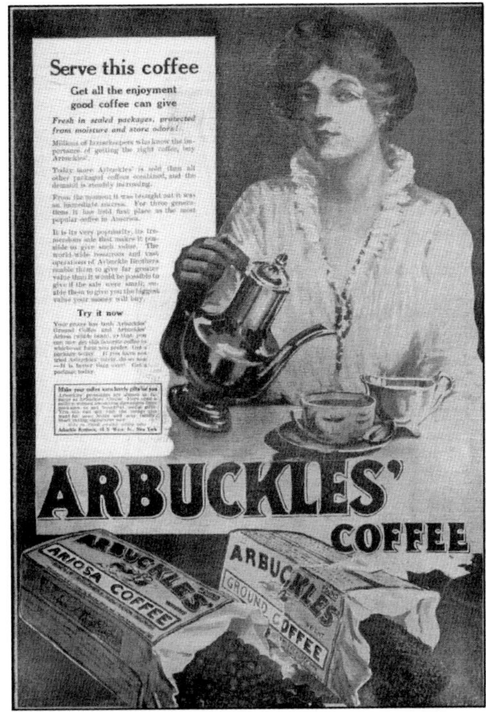

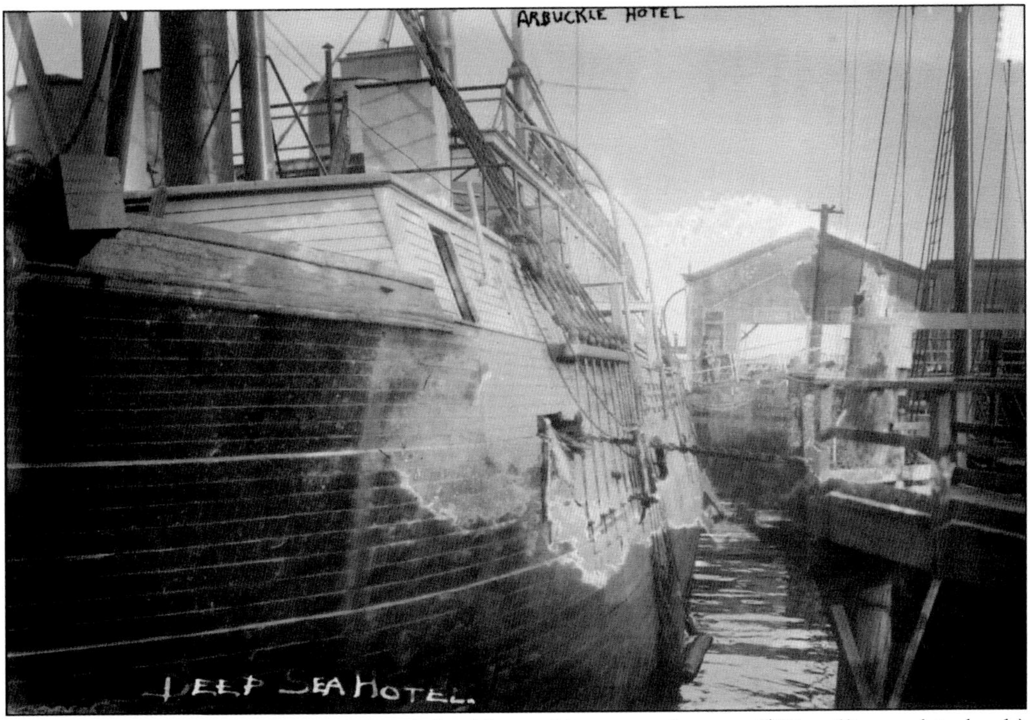

ARBUCKLE'S DEEP SEA HOTEL. John Arbuckle used his mega fortune ($33 million at his death) to give generously to the working poor, especially young women on their own. He furnished his own fully rigged ships as housing for "factory girls" and even took them for short sailing trips. (LOC.)

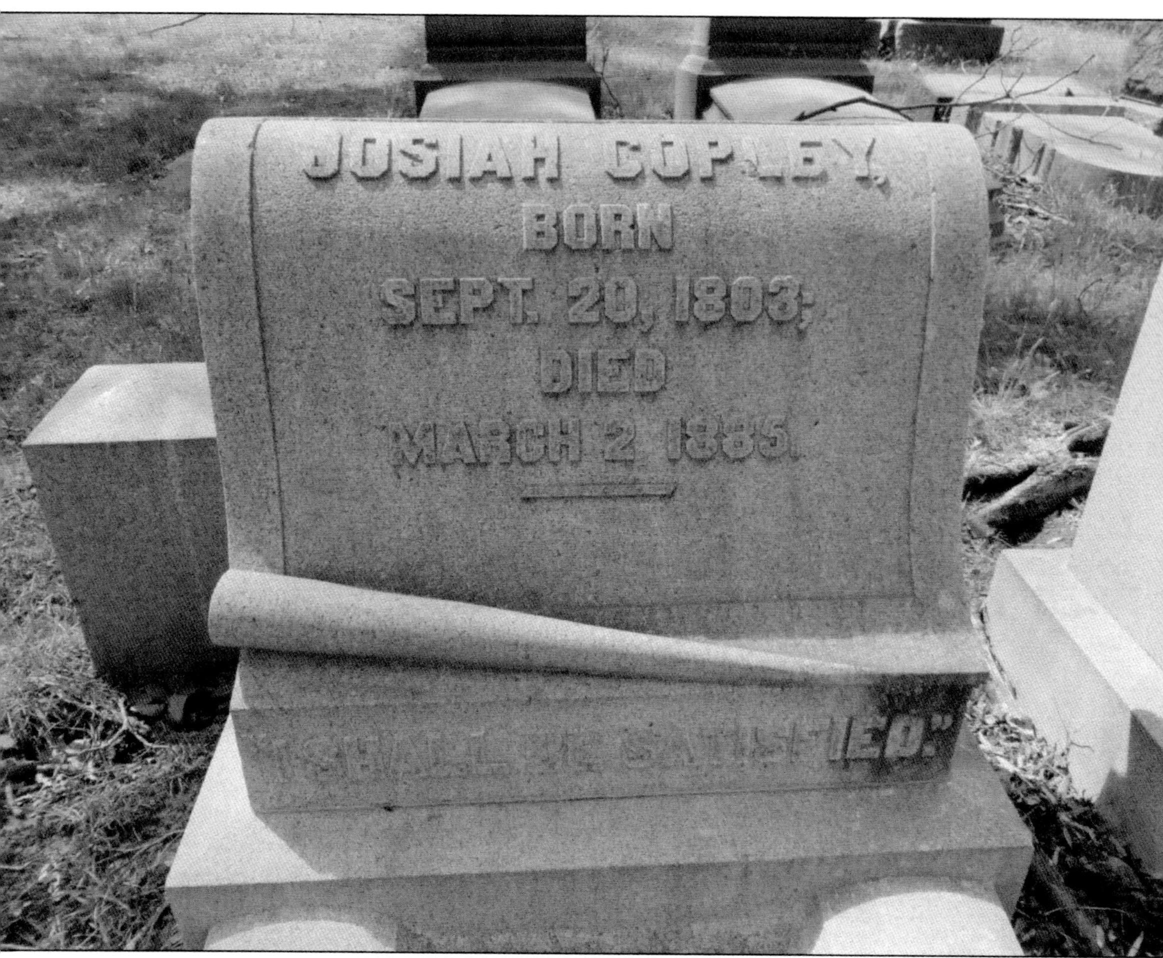

Josiah Copley (1803–1885; Section 24, Lot 38). A talented editor and writer, Josiah Copley founded the *Gazette* newspaper at Kittanning, where he lived until around 1860. He was also noted for his interests in horticulture and agriculture and owned an orchard cultivating fine fruits, apples, peaches, pears, and cherries while he continued his newspaper work with the *Pittsburgh Gazette*. Copley used this platform to advocate his abolitionist causes, in which he held a personal investment with four sons serving in the Civil War. Two of them would die on the battlefields. His daughter Mary Sibbet Copley eventually married William Thaw, producing offspring that included Harry Kendall Thaw. While Josiah Copley was well known for his business ventures, he was even better remembered for his upstanding moral character and prowess with a pen. It is said that he rarely had to correct a sentence—something that proved essential throughout his long journalistic career. (NF.)

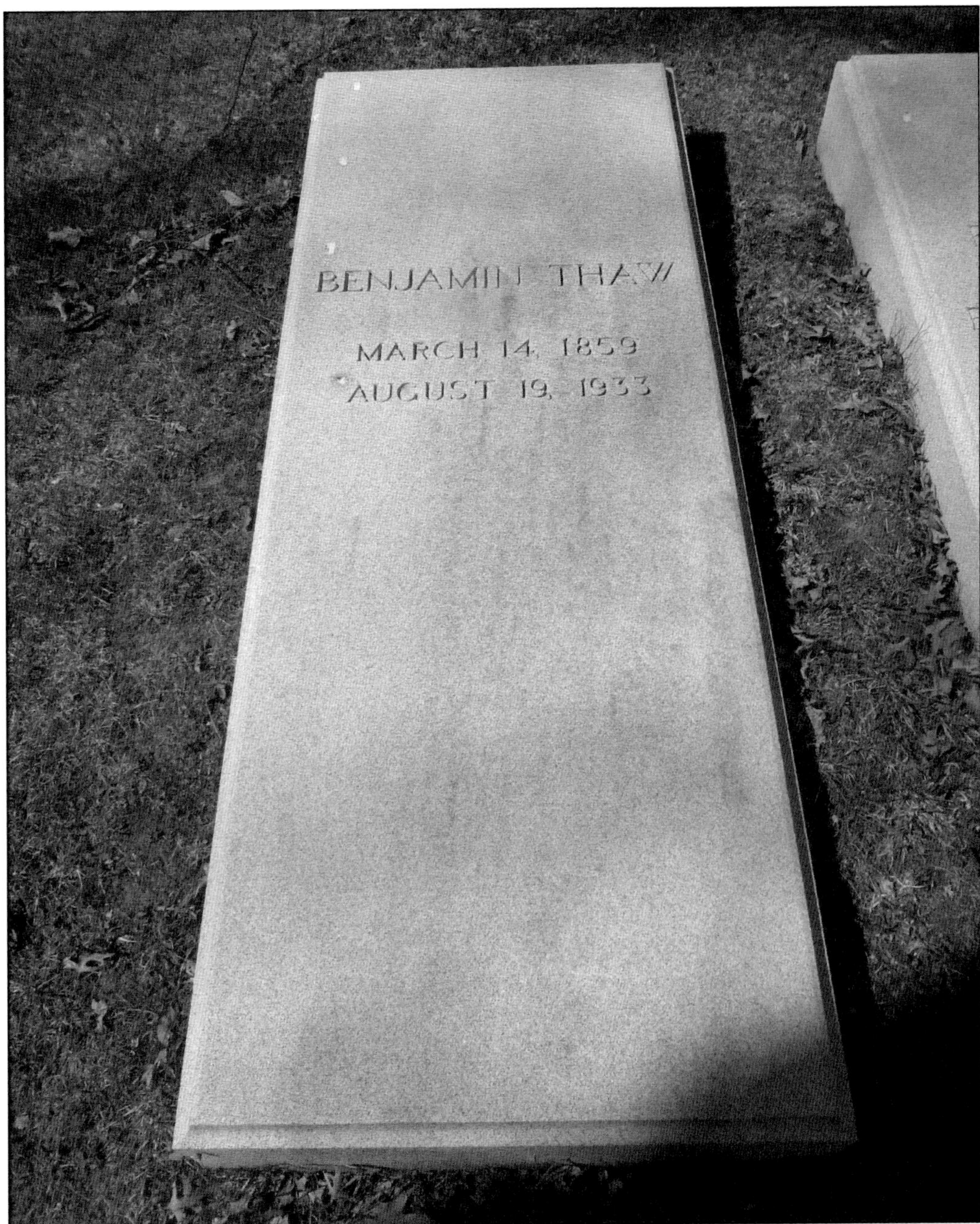

BENJAMIN THAW (1859–1933; SECTION 20, LOT 55). A wealthy banker and philanthropist, Benjamin Thaw provided a moral counterbalance for his family, given the infamous reputation of his half-brother Harry Kendall Thaw. Throughout his lifetime, Benjamin Thaw held many honors and offices, including director of the First National Bank, University of Pittsburgh trustee, and the Pennsylvania Historical Society. He served as treasurer of the YMCA board of trustees and was cofounder of the Heda Coke Company, which was later absorbed by Henry Clay Frick. In addition to these legacies, Benjamin Thaw may be most noted for the personal lineage he left behind. His two sons—Col. William Thaw (a World War I flying ace) and Lt. Alexander Blair Thaw (killed in action near St. Mihiel, France) were both well-known fighter pilots. (NF.)

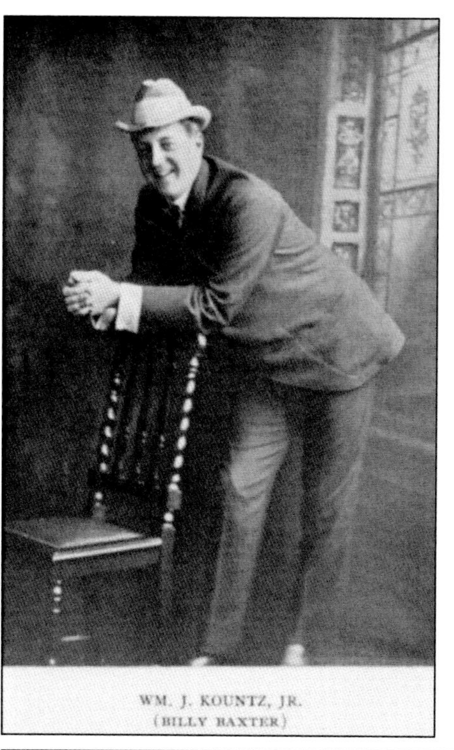

WILLIAM J. KOUNTZ JR. (1868–1899; SECTION 14, LOT 76). William Kountz had a way with words. He was a humorist, known for his short publication *Billy Baxters Letters*. Originally a promotion by the Duquesne Distributing Company, the book took a humorous approach to the mundane details of life in Pittsburgh on the eve of the 20th century, including tales of drunkenness and satire meant to lighten the mood of the reader. Kountz may have had a prolific career, but he sadly died at the young age of 32 from appendicitis. (Christopher Bailey.)

SAMUEL DIESCHER (1839–1915; SECTION 28, LOT 183). Born in Budapest in 1839, engineer Samuel Diescher immigrated to the United States in 1866. Arriving in Cincinnati, he built one of the first inclines in that area. He soon partnered with Pittsburgh engineer John Endres. They formed both a professional and personal relationship, which culminated in Diescher marrying Endres's daughter Caroline. The Dieschers both designed the Duquesne Incline. Diescher also built numerous other inclines, including the Johnstown Inclined Plane (pictured here) and the mechanics for the 1893 World's Columbian Exposition Ferris wheel. (LOC.)

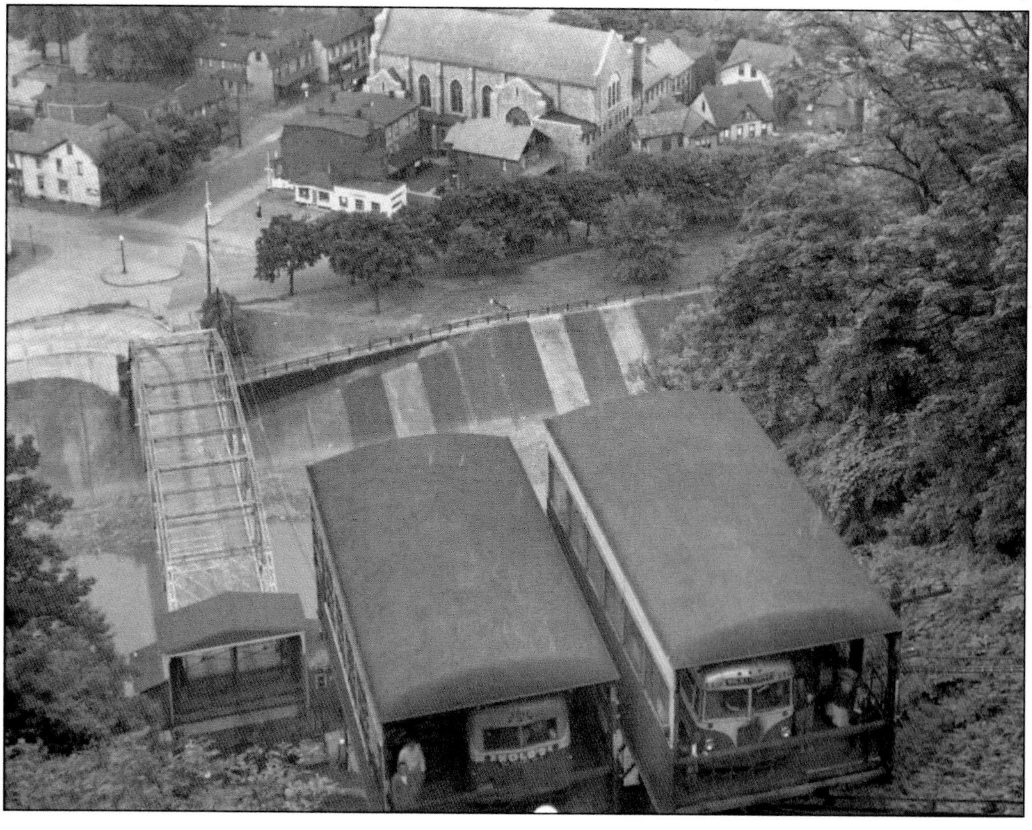

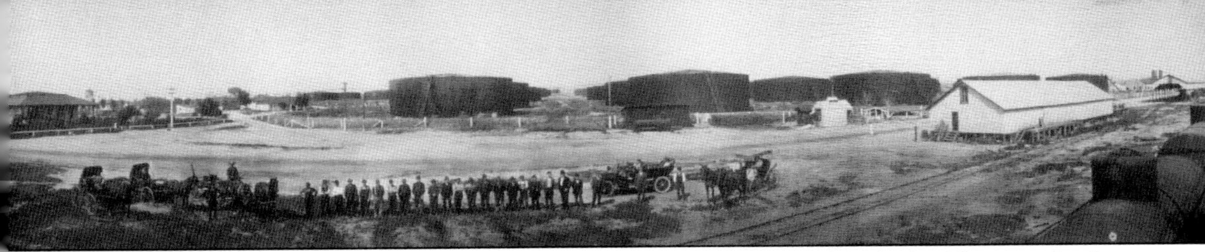

Jacob Jay Vandergrift (1827–1899; Section 8.5, Lot 24). Responsible for building much of the city that still bears his name, Vandergrift was an oil industrialist who held many prominent positions throughout his lifetime. He founded the United Pipe Line Company, Imperial Refinery, Forrest Oil Company, Prairie Oil, Union Tank Car Company, United Oil & Gas Trust, Washington Oil Company, and Oil City Trust Company. Shown here are Standard Oil tanks in Bakersfield, California, around 1910. (LOC.)

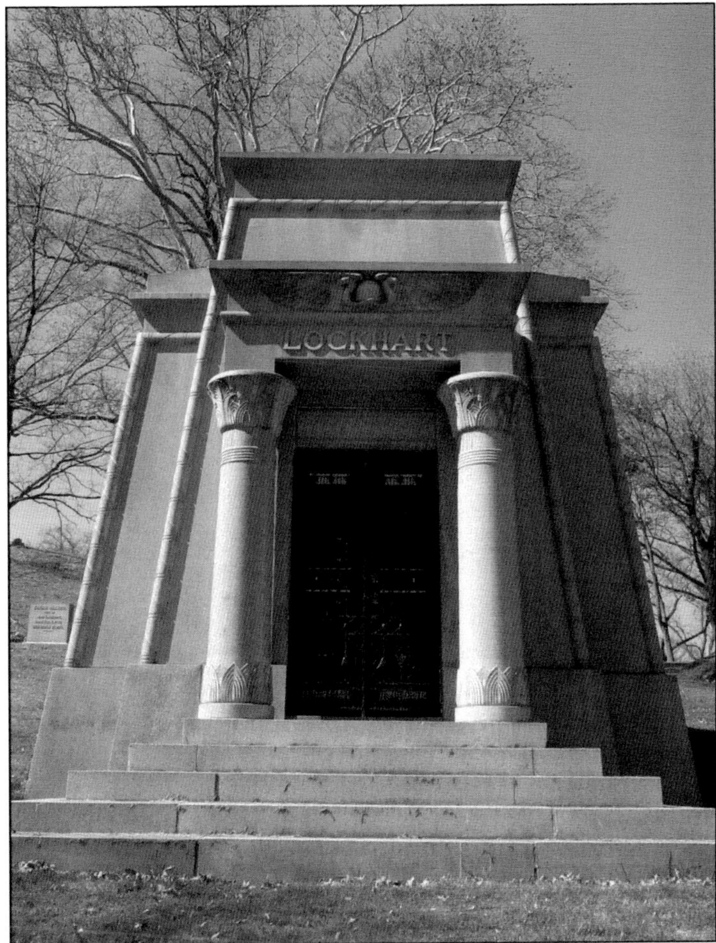

Charles Lockhart (1818–1905; Section 20, Private Mausoleum). Charles Lockhart emigrated from Scotland as a teenager and lived a long and prosperous life in America. Lockhart, Frew & Co. was a petroleum concern that shipped crude oil to Samuel Kier's refinery—the nation's first. Lockhart partnered with John D. Rockefeller in 1868 and by 1874, Lockhart, Frew & Co. had merged with Standard Oil, with Lockhart serving as director of the Pittsburgh branch. The Lockhart estate was located where Pittsburgh Theological Seminary now stands. (NF)

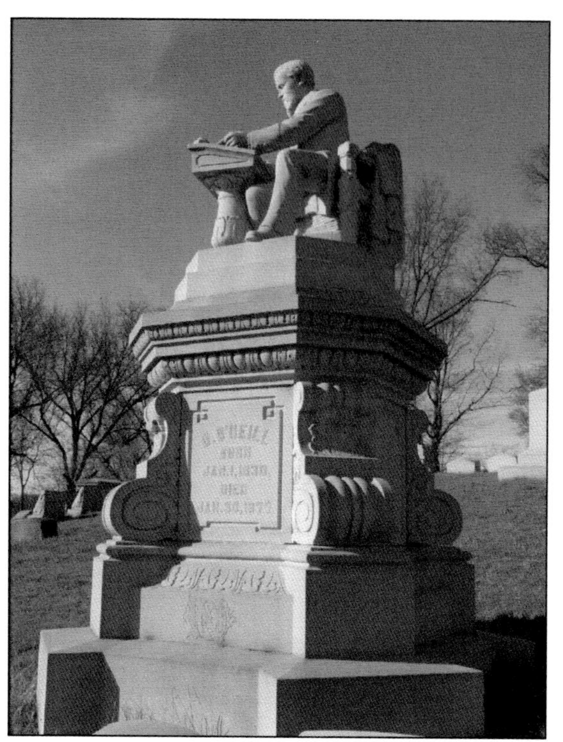

Daniel O'Neill and Alexander Rook (Section 8.5, Lot 27). As co-owners of the *Pittsburg Dispatch*, O'Neill's experience as a writer kept him in touch with the interests of the public, while Rook's experience as a printer kept their paper profitable. The *Dispatch* was a famous name in news, especially when it came to their young female journalist, Elizabeth Cochrane, whose pen name was Nelly Bly. The late reporter himself is immortalized with a stone figure in his likeness, still working at his desk, bent to the task at hand. Immediately to the right, Rook's soaring column is topped with a female figure and tablet. (NF.)

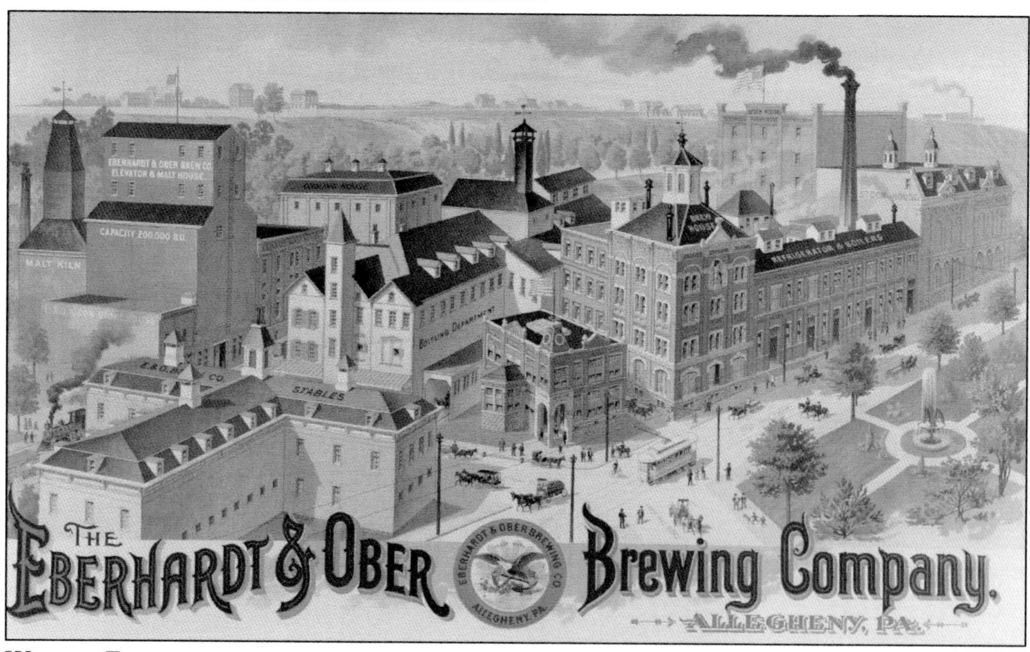

William Eberhardt and John Ober (Section 14, Lots 124 and 125). These brothers-in-law established the E&O Brewery, today's Penn Brewery. E&O beer was brewed strictly according to the German beer purity law established in the 1500s. Their familial bond is reflected in their neighboring mausoleums, which are similar in size and character. Both men used their wealth to give freely to public institutions and were remembered for their congenial kindness and jolly nature. (Case Antiques Inc.)

CHARLES FLACCUS (D. 1917; SECTION 28, LOT 287). Charles Flaccus established a glass-bottling company in 1879, which became one of the largest in the United States from the 1800s to the 1900s. Additionally, he held the first patent for glass bottles manufactured by machinery. In 1905, he built Red Gables Farm, a sprawling 100-acre estate which, though empty, still stands in Fox Chapel today. The Flaccus family was known in the equestrian community, and a 20-horse stable once stood on the property. (AC.)

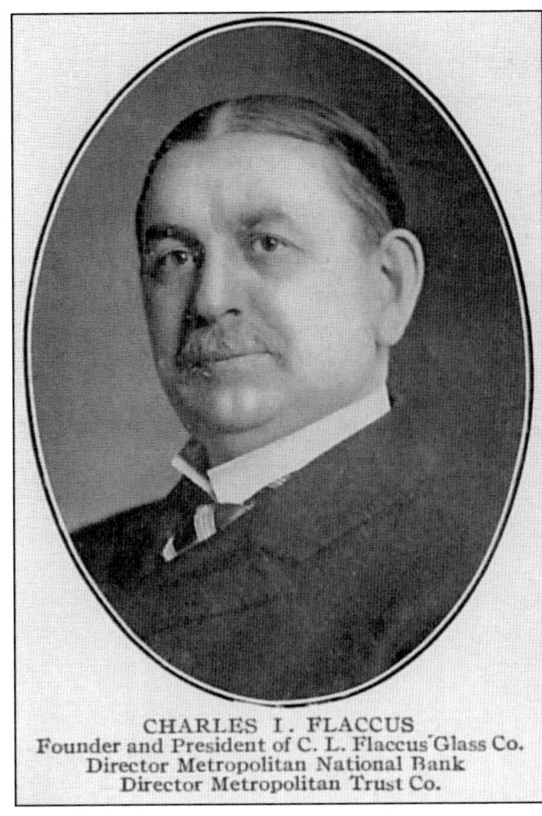

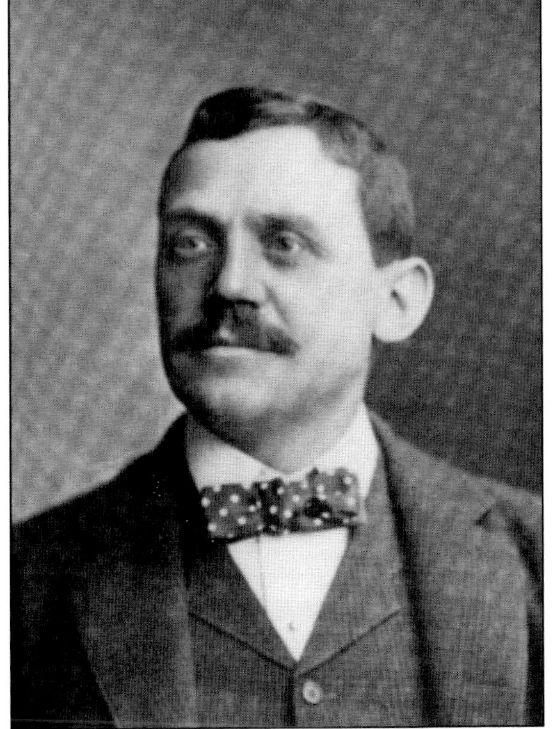

DAVID LINDSAY GILLESPIE (1858–1926; SECTION 28, LOT 177). Gillespie began his career with Western Union's telegraph office, later taking a position in his father's mill. For decades, he worked in some of Pittsburgh's best industries, including steel (Lewis, Oliver & Phillips) and gas (Westinghouse). In 1886, he followed in his father's footsteps by pursuing the lumber business. Seventeen of New York's initial skyscrapers were built using lumber from his mills. In its initial year, the company processed less than three million feet of lumber. Within 15 years, that output multiplied to more than 70 million feet. (AC.)

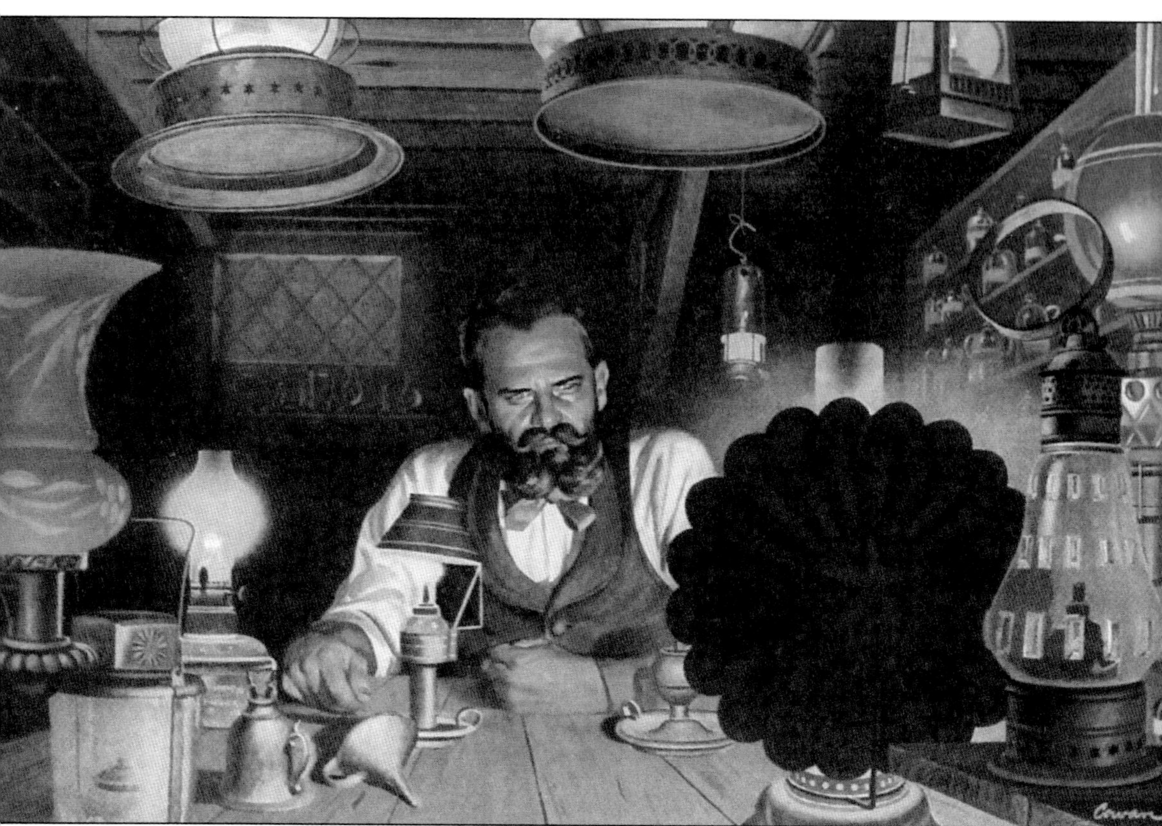

Samuel Kier (1813–1874; Section 25, Lot 57). "The Father of the American Petroleum Industry," Kier was the owner and inventor of the world's first oil refinery, right here in Pittsburgh. His discovery of crude oil was accidental, when a then-unknown substance bubbled up in his father's Tarentum, Pennsylvania, salt mine. Kier originally sold the oil as a miracle elixir, marketing it from red and gold wagons and giving presentations on its "miraculous" properties throughout the region. While it sold, it did not actually cure anything, and Kier was soon left with barrels of the goop on his hands. A mine worker's discarded match later proved the material to be flammable, and Kier set upon inventing a process to refine his "rock oil" to be burnt for light and warmth without the caustic smoke. He did not patent the method, however, believing that no one man should hold title to a process that benefitted so many. (AC.)

Five

Patriots

Each Memorial Day, a silent sea of flags gently waving among the rolling hills of Allegheny Cemetery serves as a palpable reminder. Truly, there are few places as hallowed as these grounds with respect to the debt of gratitude owed to over 12,000 veterans at rest here. These citizen soldiers rose to the occasion during every American conflict and even those prior to the birth of this nation. They repulsed the British and called themselves the first Americans. Their grandsons fought brother to brother in a Civil War whose scars are yet to heal, while newly freed slaves in the United States Colored Troops used their first moments of emancipation to maintain a nation in peril of extinction. They famously refused to give up the ship on Lake Erie in the Battle of 1812. They saw the world through gas masks, tucked in trenches under a constant threat of annihilation in the "War to End All Wars." They fought in the air, came by sea, and stormed foreign shores on foot in World War II, moving hedgerow to hedgerow, house to house, to liberate Europe from the grasp of tyranny. They fought a foe they could not see and yearned for home while in Korea and Vietnam. They sought justice for the murder of innocents after September 11, 2001, and they did it all without complaint. Those who returned home were not always whole—visibly or otherwise. Many of the men who did return home served their county in civic capacities as well; however, they were patriots first and citizens second. Thousands of their fellow countrymen are not mentioned specifically in this text. Whether called by name or not, this chapter is dedicated to each and every one of America's service men and women, their families, loved ones, and descendants. They represent the very best of us, and may their memory be a torch ever burning.

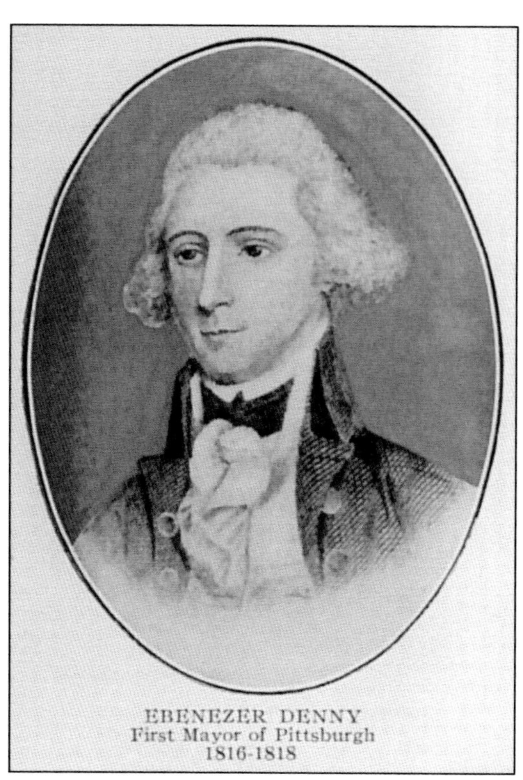

Ebenezer Denny (1761–1822; Section 11, Lot 6). A native of Carlisle, Pennsylvania, Denny crossed the Allegheny Mountains alone at age 13 through hostile Indian territory in order to relay messages to Fort Pitt. His Revolutionary War journal describes serving alongside George Washington and the surrender of the British at Yorktown. At war's end, he acquired land, married, and began a family. He aided in several Indian campaigns and at Lake Erie in the War of 1812. His status as a local hero made him a natural choice for Pittsburgh's first mayor when the city was incorporated in 1816. (AC.)

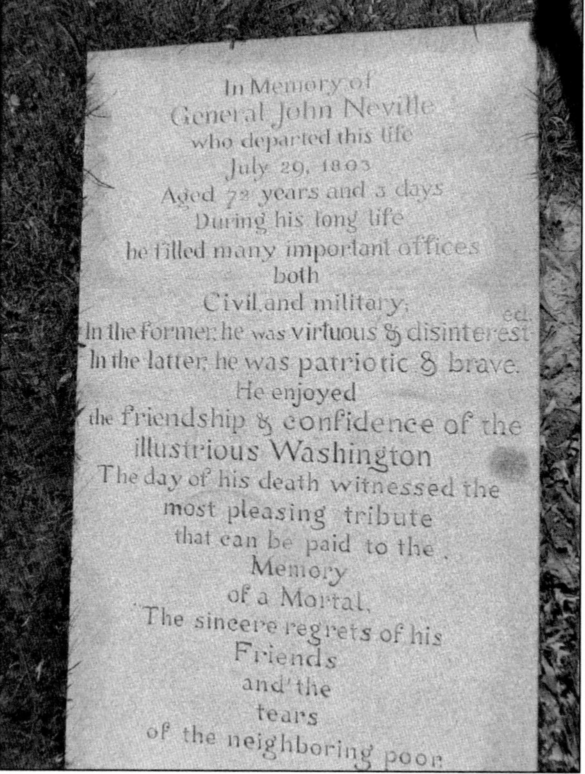

Gen. John Neville (1731–1803; Section 11, Lot 21). At 18, Neville served alongside George Washington in the French and Indian War. His Revolutionary War service includes action at Trenton, Princeton, and the notorious winter at Valley Forge. Today, he is widely remembered for his role in the Whiskey Rebellion as the region's tax collector and, thus, a natural target of the fatal uprising. In July 1794, five hundred irate farmers stormed Neville's Bower Hill estate, burning it to the ground. Neville relocated and built Woodville Plantation in present-day Collier Township, where it still stands. (NF.)

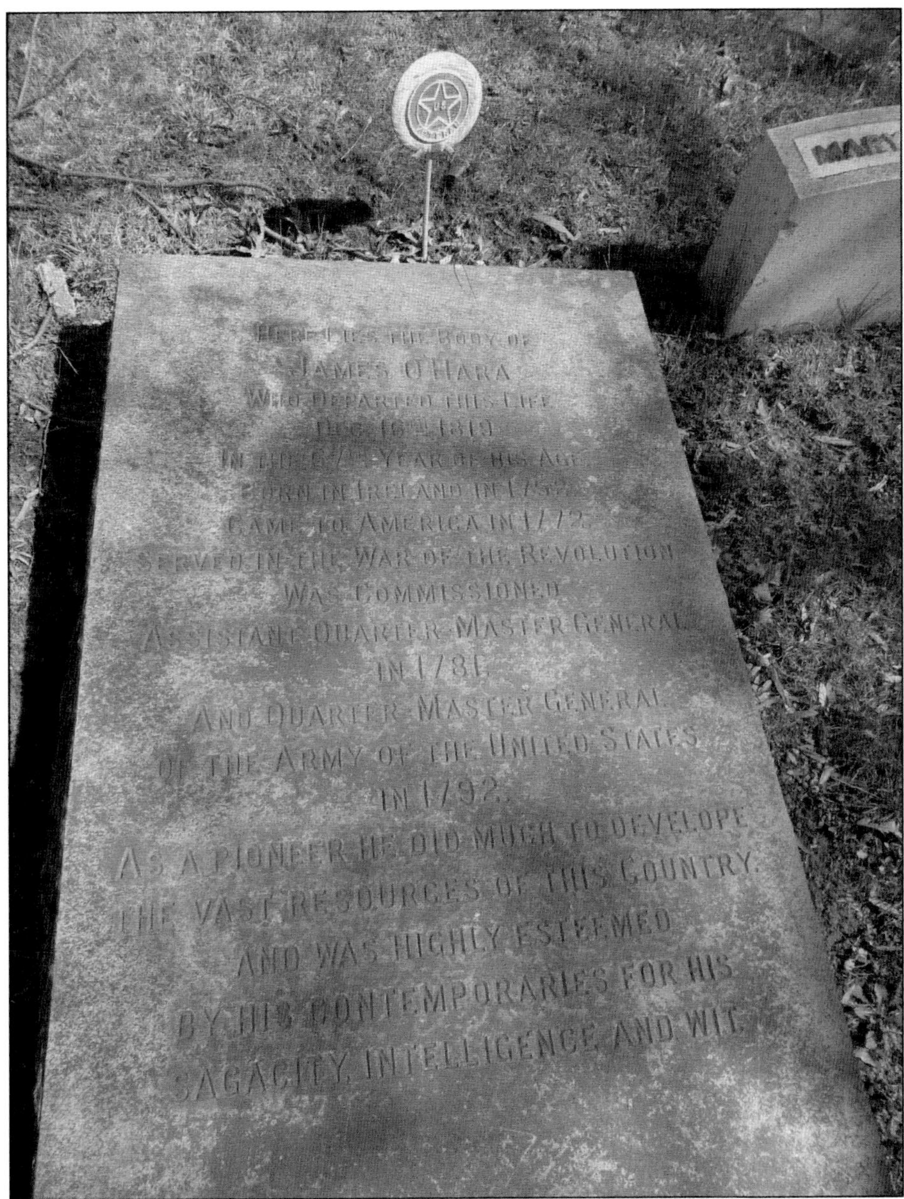

JAMES O'HARA (1752–1819; SECTION 11, LOT 6). Born in Ireland, O'Hara traveled to Pittsburgh as a frontier Indian trader, using his knowledge of French to communicate with natives and learn their dialect in turn. When the Revolutionary War came, Washington appointed him quartermaster general, and he served at Fort Pitt and Fort Kanawha in present-day West Virginia. He settled in Pittsburgh after the war and set about becoming one of the largest landowners in the region, including most of the downtown area and the Point. He resided there in a handsome log home built for his bride, Mary Carson, on a hill overlooking the three rivers, amid a splendid 60-acre orchard originally planted by loyalists in the name of the king. His daughters married into the familiar pioneer families of Croghan and Denny and, in the next generation, Schenley. In 1797, O'Hara established Pittsburgh's first glassworks with a fellow veteran, Isaac Craig. The O'Hara fortune grew exponentially, and their joined families established several country estates where famous guests were entertained in lavish comfort. (NF.)

Beneath this stone are deposited
the mortal remains of
Major ISAAC CRAIG
a soldier of the revolution who served his country faithfully by sea and by land from the first call to arms to the close of the struggle for independence.
Born near Hillsborough in Ireland A.D. 1741 emigrated to America in 1768 and died on Montour's Island near Pittsburgh on the 14th day of May 1826. Having earned and enjoyed the reputation of an honest man, a useful citizen, a kind husband and an affectionate parent.

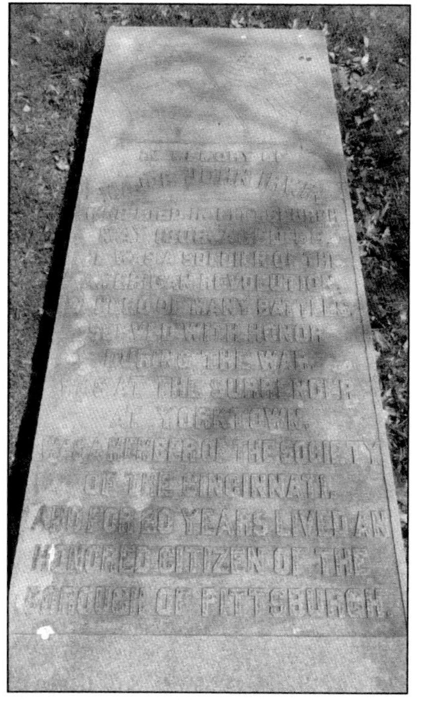

Maj. Isaac Craig, Quartermaster General (1741–1826; Section 11, Lot 21). A native of Ireland, Craig enlisted in the Continental Army, crossed the Delaware with Washington, and fought at Princeton, Trenton, and Brandywine. Afterward, Craig was sent to Fort Pitt to guard the frontier and became one of the first two men to purchase land from William Penn. As owner of the Point, Craig traded with the Indians and built a sawmill, distillery, saltworks, and later a glassworks with James O'Hara. Craig married Amelia Neville, daughter of General Neville, and raised their family on Neville Island. (NF.)

John Irwin (1752–1808; Section 11, Lot 40). Enlisting in the cause of freedom in 1776, Irwin served as lieutenant under the infamous traitor Benedict Arnold and then as an adjutant officer under Gen. "Mad" Anthony Wayne. Irwin was among the wounded who were slaughtered by the British in the Paoli Massacre. Repeated stabs by bayonet were assumed to have killed the grievously mangled Irwin, who survived, recovered under the care of Washington's personal staff, and witnessed the British surrender at Yorktown. (NF.)

Dr. Felix Brunot (1752–1838; Section 13, Lots 42 and 43). Brunot was raised in the estate shown here as the foster brother of the famed Marquis de Lafayette. The brothers traveled to the colonies to serve under Washington, with Brunot serving as a surgeon in Lafayette's expeditionary force. After the war, he married and raised his family of six sons on Brunot's Island, a 300-acre estate where he made his own medicines and entertained many famous people, including Lewis and Clark on their journey west. The Brunot mansion in Allegheny City (North Side) was designed for use in the Underground Railroad. (LOC.)

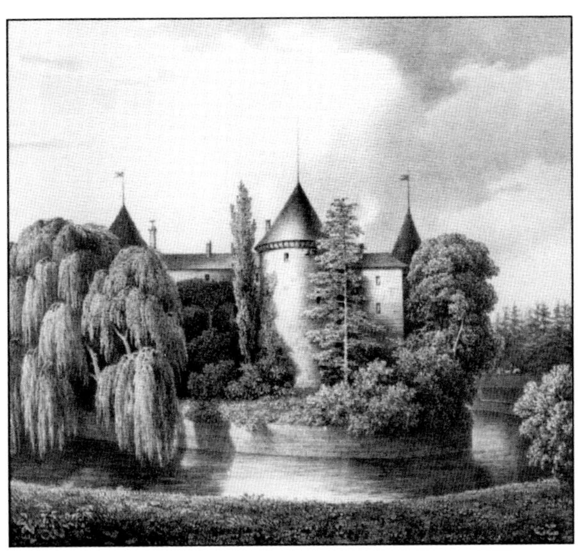

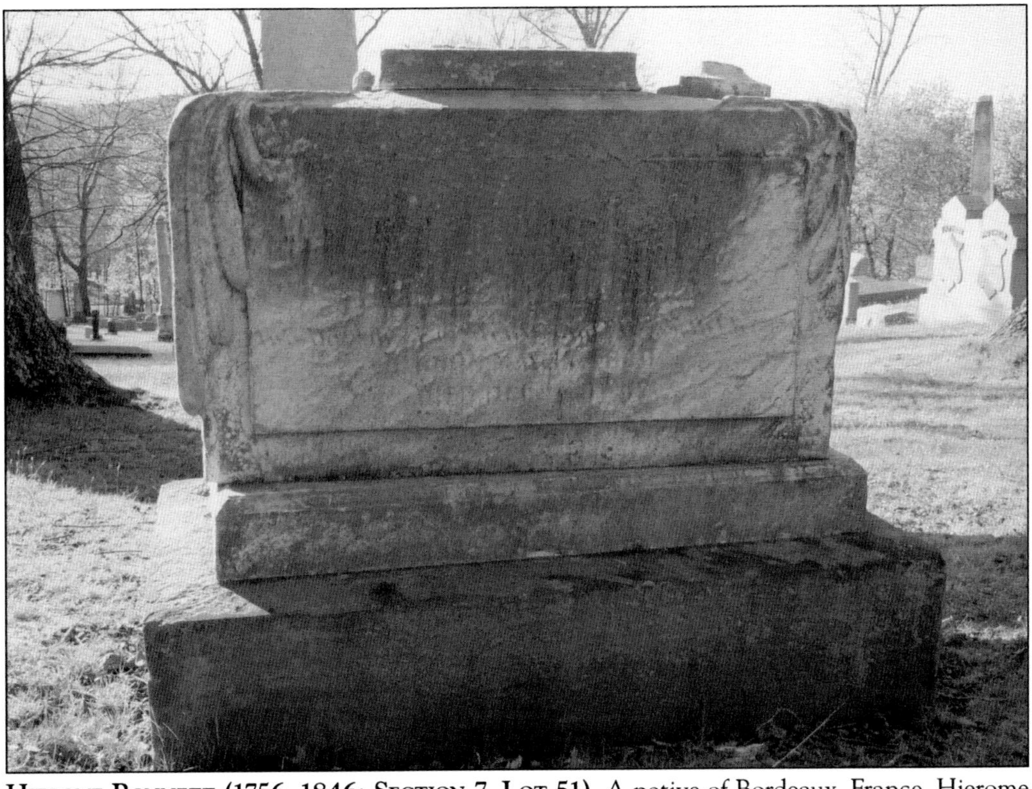

Hierome Bonnett (1756–1846; Section 7, Lot 51). A native of Bordeaux, France, Hierome Bonnett was dedicated in both his military service and patriotism. When he died in 1846, his obituary noted that "he came to the United States in the suite of Lafayette, and was one of the brave band who gave their services in the cause of American Liberty." Active in battles such as Germantown, at the conclusion of the fighting, Bonnett made Pittsburgh home and became a successful merchant in the city for many years. (NF.)

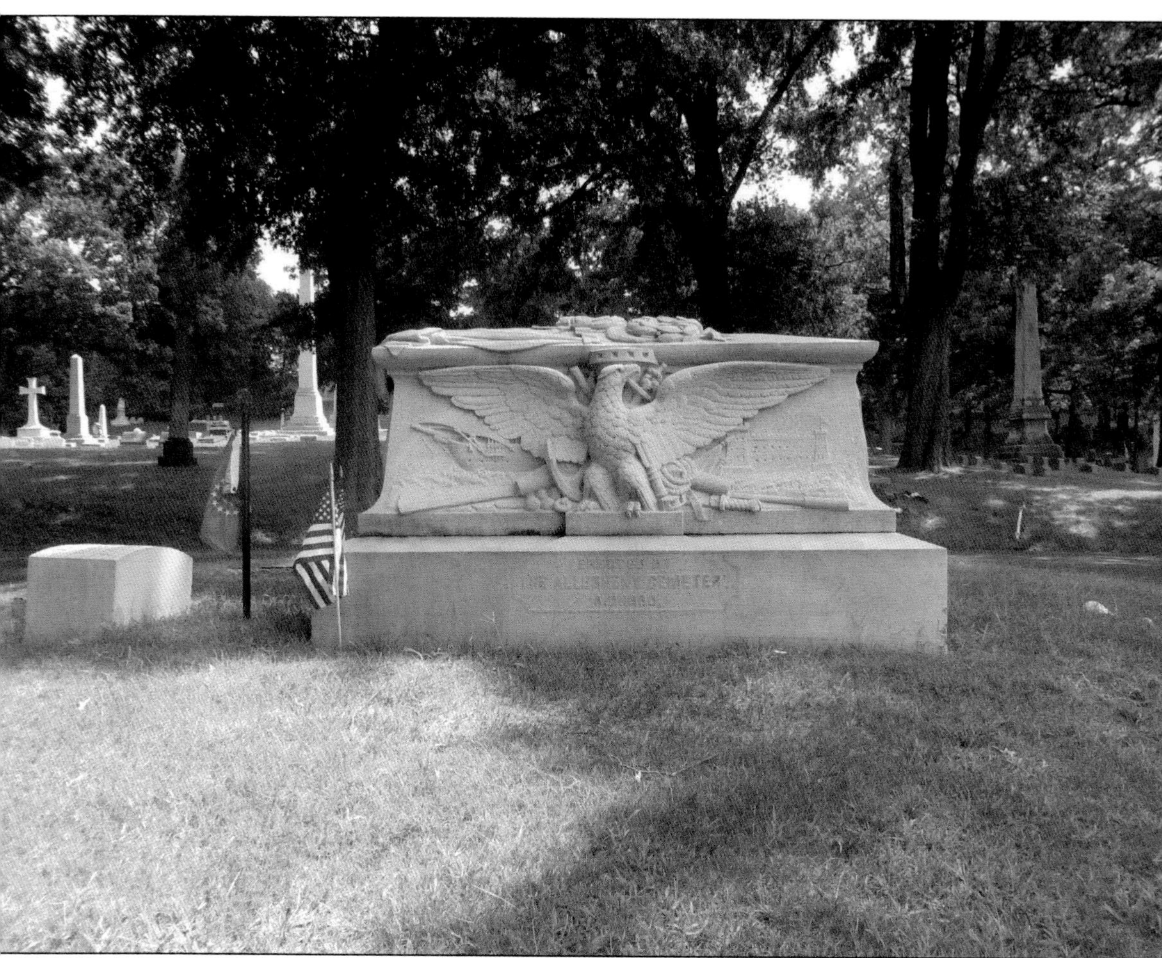

Commodore Joshua Barney (1759–1818; Section 8.5, Lot 1). Navigating a vessel by age 16 and participating in the capture of British stores by age 17, it seems that Commodore Barney was destined for great things. Awarded the rank of lieutenant for gallantry in action, he was taken prisoner and released on no fewer than four separate occasions. In 1794, he entered into the service of the French government, which gave him a captain's commission and command of a squadron. Years later, he returned to America and in 1814 was called to defend Washington. He was severely wounded and taken prisoner during the Battle of Bladensburg, which left shrapnel in his thigh that was never removed. In 1818, he was on his way through Pittsburgh to his newly purchased farm in Kentucky when he was suddenly taken ill and died. He was buried in Pittsburgh and was moved to Allegheny Cemetery in 1848. (NF.)

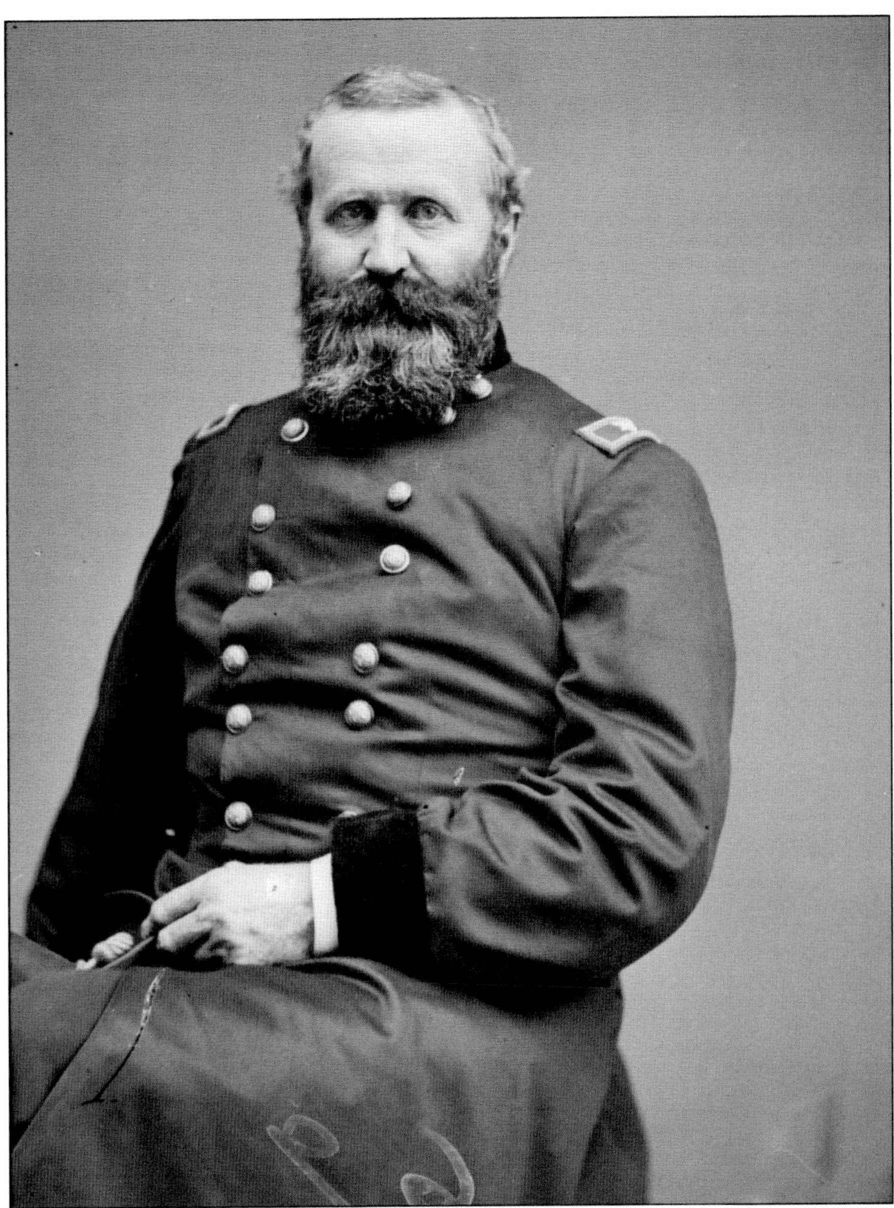

Gen. Alexander Hays (d. May 5, 1864; Section 8, Lot 149). Hays was educated at West Point, where he became a close personal friend of Ulysses S. Grant. Promoted twice for gallantry in the Civil War, Hays was severely injured at Second Bull Run and was largely responsible for repulsing Pickett's charge at Gettysburg, where a prominent bronze statue now stands in his honor. Nicknamed "Fighting Elleck," the fiery, red-haired warrior chose to fight alongside his men, often cheering and swearing oaths in the midst of the fury and once dragging a captured Confederate flag through the mud while riding down the front line. While he was encouraging troops at the Battle of the Wilderness, a sniper's bullet found his head, killing him instantly. On the day of his funeral, businesses closed, the streets filled with people, and cannon fire sounded from the hills. During his 1869 presidential visit to the city, Grant personally requested to be taken to the grave of his fallen comrade. After once circling the monument in contemplative silence, he sat upon an inverted cannon and openly wept. (LOC.)

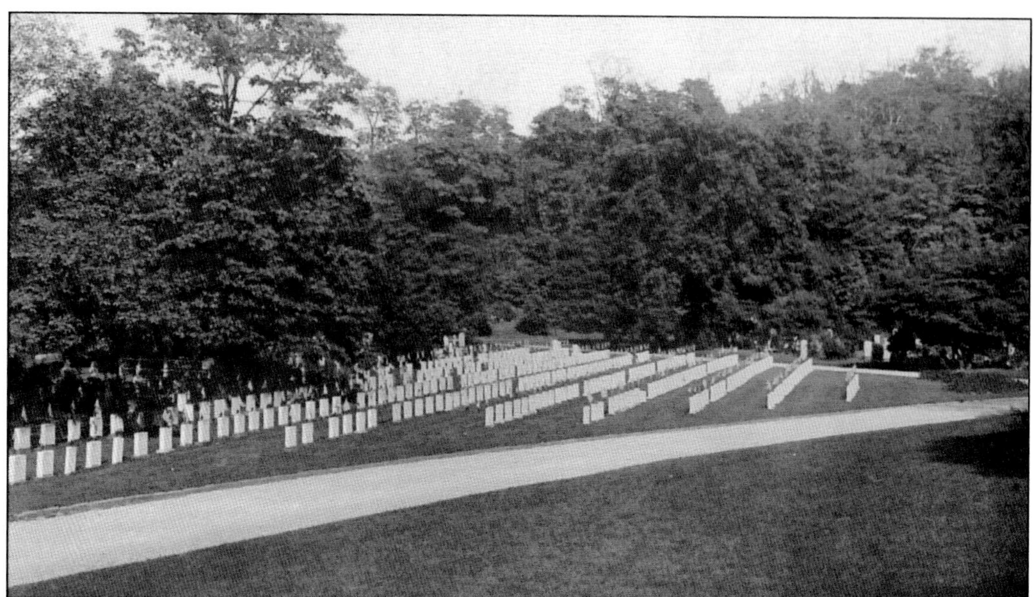

Grand Army of the Republic Lots (Sections 33 and 35, Lots 1, 65, 231, and 232). The Grand Army of the Republic, or GAR, was an organization of Union veterans who met regularly, held fundraising galas to benefit survivors and their families, and also made plans for proper burial and memorialization of departed comrades. Upon request, Allegheny Cemetery donated lots set apart just for them, as time and space required, in recognition of the debt of gratitude owed by all citizens of the United States. (AC.)

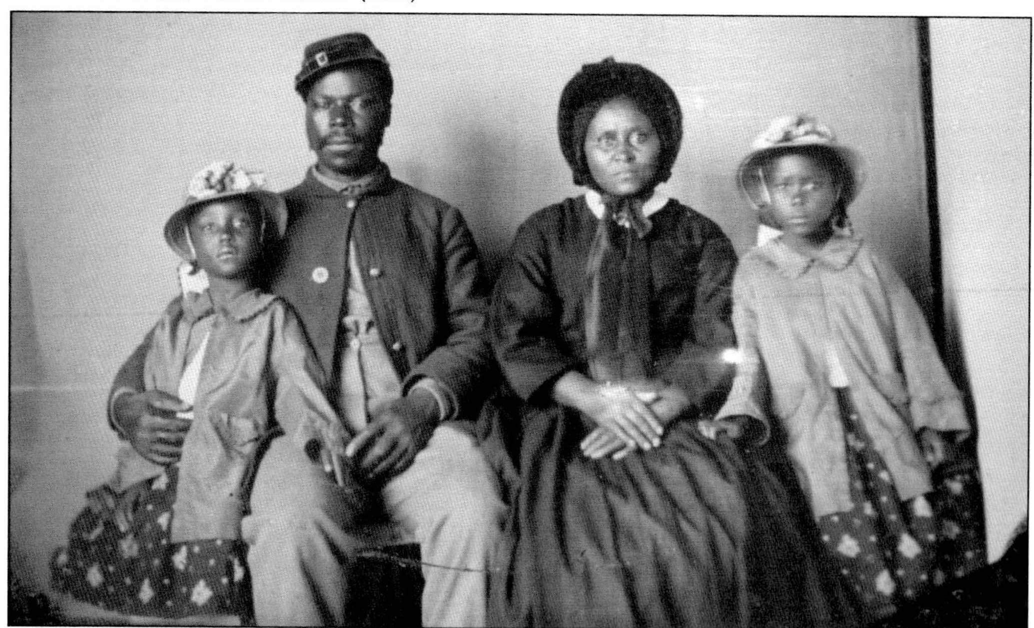

United States Colored Troops (Section 33, Lots 231 and 232). Most of these soldiers were former slaves who enlisted in the cause of the Union following the January 1, 1863, Emancipation Proclamation. Men who would rather die free than live enslaved fought and fell alongside their white brethren and are buried shoulder to shoulder with them as members of the Grand Army of the Republic. Over 140 United States Colored Troops rest at Allegheny. (LOC.)

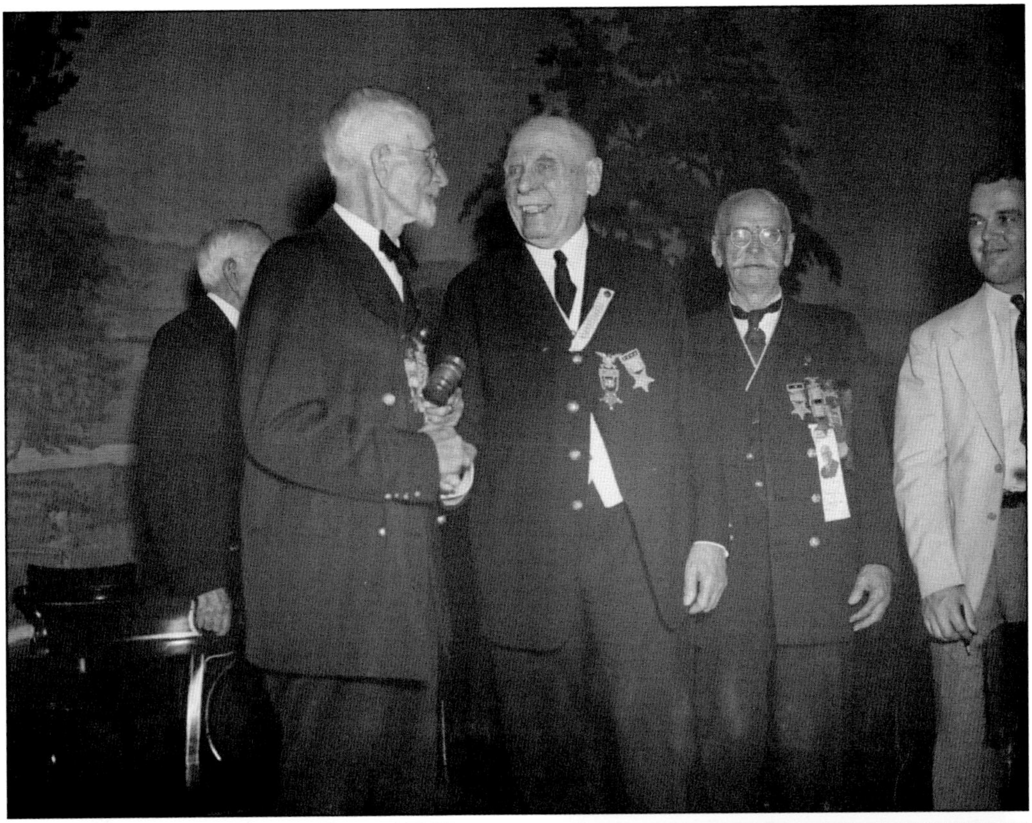

Gen. Carl Henry William Ruhe (1849–1942; Section 34, Soldiers Memorial). General Ruhe was 87 years old when he was elected commander in chief of the Grand Army of the Republic. Prior to that, he served with the 4th Pennsylvania Cavalry. The regiment was active from October 1861 to June 1865 and saw 98 men killed or mortally wounded while another 260 died from disease. The unit was commanded by Col. James Childs beginning in 1862 and served in places such as Fredericksburg, Gaines Mill, and Antietam. (LOC.)

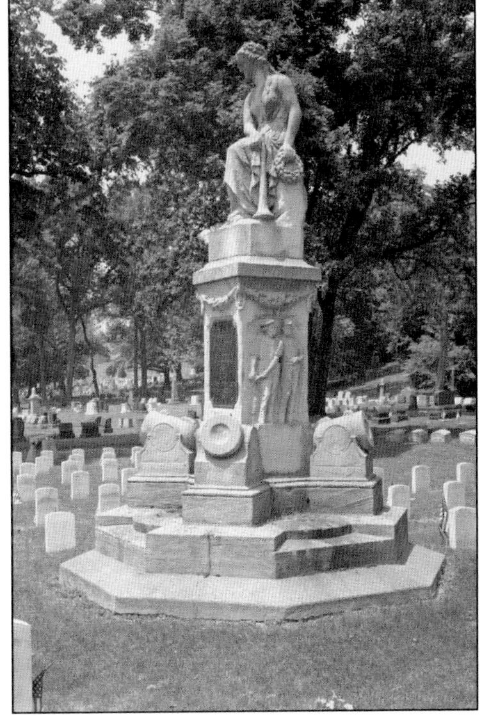

Civil War National Cemetery (Section 33, Lot 66). This lot, which contains the graves of 298 Union and 5 Confederate soldiers, was donated in 1862, upon request, to the government of the United States for veterans of the Civil War. Two authentic, combat-worn Union cannons are mounted at the head of this lot. A seated female figure in sandstone was commissioned and placed in 1876 by the Ladies' Monumental Association of Allegheny County and features reliefs of soldiers from both sides of the conflict and an inscription (AC.)

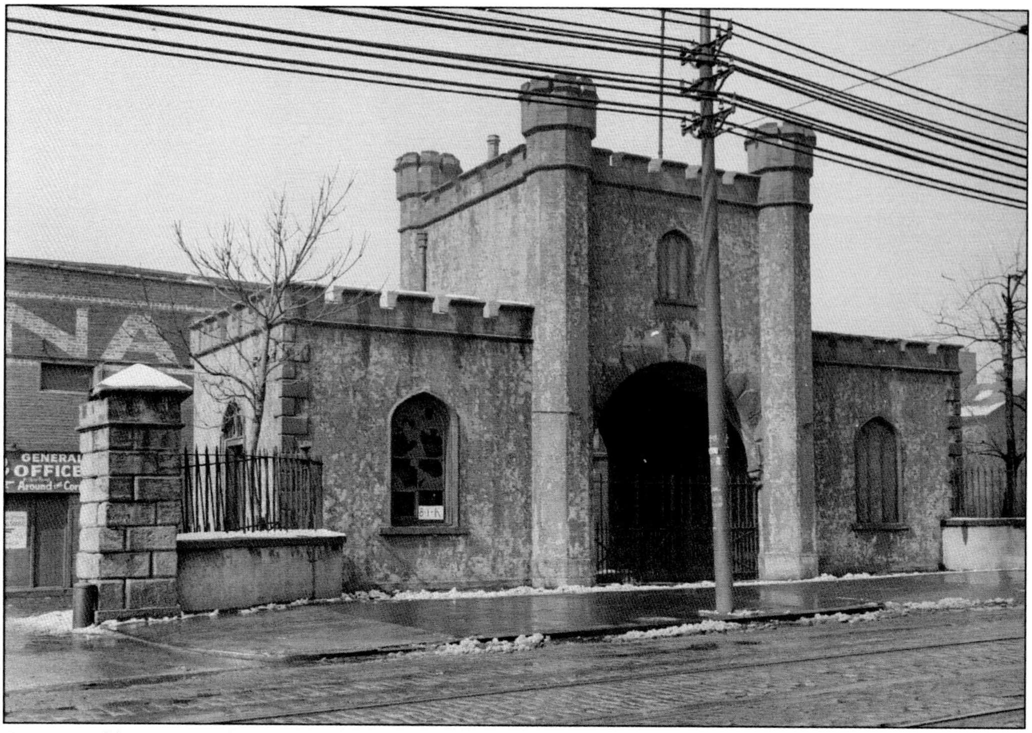

ARSENAL EXPLOSION MONUMENT. September 17, 1862, is marked in history with more blood and tears than most. At Antietam, nearly 23,000 casualties were suffered in a single day. That same day, the greatest civilian casualty of the Civil War unfolded at Pittsburgh's Allegheny Arsenal (shown here). Explosions rocked the arsenal, with nearly all victims being women or children, unidentifiable due to their injuries. The incident was likely caused by a horseshoe spark igniting gunpowder between the cobblestones. Allegheny Cemetery addressed the immediate need, donating the land in which 45 of the 78 victims now rest. (LOC.)

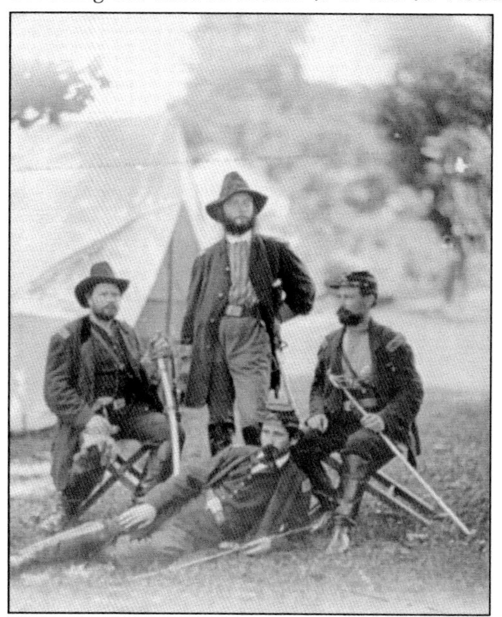

COL. JAMES HARVEY CHILDS (1834–1862; SECTION 20, LOT 1). Colonel Childs fell in the line of duty in the Battle of Antietam when a cannonball struck his right hip, knocking him from his horse and disemboweling him. His last conscious moments were spent reorganizing command of his men and imparting these final words to his eldest son, "Tell Howe to be a good boy, and a good man, and true to his country." The Howe-Childs family estate still stands on Fifth Avenue. Restored by Chatham University, it is the oldest surviving home along Pittsburgh's Millionaire's Row. (LOC.)

Archibaold Rowand Jr. (1845–1913; Section 23, Lot 62). "Arch" was a teenager when he served as a spy for the Union army, delivering information on enemy ordnance and strength directly to Gen. Ulysses S. Grant. A soldier of the 1st West Virginia Cavalry, Rowand was a member of Jessie's Scouts, an elite group of Yankees who would dress in disguise, infiltrate enemy camps, and relay intelligence to fellow spies in code. Under threat of execution should he be discovered, Rowand managed to succeed in every mission, earning him a Congressional Medal of Honor from General Sheridan. (AC.)

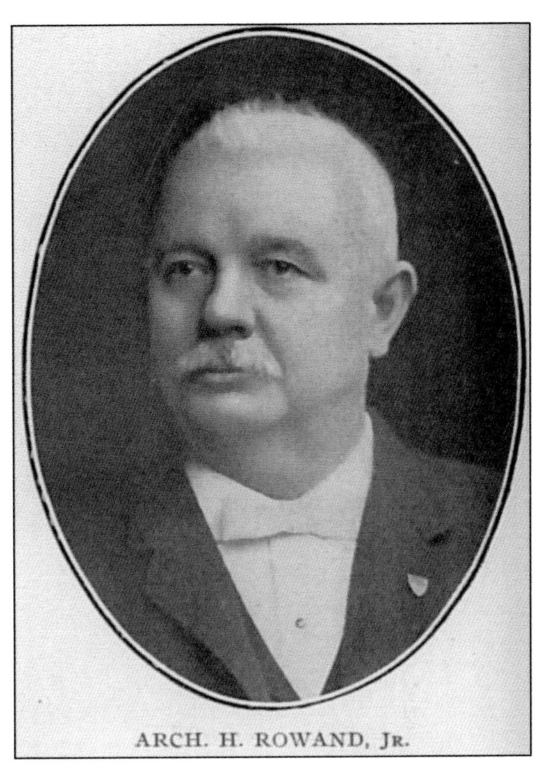

ARCH. H. ROWAND, JR.

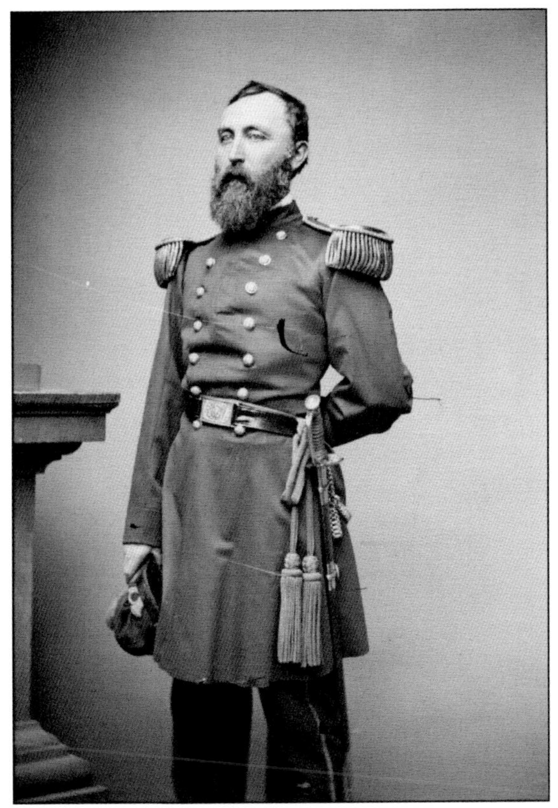

Civil War Generals. Allegheny's Civil War heritage has been nationally recognized, though regionally, many of these soldier's names have become local legend. Eight known Civil War generals rest in these hallowed grounds—Frederick H. Collier (Section 29, Lot 32), Alexander Hays (see page 55), Conrad Feger Jackson (Section 31, Lot 70), James Scott Negley (Section 19, Lot 23), Alfred L. Pearson (Section 2, Lot 70), Thomas A. Rowley (Section 7, Lot 102), David Henry Williams (Section 16, Lot 5), and Jacob Bowman Sweitzer (Section 14, Lot 10, pictured here). (LOC.)

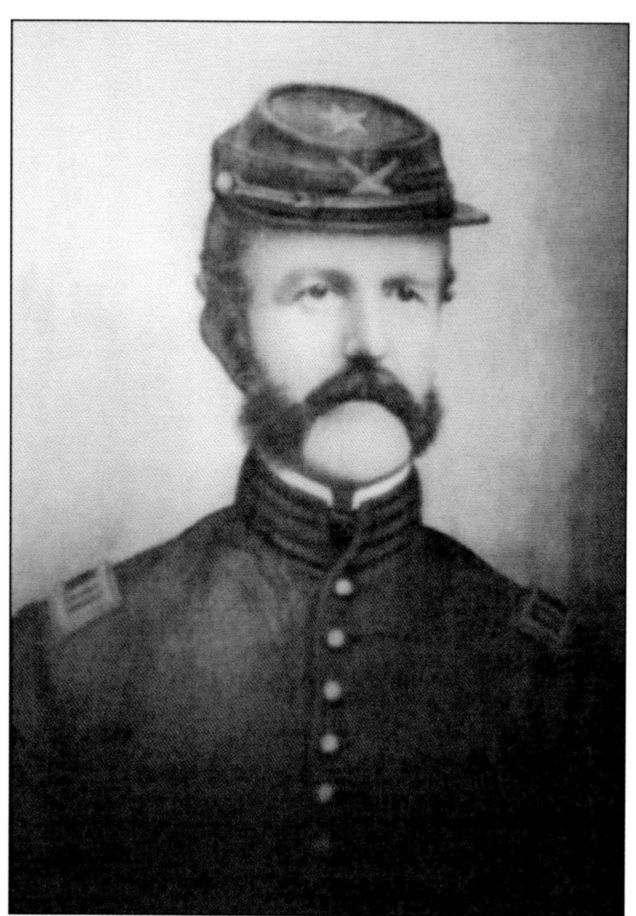

Capt. Robert B. Hampton (1814–1863; Section 14, Lot 91). Captain Hampton's devotion to public service was borne of the lawlessness during the California Gold Rush, when he was both a prospector and an officer of the First California Guard. In the Civil War, he organized Hampton's Battery F, which became widely noted for its service in significant engagements, including Bull Run and Antietam in 1862. Hampton fell in the Battle of Chancellorsville on the morning of Sunday, May 3. His men went on to fight in Gettysburg, where 14 of them would fall repulsing Pickett's Charge, in the Peach Orchard, and on Cemetery Ridge. There are two monuments dedicated to Hampton's Battery near the Pennsylvania Memorial. Survivors held reunions both at Gettysburg and Allegheny Cemetery, where they remembered their beloved captain and regaled each other with songs and stories of their service under him. (Left, Jimmy Brown; below, LOC.)

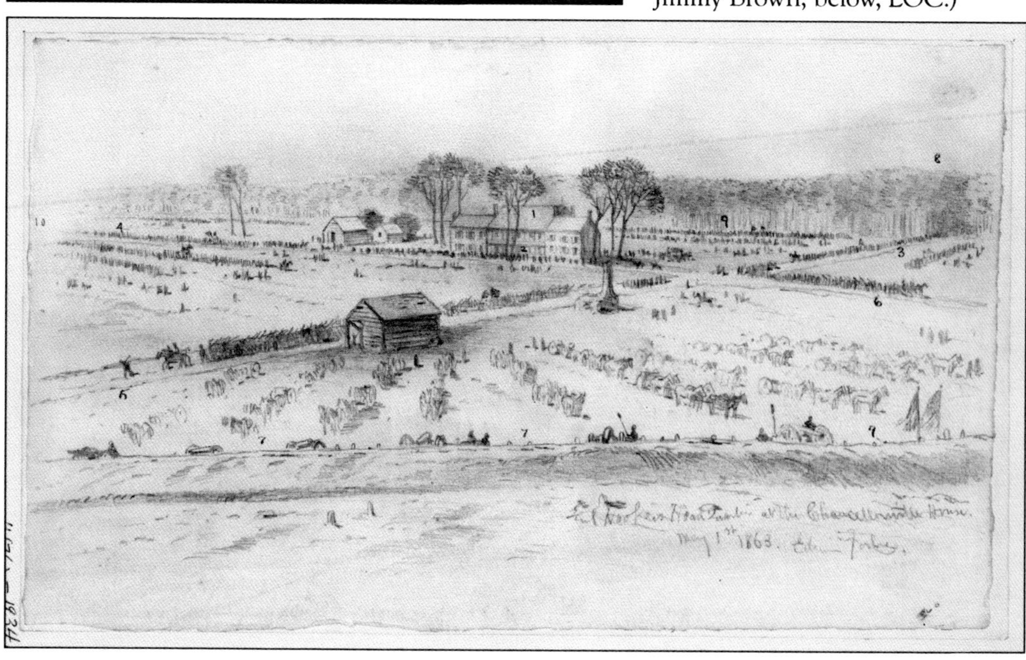

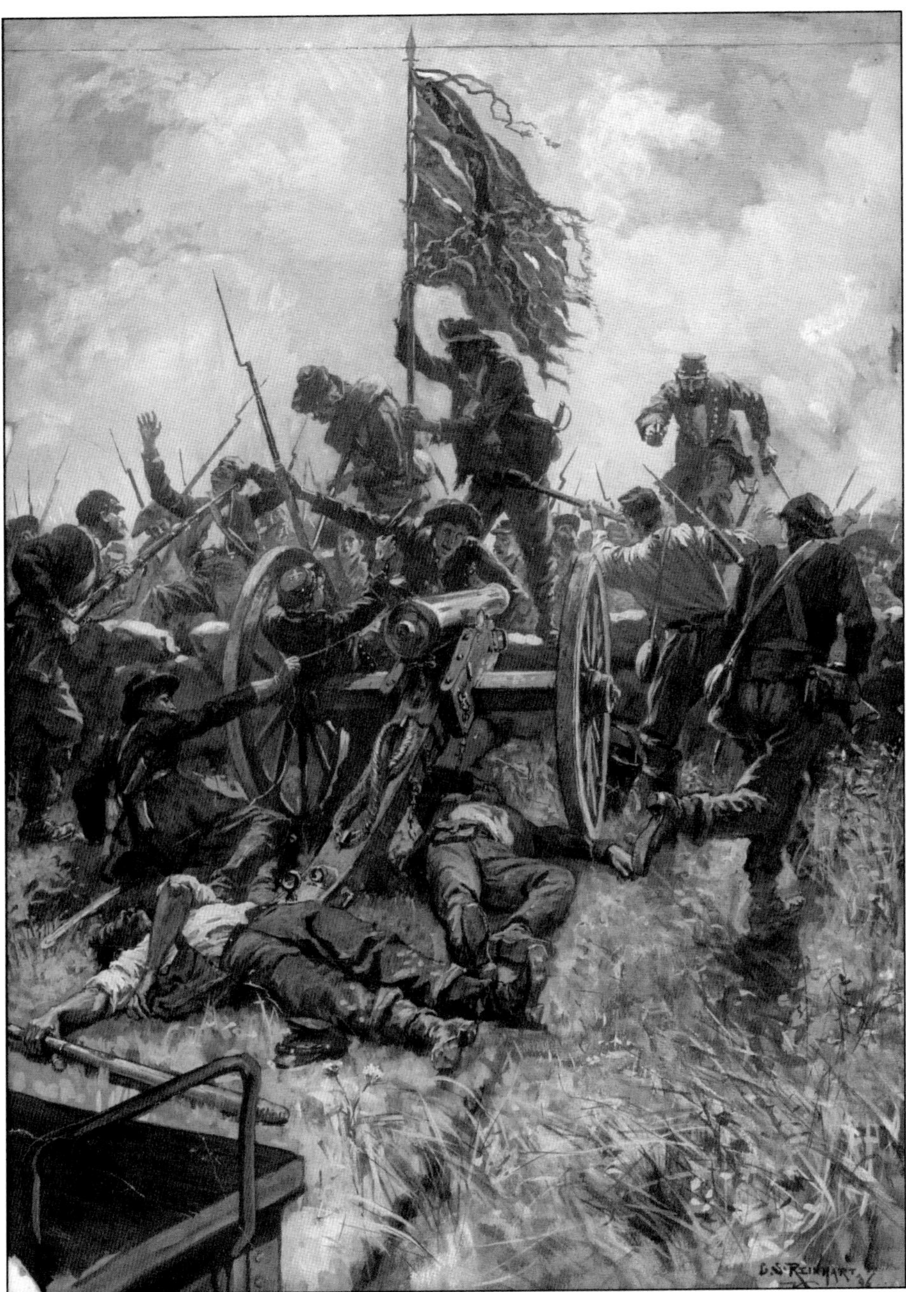

GETTYSBURG DEATH GRIP EXTENDS BEYOND BATTLEFIELD. Second Lt. Joseph Miller, 21-year-old son of longtime Allegheny Cemetery manager Reuben Miller Jr., was wounded July 3, 1863, and died on August 9 of that year (Section 8.5, Lot 7/8). First Lt. Joseph B. Todd, a Lawrenceville native, was wounded July 2, 1863, and ultimately succumbed to his wounds in March 1865 (Section 13, Lot 1). A prominent stone, named Hampton's Battery Rock, still lies on the battlefield and is documented as the location where the wounded and dying of this famed unit were sheltered from further violence during the fray. Artist Charles Stanley Reinhart's rendition of the *High Water Line at Gettysburg* depicts the exact location and engagement of these men. Reinhart himself is buried at Allegheny Cemetery (see page 92). (LOC.)

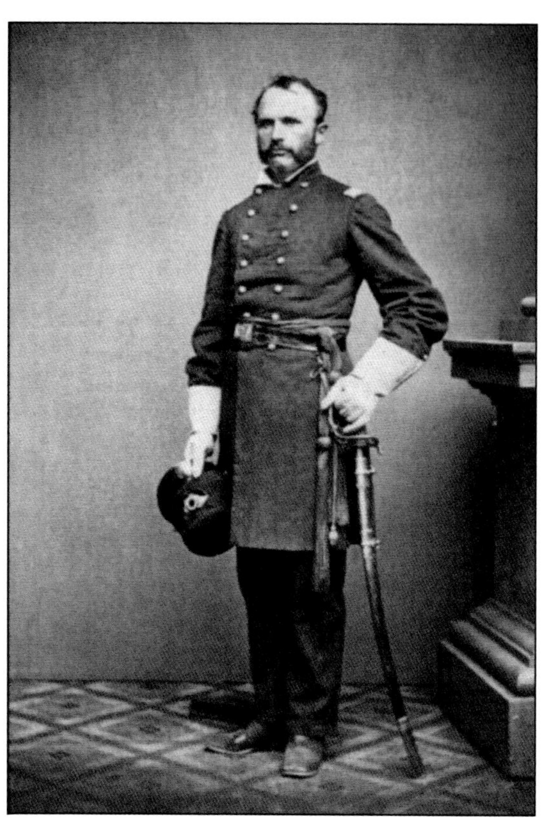

Col. Samuel W. Black (1816–1862; Section 4, Lot 18). A lieutenant colonel in the Mexican War, Black eventually served as governor of the Nebraska Territory. In 1861, he resigned his governorship, believing so strongly in the Union cause that he was willing to fight and die for it. After achieving the rank of colonel, he was killed in battle at Gaines Mill, Virginia, on June 27, 1862, leaving behind his wife and only son. His marker reads: "*Dulce et decorum est pro patria mori*," meaning "It is sweet and glorious to die for one's country." (AC.)

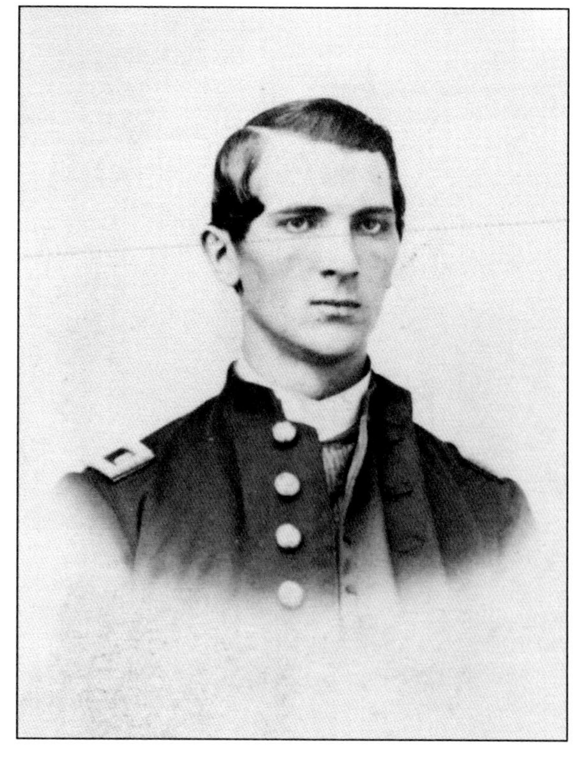

Charles Atwell (1841–1863; Section 12, Lot 50). Charles Atwell served in the Union army, initially as first lieutenant in Knap's Battery E, Pennsylvania Volunteer Light Artillery. In 1862, he commanded a unit during the Spring Peninsular Campaign. He received shoulder wounds at the Battle of Chancellorsville. Later promoted to captain, he was leading soldiers at Tennessee's Battle of Wauhatchie when, on October, 29, 1863, he was severely wounded. Days later, he died of those wounds and was returned to Pittsburgh for an honorable burial at the age of 22. (LOC.)

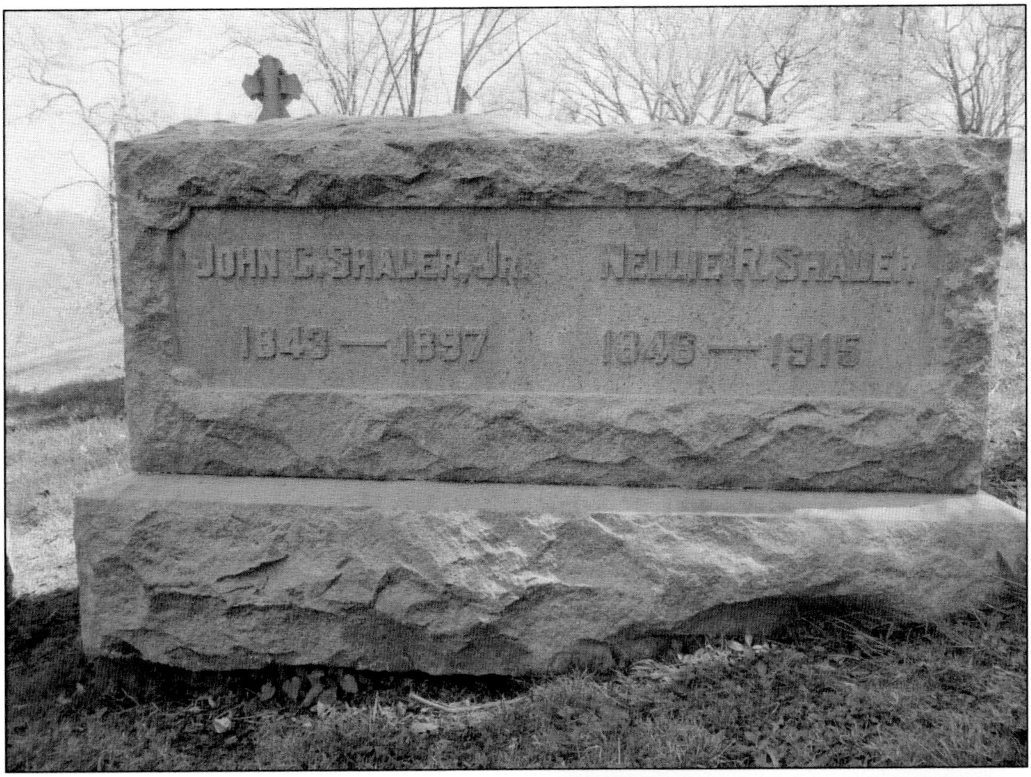

John Conway Shaler (1843–1897; Section 25, Lot 12). In his Civil War journal, a teenaged Shaler gives insight into the daily life of a soldier in Hampton's Battery F. Entries describe walking 12–20 miles per day and "scenes both amusing and revolting all along the road." A line written October 3, 1862, notes "aurora borealis after dark this evening" while encamped at Capitol Hill, DC. Though many men in his unit did not survive, Shaler returned home to Pittsburgh to marry, operate his own glassware business, teach Sunday school, and raise a family. (NF.)

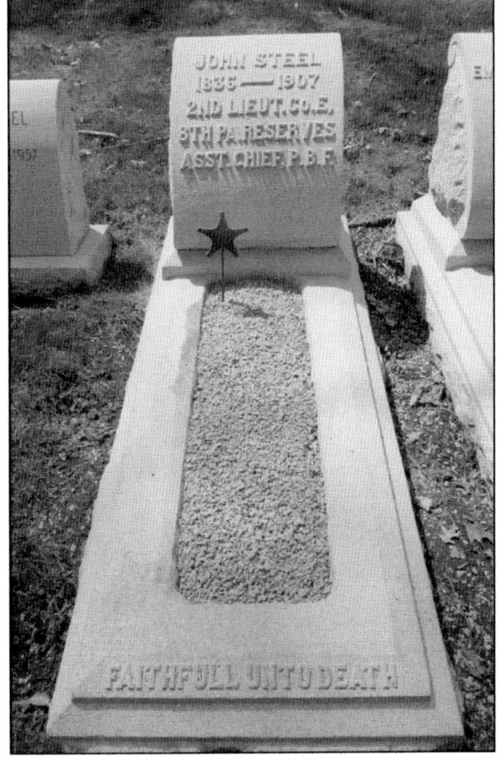

Steel Brothers (Section 24, Lot 25). John and James Steel were both volunteers in the Niagara Fire Company before enlisting for service in the Civil War. James was 21 when he was killed September 17, 1862, at the Battle of Antietam, though it was not until 1864 that his remains were able to be returned home for burial. John served gallantly through the war and returned home to marry and have a family, living until 1907. He served as assistant fire chief in the company and was said to remember his brother often and with emotion. (NF.)

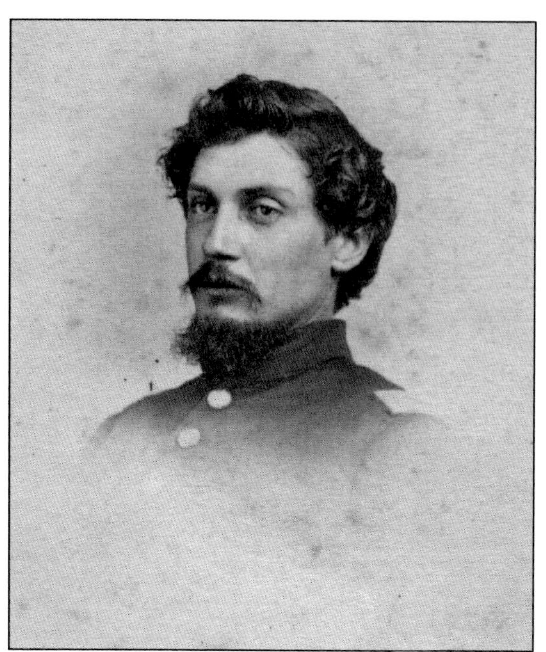

Col. William McIlwaine (Section 13, Lot 39). McIlwaine organized Company F of the 102nd Pennsylvania Volunteer Infantry, recruiting men of the 9th and 10th Wards, as well as fellow members of the Niagara Fire Engine Company. His regiment was noted for gallantry at Chancellorsville and was nearly decimated in the Battle of the Wilderness. William fell in fierce fighting on June 9, 1864, at the Battle of Cold Harbor, Virginia. His brother Andrew sought vengeance for his death, only to fall in the same battle. Of three brothers, Capt. Hugh McIlwaine returned home alone. (LOC.)

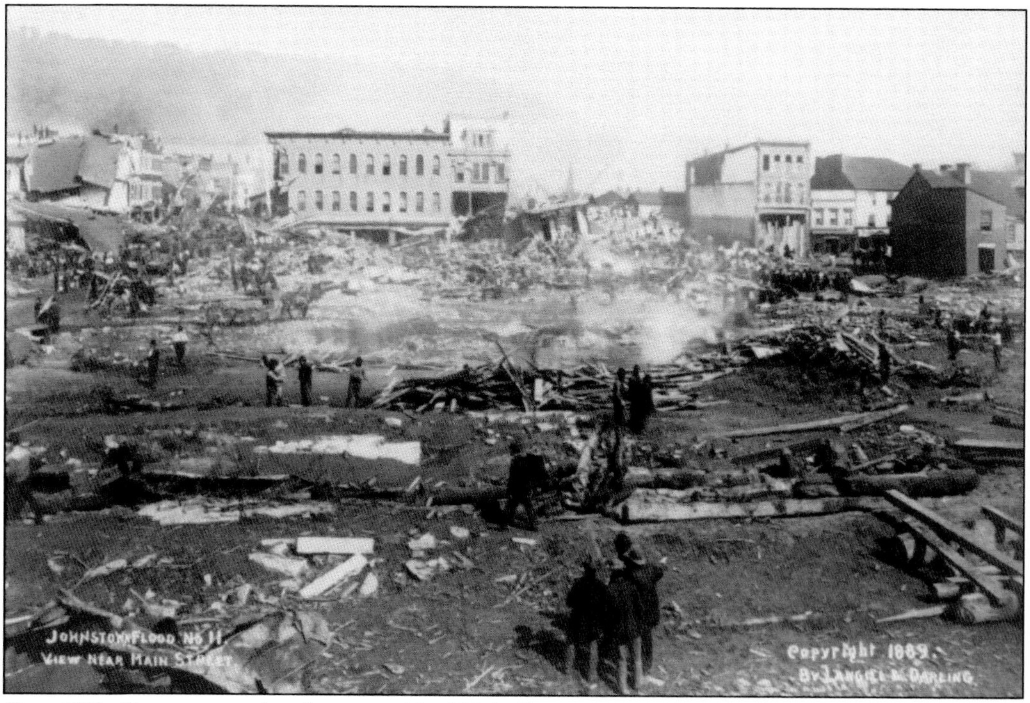

Col. P.D. Perchment (d. August 15, 1894; Section 28, Lot 111). Colonel Perchment is remembered for his unit's role in protecting the surviving citizens in the aftermath of the devastating Johnstown flood. John A Wiley, brigadier general, wrote his expression of gratitude, stating that "you have won the commendation of every officer and citizen that has come in contact with you." Newspaper accounts speak of the thousands who paid tribute to Colonel Perchment upon his death. He died following a five-month encampment at Johnstown from malaria, heart trouble, dropsy, and Bright's disease. He was 36 years old. (LOC.)

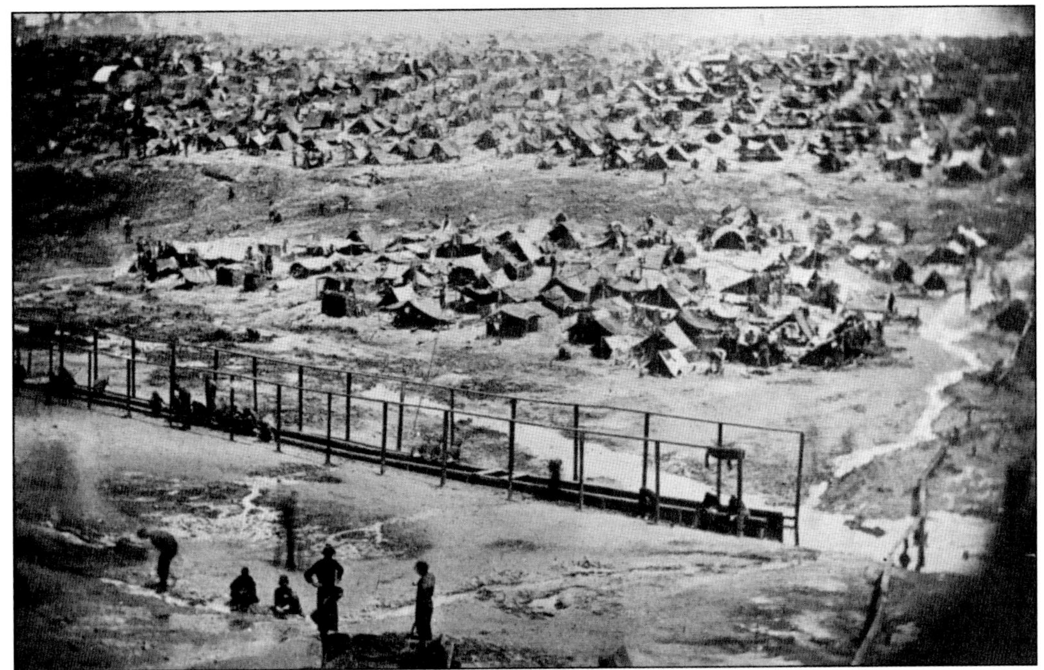

William H. Bryers (Section 9, Lot 206). Bryers's official cause of death reads, "Died from effects of starvation while prisoner . . . in hands of Southern Devils." A soldier in the local 102nd Pennsylvania Infantry, he was captured in Petersburg, Virginia, in June 1864 and sent to Andersonville Prison in Georgia, where he was one of over 33,000 men being held in a space of about 500 acres. Over 13,000 Union prisoners perished from malnutrition and disease as a result of the conditions at Andersonville; this was ruled a war crime, for which the prison commandant was later tried and hung. (LOC.)

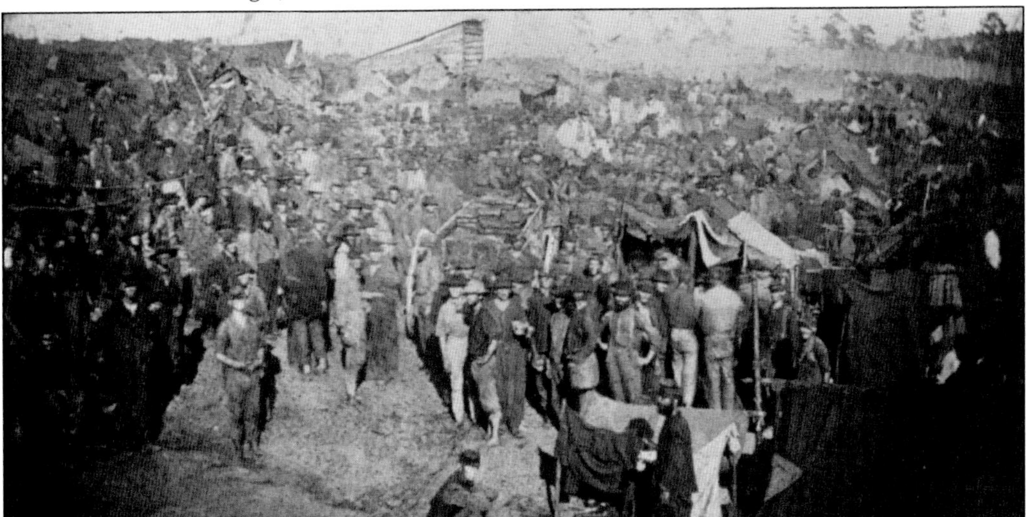

Cruelty At Andersonville Claims More Lives. Other victims who died from malnutrition, disease, and suffering at Andersonville include 45-year-old William Lutz (d. December 27, 1864; Section 31, Lot 238), 43-year-old William H. Anshutz (d. December 22, 1864; Section 19, Lot 113), 21-year-old Robert Wightman Jr. (d. March 30, 1865; Section 29, Lot 137), and 22-year-old John S. Rogers (d. March 1, 1865; Section 8, Lot 77). (LOC.)

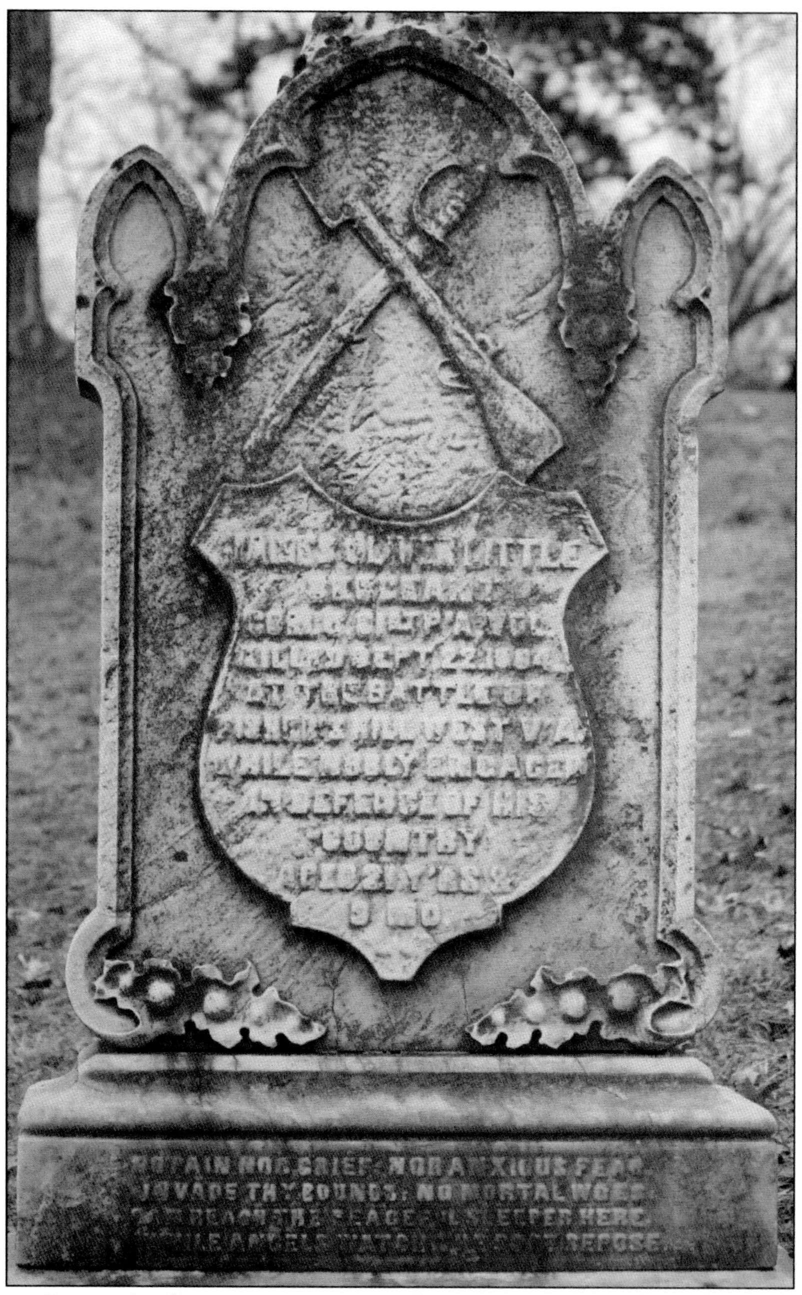

James Oliver Little (d. September 22, 1864; Section 21, Lot 44). In the midst of his 21st year, James Oliver Little found himself in the middle of a fierce battle raging during the course of the Civil War. Fought near Strasburg, Virginia, the Battle of Fisher's Hill pitted the Confederate troops of Lt. Gen. Jubal Early against Maj. Gen. Philip Sheridan's Union troops. Sergeant Little fought on behalf of the Pennsylvania Volunteers and was killed in action on the second day of the battle (September 22, 1864). Months later, the bloody war that tore America apart would finally end. Sergeant Oliver's headstone bears a striking inscription underneath the crossed sword and rifle signifying his death in battle. It reads: "No pain, nor grief, nor anxious fear, invade thy bounds, no mortal woes can reach the peaceful sleeper here, while angels watch the soft repose." (LS.)

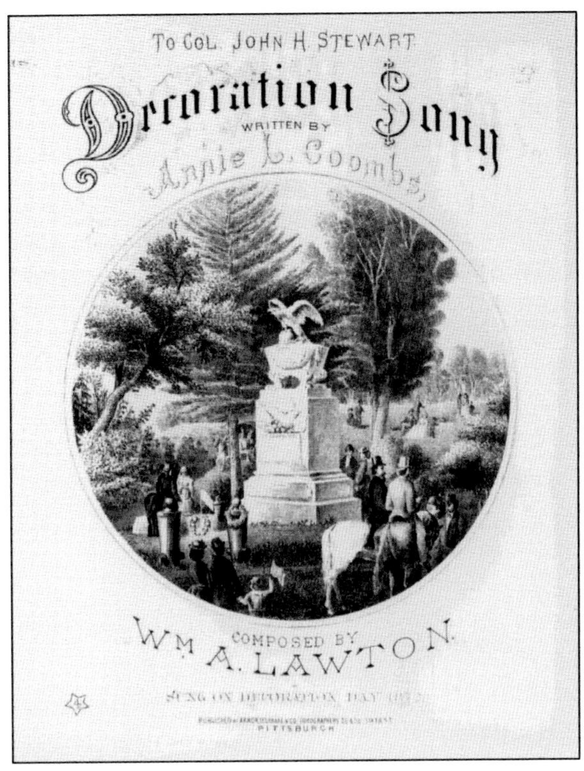

Decoration Day At Allegheny Cemetery, 1872. This sheet music cover depicts a Decoration Day gathering at the gravesite of Gen. Alexander Hays, who fell in the Battle of the Wilderness (see page 55). This is the earliest known evidence of such ceremonies at Allegheny, predating newspaper coverage of the 1875 observation. The opportunity to decorate graves of fallen soldiers was of significant cultural importance to a nation still mourning the loss of over 600,000 lives in the Civil War, and this is especially meaningful when considering that over 40 percent of Civil War dead were never identified or returned to families for private burial. (LOC.)

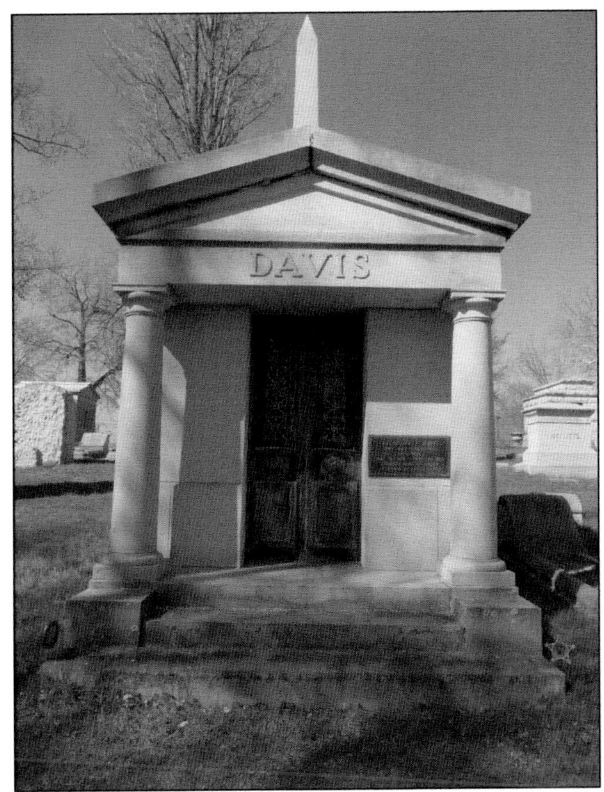

Maj. Augustus P. Davis (1835–1899; Section 28, Lot 35). Davis served with the 11th Maine Infantry and was injured in the Battle of Fair Oaks. He settled in Pittsburgh after the war, was an active member of the Grand Army of the Republic, and in 1881 founded what is now the Sons of Union Veterans of the Civil War, which was similar in purpose and organization. When the last living GAR member died in 1954, all property was signed over to the Sons, which is still active today. (NF.)

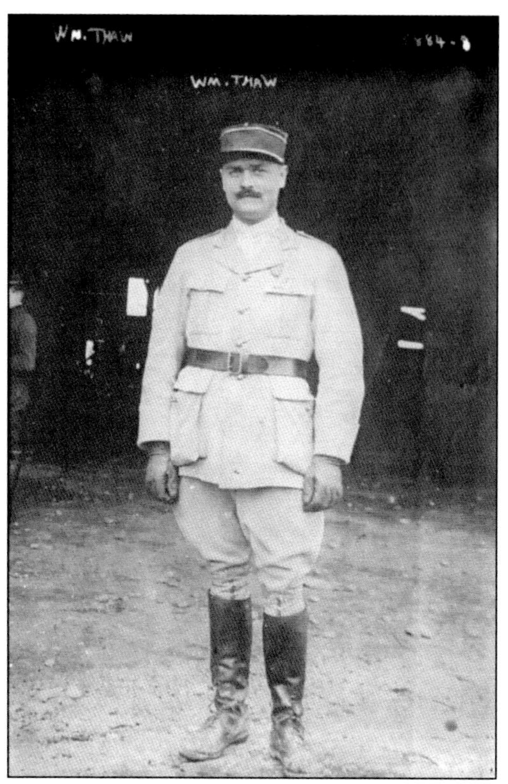

COL. WILLIAM THAW (1893–1934; SECTION 20, LOT 55). Thaw, a gentleman by birth, was the only surviving founder of the Lafayette Escadrille, an elite group of American pilots who volunteered for duty in France prior to the United States' involvement in World War I. Initially rejected by the French Air Service, the audacious young Yankee donated his personal plane to the cause and spent four months in front-line trenches before hiking 32 kilometers to the nearest air base to demand they reconsider. Colonel Thaw was awarded the Legion D'Honneur for showing contempt for danger at Verdun, where he was shot through the arm but continued the dogfight to the death, earning him his first confirmed victory and making headlines back home. Quickly achieving status as an Ace, Thaw became squadron commander and earned two additional medals for extraordinary heroism and gallantry by war's end. The never flustered young officer kept two pet lion cubs, Whiskey and Soda, who were given to the Paris zoo after the war. It is said that upon visiting years later, both lions immediately recognized him. (Left, LOC; below, NF.)

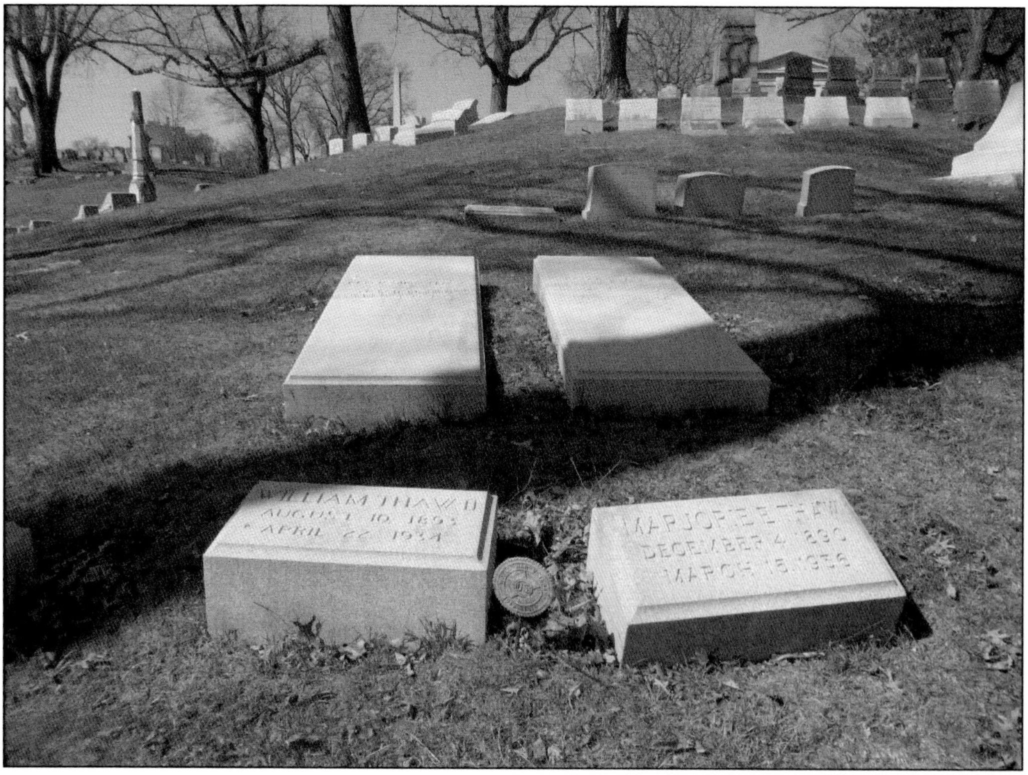

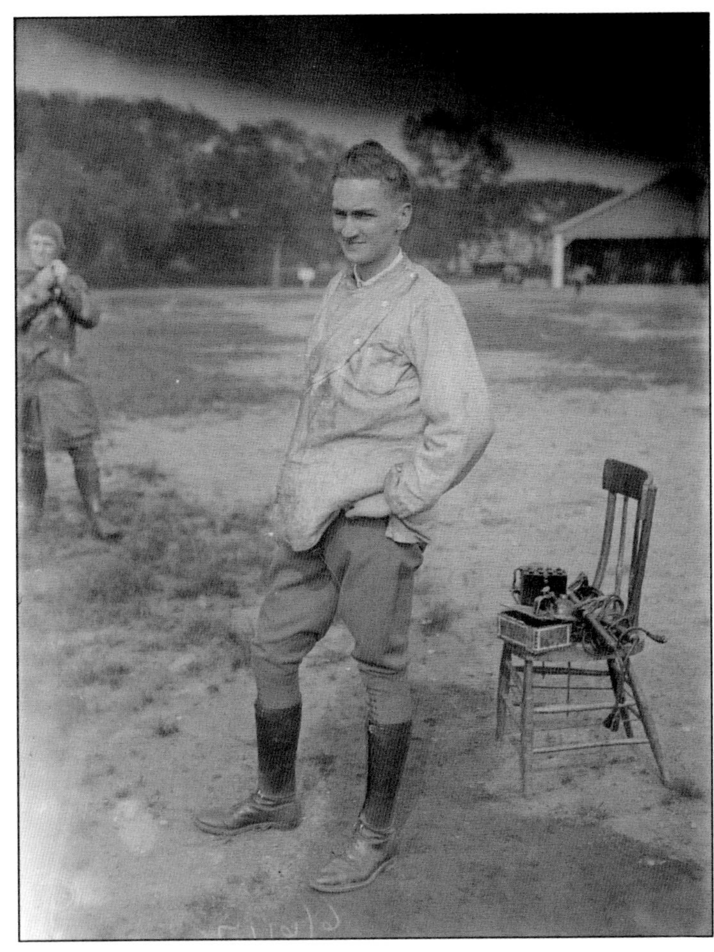

1st Lt. Alexander Blair Thaw (1898–1918; Section 20, Lot 55). The August 23, 1918, *Altoona Tribute* noted: "Lieutenant Blair Thaw, of Pittsburg, member of the American aviation service, was killed . . . when his airplane fell as the result of engine trouble. Lieutenant Thaw . . . was traveling in a pursuit group near the front toward Paris. Thaw . . . had just been promoted . . . and was on his way to take over the squadron when he fell to his death." His body was buried in St. Mihiel, France, with a cenotaph honoring his memory at home. (LOC.)

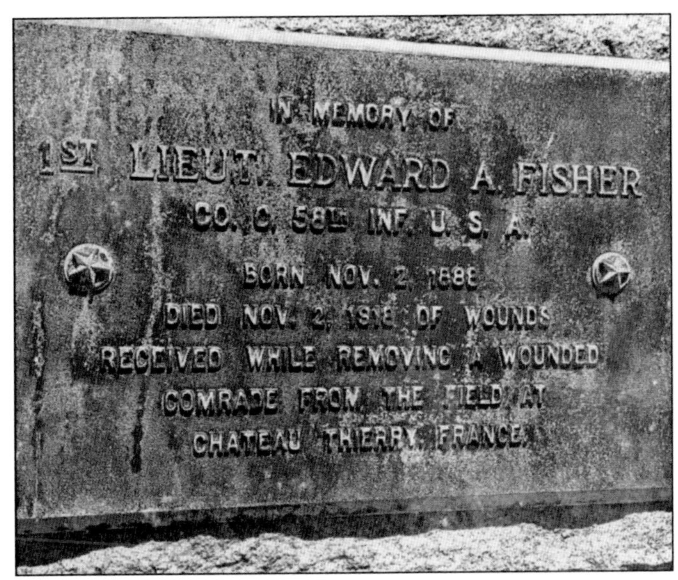

Edward A. Fisher (d. November 2, 1918; Section 9, Lot 874). Lieutenant Fisher died from injuries received removing a wounded comrade from a battlefield in Château-Thierry, France. The July 18, 1918, battle was one of the first engagements for the American Expeditionary Forces. His life ended on his 30th birthday. Far from home, with strangers turned brothers, he selflessly gave his life. Lieutenant Fisher and the countless others who served alongside him, never again to return home, are honored by everyone. (LS.)

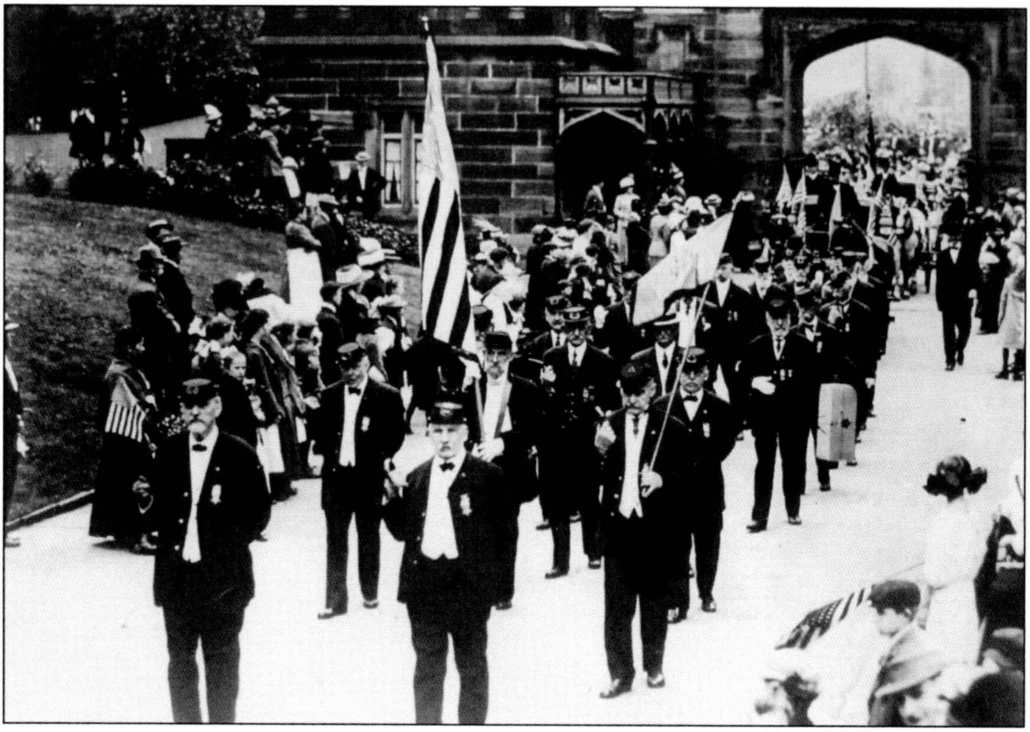

Memorial Day 1918. Pittsburgh's Memorial Day tradition began here in 1872. Surviving Grand Army of the Republic veterans organized the original Butler Street procession into the cemetery, with memorial services and full military honors in Section 33 (at the current Soldier's Memorial). Here, in 1918, cemetery manager Conrad C. Arensberg is seen leading the procession (front left). This tradition continues with the St. Mary's and Allegheny Cemetery annual parade, the largest in Pittsburgh and one of the oldest Memorial Day observances in the nation. (AC.)

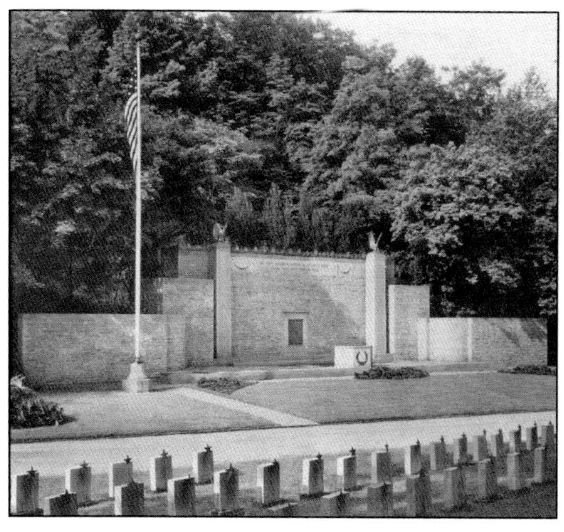

Soldier's Memorial, 1937 (Section 33). Overlooking rows of honored war dead is a 116-foot-wide, 30-foot-tall wall built of solid stone quarried from the cemetery's own hills. Architect Brandon Smith's design was chosen to reflect that "simplicity in its monuments is the choice and not the necessity of the Nation." Two bronze eagles, "poised ready for flight, symbolizing the vigilance of a free people in defense of their soil, their homes and their liberties" flank Lincoln's resolution, which reads: "We here highly resolve that these dead shall not have died in vain." Two of only 48 surviving Confederate cannons were put on display at the memorial in 1988. (AC.)

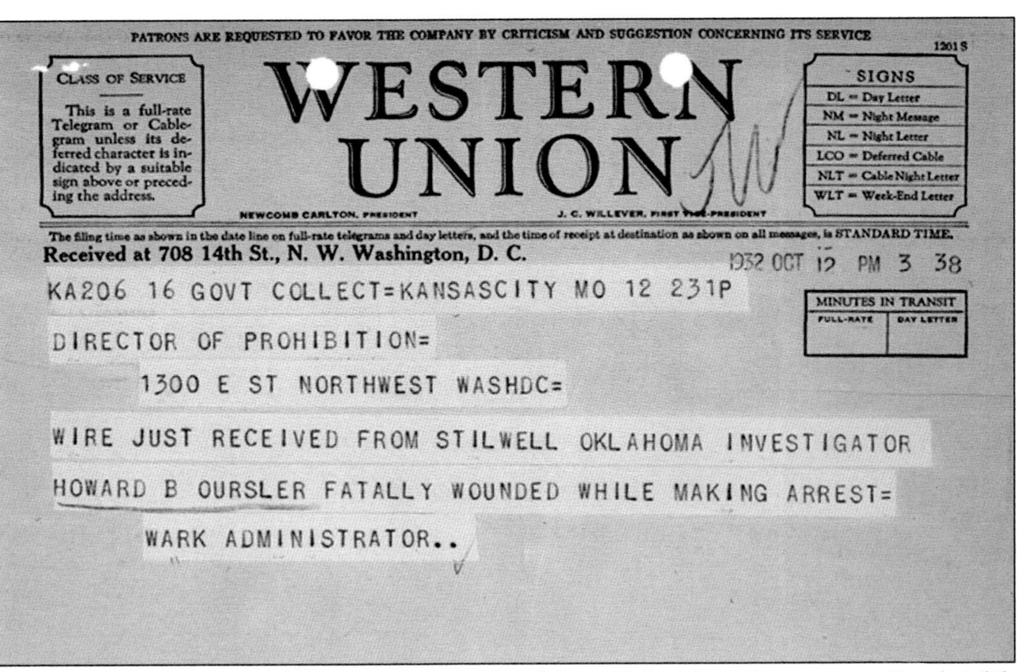

PATRONS ARE REQUESTED TO FAVOR THE COMPANY BY CRITICISM AND SUGGESTION CONCERNING ITS SERVICE

1201 S

CLASS OF SERVICE

This is a full-rate Telegram or Cablegram unless its deferred character is indicated by a suitable sign above or preceding the address.

WESTERN UNION

NEWCOMB CARLTON, PRESIDENT J. C. WILLEVER, FIRST VICE-PRESIDENT

SIGNS

DL = Day Letter
NM = Night Message
NL = Night Letter
LCO = Deferred Cable
NLT = Cable Night Letter
WLT = Week-End Letter

The filing time as shown in the date line on full-rate telegrams and day letters, and the time of receipt at destination as shown on all messages, is STANDARD TIME.

Received at 708 14th St., N. W. Washington, D. C. 1932 OCT 12 PM 3 38

MINUTES IN TRANSIT | FULL-RATE | DAY LETTER

KA206 16 GOVT COLLECT=KANSASCITY MO 12 231P

DIRECTOR OF PROHIBITION=

1300 E ST NORTHWEST WASHDC=

WIRE JUST RECEIVED FROM STILWELL OKLAHOMA INVESTIGATOR HOWARD B OURSLER FATALLY WOUNDED WHILE MAKING ARREST=

WARK ADMINISTRATOR..

COL. HOWARD B. OURSLER (1874–1932; SECTION 16, LOT 134). A Prohibition agent, Oursler's life ended while attempting to arrest a known whiskey distributor in the streets of Stillwell, Oklahoma, in broad daylight. The outlaw Edward Dudley attempted to flee, which ended in a tussle between the men, during which Dudley managed to grab Oursler's pistol and used it against him with a point-blank shot to the gut. Oursler died several hours later, but not before identifying his killer, who was apprehended by a government posse in a hillside hideout. (ATF Archives.)

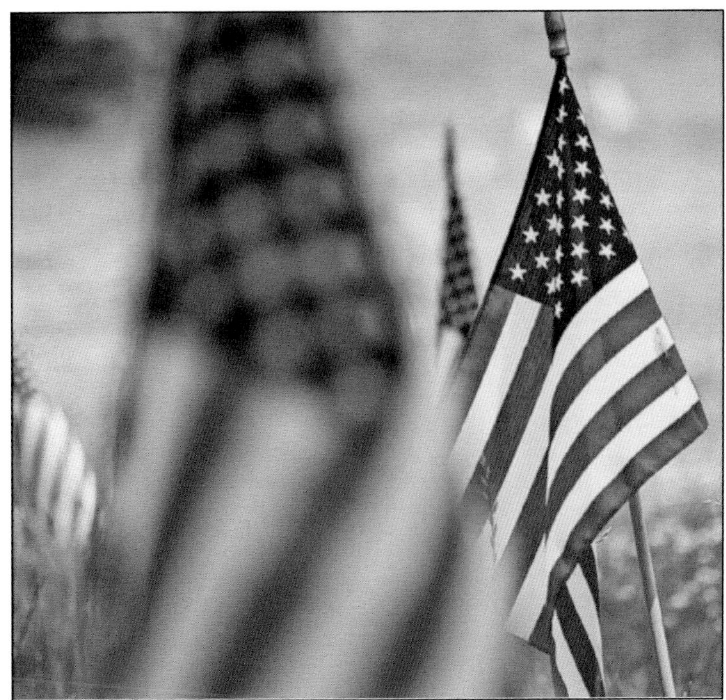

ALLEGHENY COUNTY SOLDIERS LOTS (SECTION 38, LOTS 300–309; SECTION 43, LOTS 31 AND 311). Allegheny County established its first lots in the cemetery in 1944 to provide burial for World War II veterans. As initial space continued to fill, and as the United States entered into conflicts with Korea and Vietnam, several more were added, amounting to over 3,500 burials in this area today—each of them receiving a government-issued flag placed lovingly by volunteer veterans each May in observance of Memorial Day. (AC.)

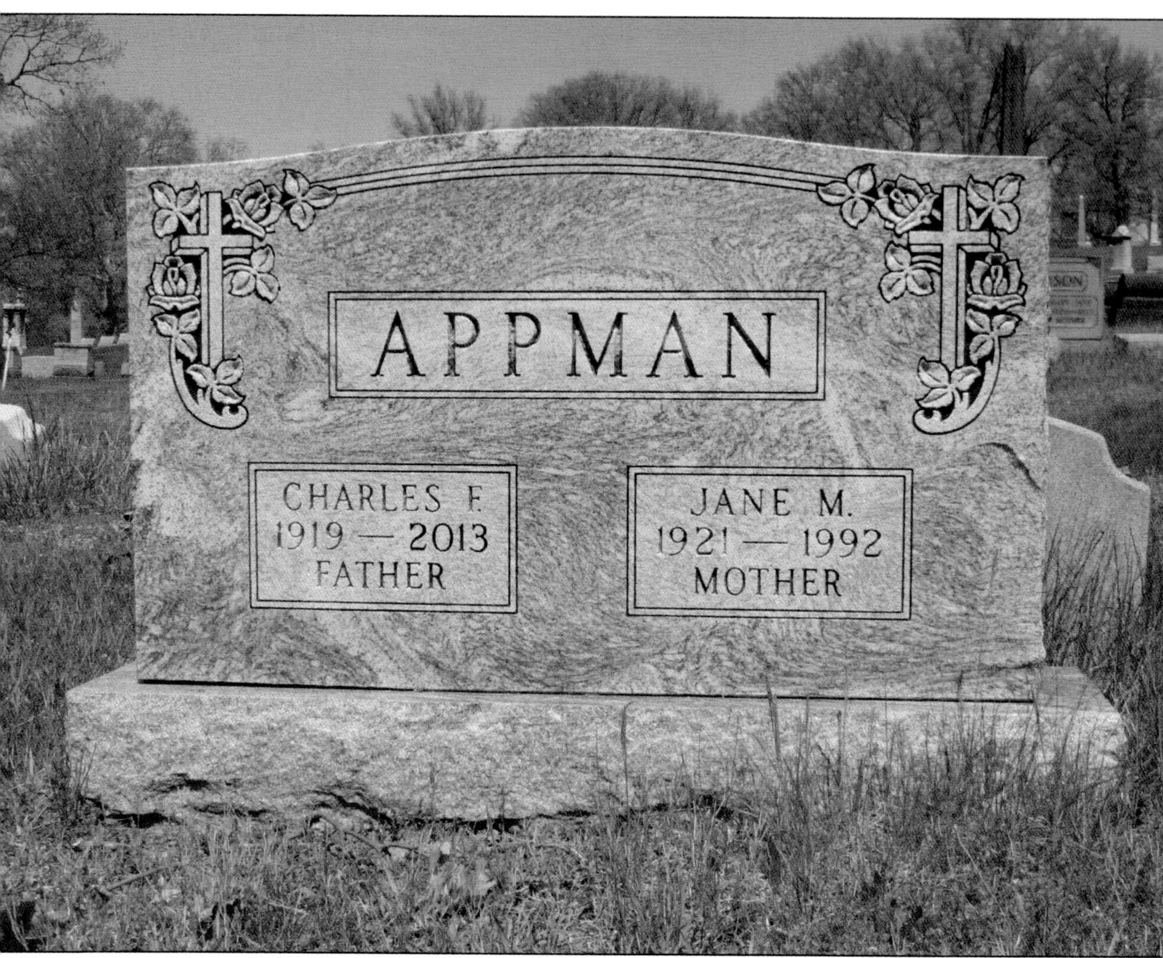

CHARLES APPMAN (1919–2013; SECTION 9, LOT 820). Many men speak of the atrocities of war; few survive them. Charles Appman was one such survivor. The Malmedy Massacre took place in Germany in 1944. During the incident, German soldiers murdered 84 soldiers in Appman's unit. Only 43 survived. A forward observer in Battery B of the 285th Field Artillery, Appman gave his account of the incident shortly after the war. In order to survive, he played dead while the Germans systematically shot his fellow soldiers, including one that had fallen atop Appman. He stayed there for over an hour, covered in the blood of others, until the shooting stopped. He was later rescued by an engineering battalion, only to discover a bullet hole that had gone through his coat and sweater without injuring him. In recounting the incident, Appman said he saw a bright white light, "knew it was God, and it calmed me, and I stopped shaking." (NF.)

Six

Civic Leaders

Allegheny Cemetery has a rich heritage of civic leaders among her ranks, many of whom are credited with far reaching improvements to the city of Pittsburgh, held public offices in various capacities, or gave freely of themselves to aid the less fortunate. Many of their names appear on public buildings and civic institutions that have made this region culturally vibrant and a "most livable" city. There are 28 Pittsburgh mayors at Allegheny, beginning with Ebenezer Denny, who appears in the previous chapter, while three more mayors appear here. Some of these men were abolitionists during a time when this sociopolitical stance was unpopular and often dangerous. At grave personal risk, they would use their own homes and businesses as stops along the Underground Railroad. Under the Fugitive Slave Law of 1850, any personal property could be searched and seized without warning, should owners be suspected of aiding in the cause of freedom. These men have also made advances in the field of science, medicine, and legislation, and while some have been long forgotten, their lasting contributions to society live on.

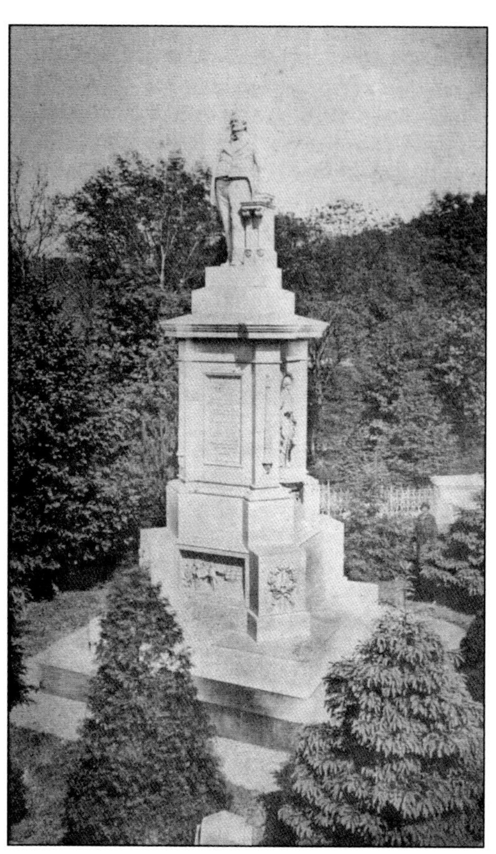

CHARLES AVERY (1784–1858; SECTION 3, LOT 11). In 1812, Avery arrived in this nascent country. The cotton industry of the South highlighted the plight of slave families. Avery worked tirelessly, providing opportunity where he saw oppression. Returning north, Avery assisted slaves escaping into Canada. He established the Allegheny Institute and Mission Church (later Avery College), which was a stop on the Underground Railroad as slaves traveled through Pittsburgh. When he died in 1858, Avery left much of his $800,000 fortune to fighting racial injustice, for the betterment of freed slaves. (AC.)

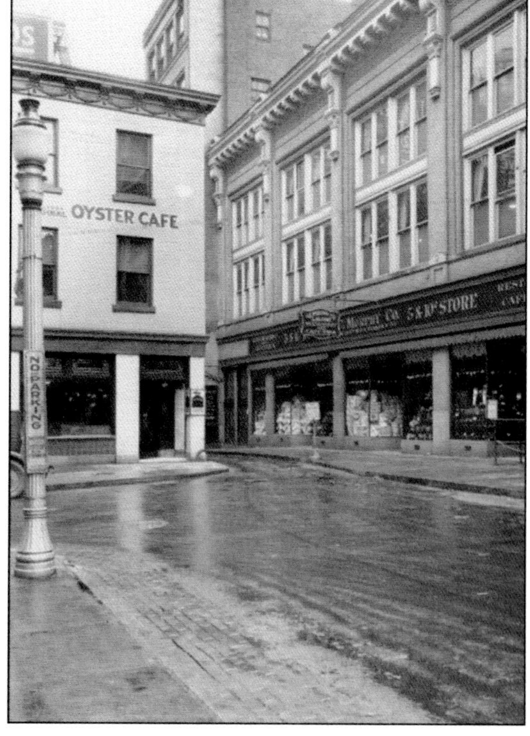

REV. JOHN C. PECK (1802–1875; SECTION 29, LOT 225). Reverend Peck was a free man of color and an outspoken abolitionist, along with his son David. Both were friends of Charles Avery and Frederick Douglass. The Original Oyster House, established by Peck and still located in Market Square, was an invaluable stop along the Underground Railroad for countless slaves pursuing freedom. Escapes were planned for servants staying with their masters at the Monongahela House, where they were ushered out in disguise and hidden in Peck's Original Oyster House until river transportation could be arranged. (ASC.)

Dr. Jonas Roup McClintock (1808–1879; Section 18, Lot 71). The original "Boy Mayor," McClintock was elected to office at age 28, serving from 1836 to 1839, during which time he established the Pittsburgh Police Department. Dr. McClintock was beloved for providing free health care to the poor and is credited with saving countless lives during the fatal cholera epidemic of 1832. In peacetime, he was a founding member of the Duquesne Grays (a citizens' safety brigade) and during the Civil War, he achieved the rank of adjutant general, raising a company of 3,500 men and performing lifesaving surgeries on the field of battle while refusing to be paid. (AC.)

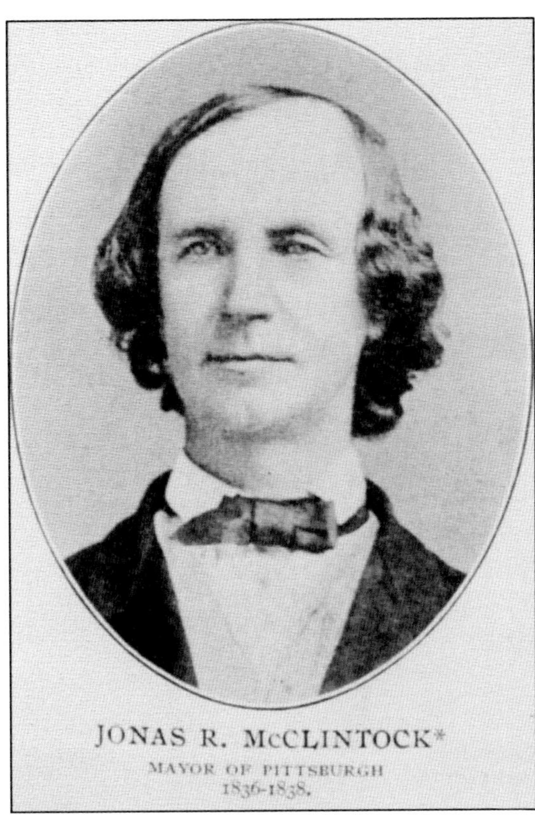

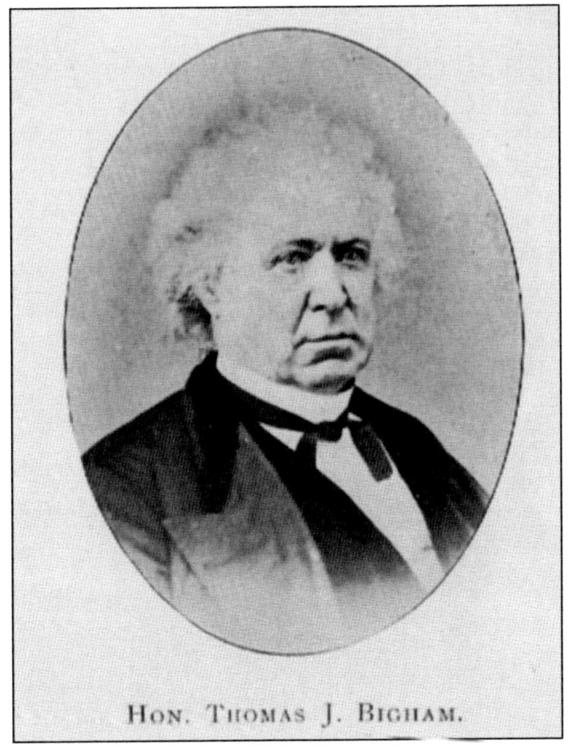

Thomas Bigham (1810–1884; Section 25, Lot 123). Bigham was a founding corporator of Allegheny Cemetery, as well as a lawyer, senator, and noted abolitionist who used his own home as a crucial stop on Pittsburgh's Underground Railroad. Widely respected in his day and dubbed "the Sage of Mount Washington," Bigham founded Grace Episcopal Church there. His historic home is used now as a clubhouse in Chatham Village. (AC.)

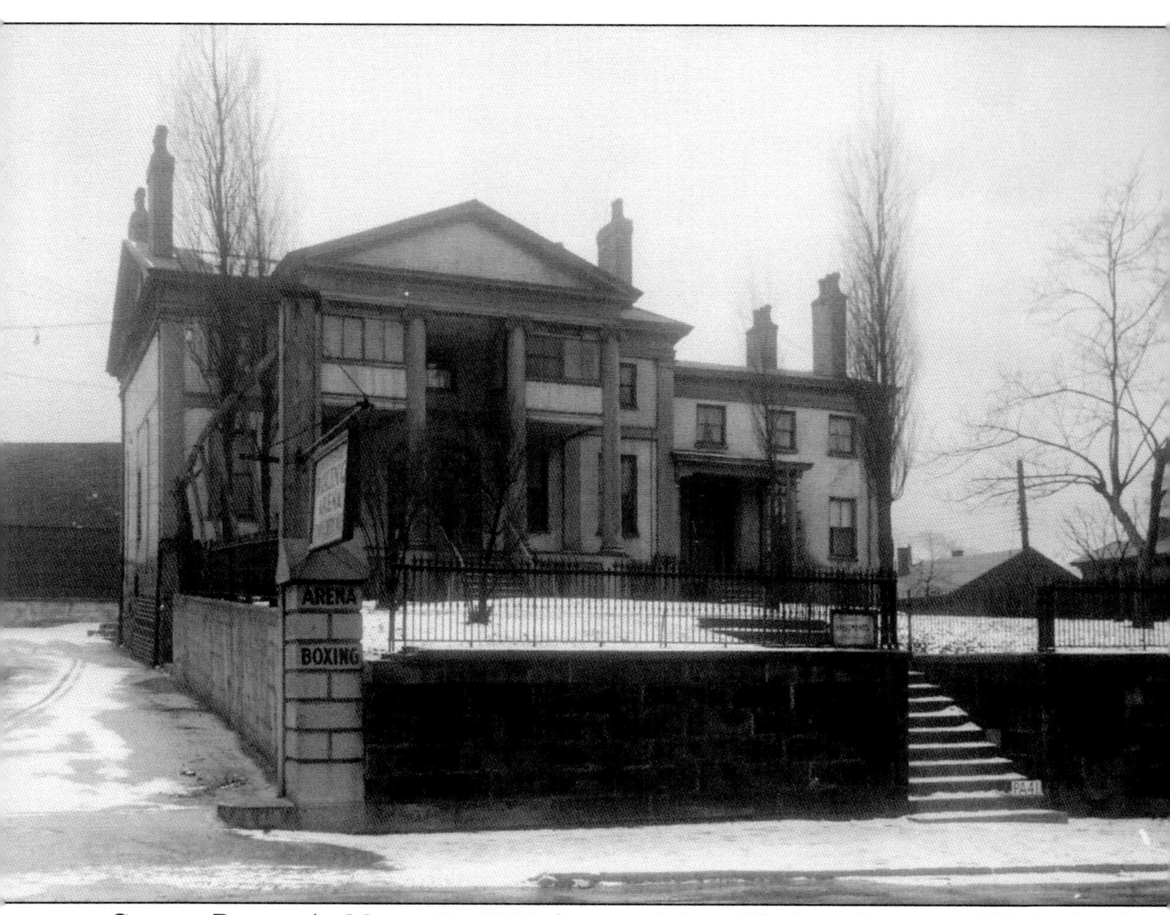

Charles Brewer (d. March 31, 1860; Section 4, Lot 47). According to an 1891 *Pittsburgh Dispatch* newspaper account, Charles Brewer was "a wealthy and philanthropic Pittsburgher who left a fund which still supplies the poor of the city with coal in the winter." That fund was administered by the Western Pennsylvania Hospital for nearly 50 years because Brewer did not wish to be known as its benefactor. During that time, the distributed funds totaled over $130,000, and Brewer's benevolence did not end there. His residence (pictured here) in Pittsburgh's North Side held yet another testament to the character of the man. Years after his passing, tunnels were found underneath his house leading to the nearby Allegheny River. Based on that, it is believed he opened his home as a stop on Pittsburgh's Underground Railroad and may have aided as many in secrecy as he did publicly. Additionally, Brewer endowed funds for the Orphan Society of Pittsburgh and the Episcopalian Church Home. When he died, Brewer dictated that the key to his mausoleum be used to lock the doors one final time and then thrown into the Allegheny River, where it likely still rests today. (LOC.)

Rev. Francis Herron, DD (1774–1860; Section 3, Lots 23 and 24). Herron studied theology at Dickinson College and began preaching at age 23. He brought the gospel to remote backwoods communities and traveled through Pittsburgh when it was but a pioneer outpost before camping with Native Americans during his missionary journey through Ohio. Herron settled in Pittsburgh and become its moral and ethical leader. He served for 50 years as pastor of the First Presbyterian Church downtown and later established the Third Presbyterian Church in Shadyside—both vastly important social and cultural institutions to this day. (AC.)

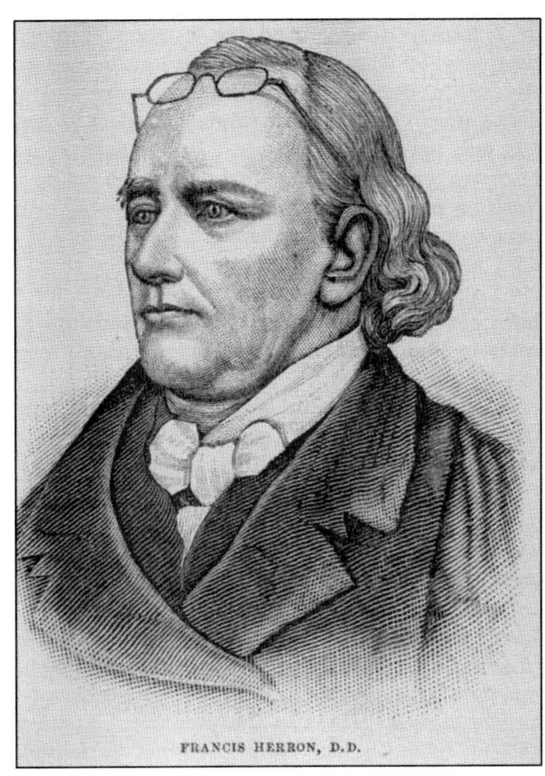
FRANCIS HERRON, D.D.

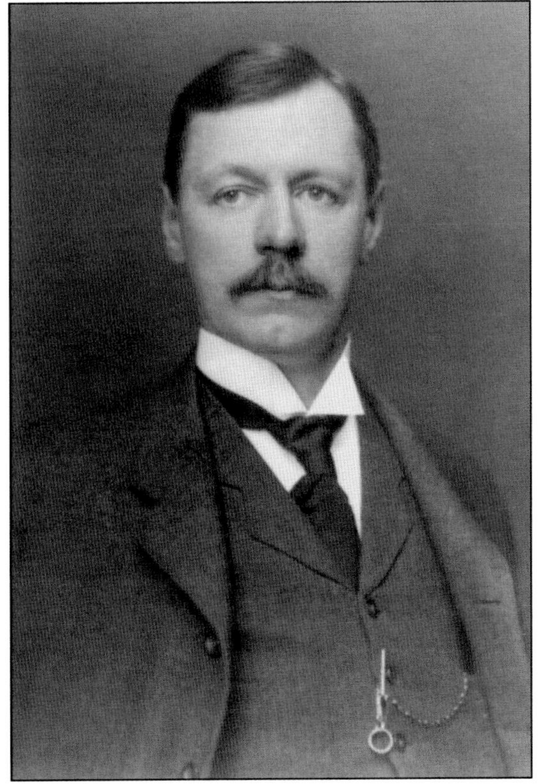

George Shiras Jr. (1832–1924; Section 2, Lot 91). Shiras's grandfather of the same name traveled to Pennsylvania on orders from President Washington to suppress the Whiskey Rebellion and afterward, ironically, purchased Fort Pitt from Isaac Craig to operate a brewery there. Shiras's family was well connected—he himself was the nephew of Rev. Francis Herron, and his brother Charles was Stephen Foster's best childhood friend. After graduating from Yale in 1853, he practiced law until 1892, when Pres. Benjamin Harrison appointed him associate chief justice of the Supreme Court, a seat he held until 1903. (LOC.)

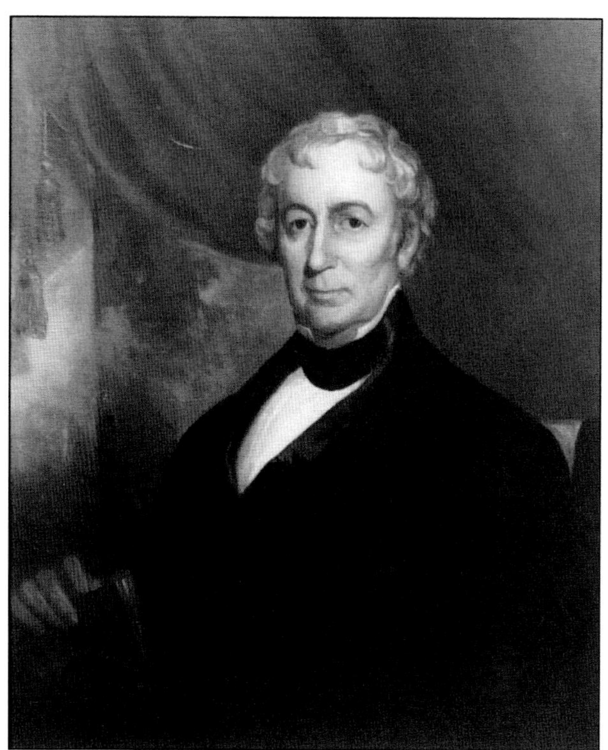

Rev. Robert Bruce (1776–1846; Section 8, Lot 63). Reverend Bruce was born in Scotland and educated at the University of Edinburgh. In Pittsburgh, he is remembered as the first chancellor of what is today the University of Pittsburgh, where he taught natural history, chemistry, and mathematics from 1820 to 1846. He was also pastor of the First United Presbyterian Church and the husband of Margaret Gausman, with whom he raised a family of 10 children. (ASC.)

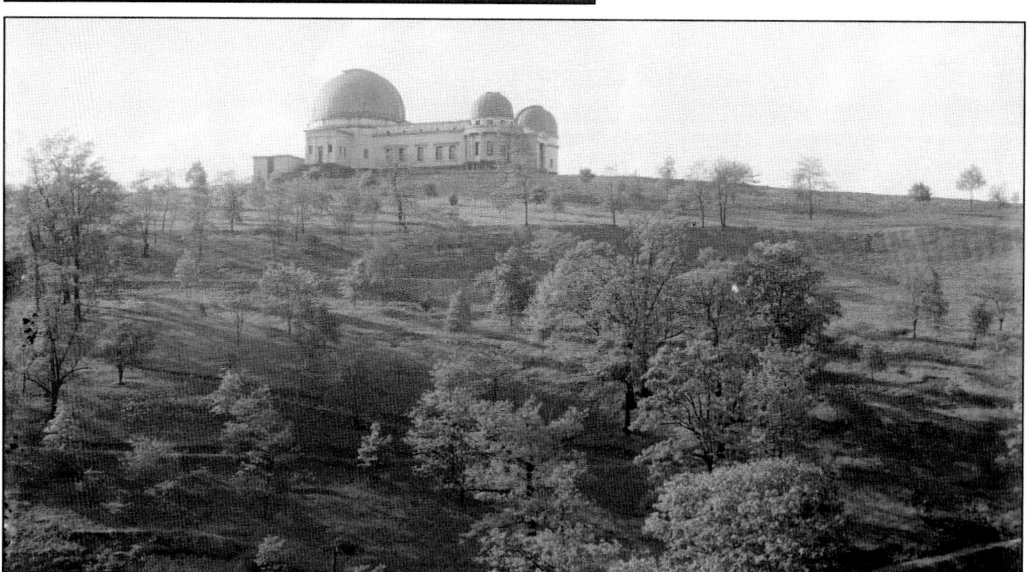

Allegheny Observatory Founders. Two of the three founders of the Allegheny Observatory rest here. Harvey Childs in Section 14, Lot 95, and Josiah King in Section 16, Lot 133. The 1858 appearance of Donati's Comet inspired Childs and King, who met at the home of the renowned professor Louis Bradley and resolved to purchase a telescope and erect an observatory to house it. This original structure was deeded to the University of Pittsburgh in 1867, but its successor still stands in Riverview Park. William Thaw Sr., father of the notorious Harry Kendall Thaw, is also buried at Allegheny and heavily financed the new building; the Thaw Telescope is named for him. (LOC.)

FELIX R. BRUNOT (1820–1898; SECTION 13, LOTS 42 AND 43). Felix Reville Brunot was a civil engineer who invested in steel and became wealthy. Like his grandfather, Brunot volunteered for the Union army as a surgeon, saving countless lives on the field of battle at Shiloh and Gaines' Mills before being taken captive and held briefly as a prisoner of war. He was chairman of the 1864 Sanitary Fair, an 18-day fundraising effort held in Market Square, during which over $320,000 in proceeds were netted for the benefit of soldiers and their families. (LOC.)

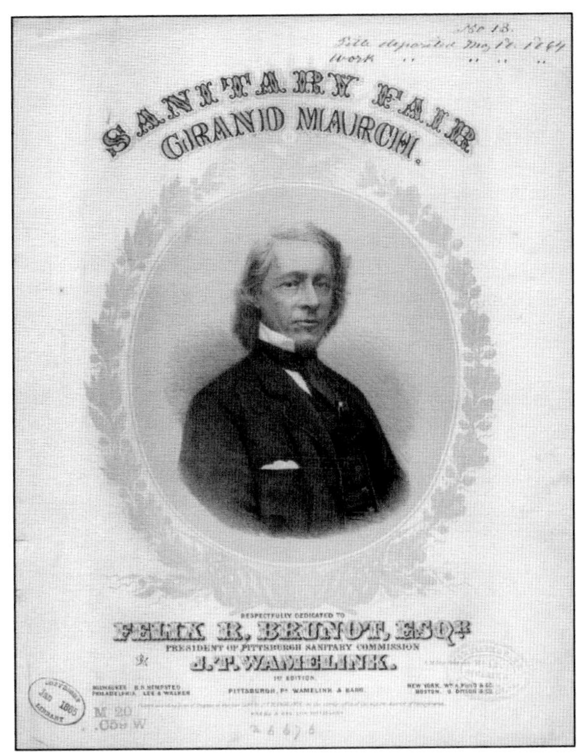

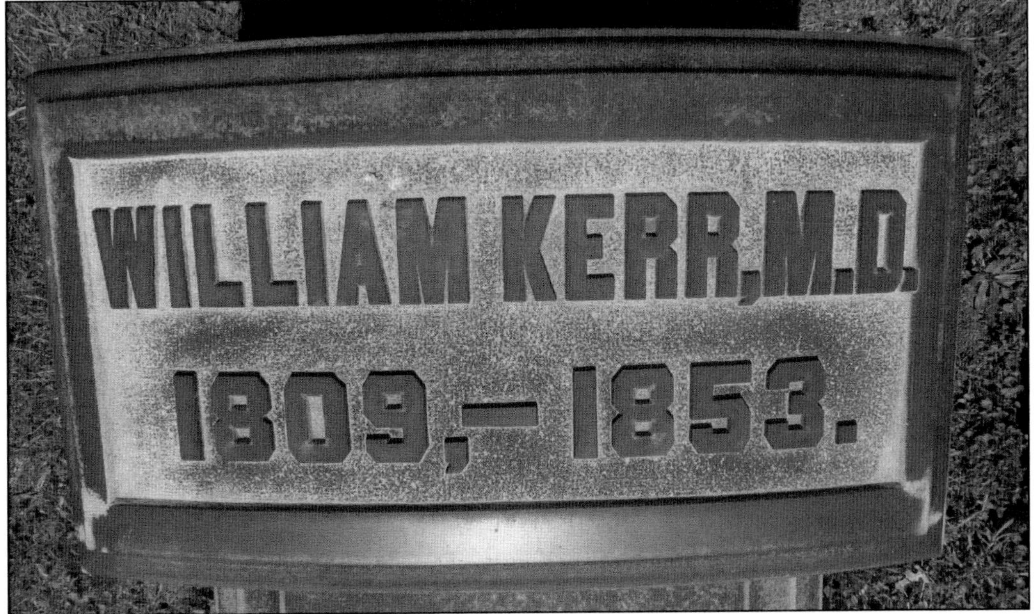

DR. WILLIAM KERR (1809–1853; SECTION 5, LOT 42). Kerr studied medicine at the University of Pennsylvania and operated a physician's office on Liberty Avenue and an apothecary on Wood Street. He was elected the 14th mayor of Pittsburgh (1846–1847), during which time he devoted himself to rebuilding the city after the devastating fire of 1845. Previously a metropolis of wooden clapboard buildings, Mayor Kerr's Pittsburgh rose from the ashes as a city of stone and brick. Dr. Kerr died young at age 44 from effects of consumption, later known as tuberculosis. (NF.)

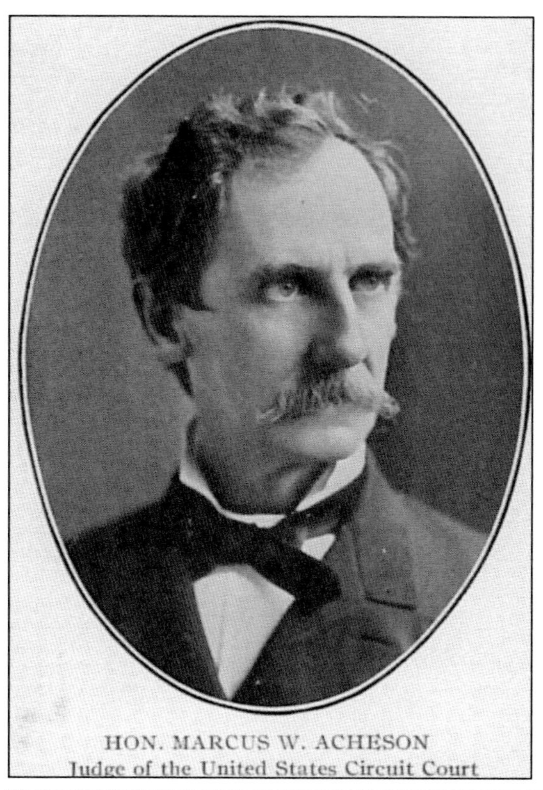
HON. MARCUS W. ACHESON
Judge of the United States Circuit Court

Marcus Wilson Acheson (1828–1906; Section 25, Lot 105). Born in nearby Washington County, Pennsylvania, Marcus Acheson spent his life in pursuit of liberty and justice. In 1852, he began to practice private law in Pittsburgh. In January 1880, Pres. Rutherford B. Hayes appointed Acheson to a seat on the US District Court for the Western District of Pennsylvania. A few days later, he was confirmed by the Senate and served in that position for the greater part of the next decade. In 1891, he was appointed by Pres. Benjamin Harrison to a seat on the US Circuit Court for the Third Circuit and concurrently to the newly created US Court of Appeals for the Third Circuit. He held those positions for the rest of his life, until his death at age 78 in 1906. (Left, AC; below, NF.)

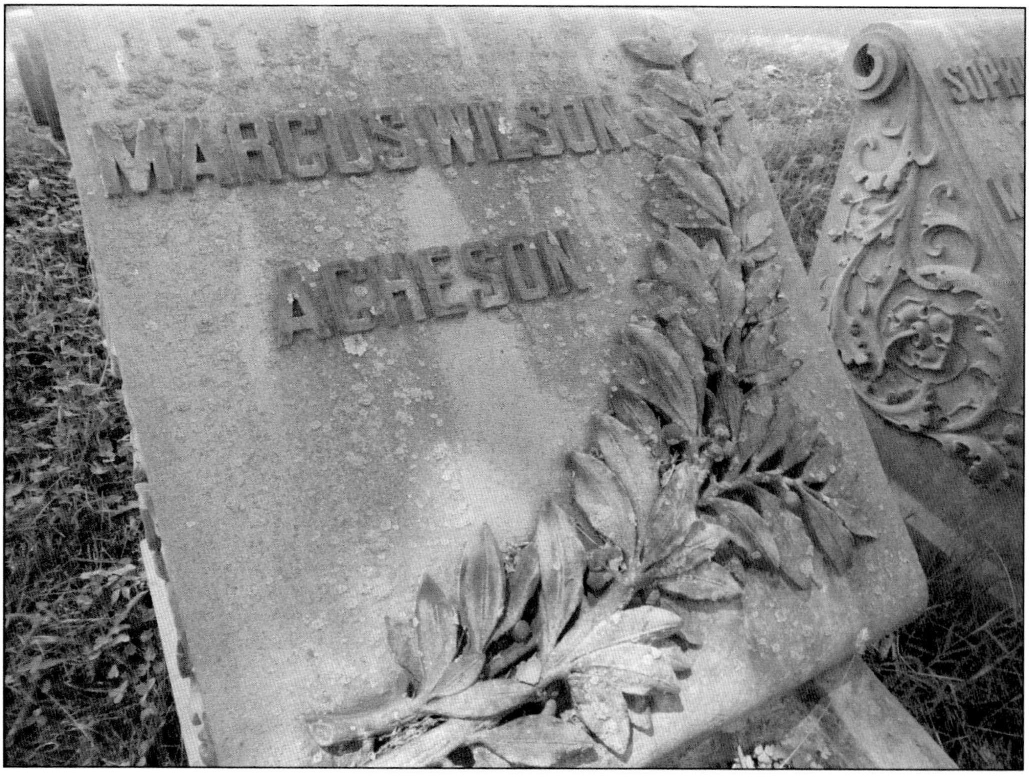

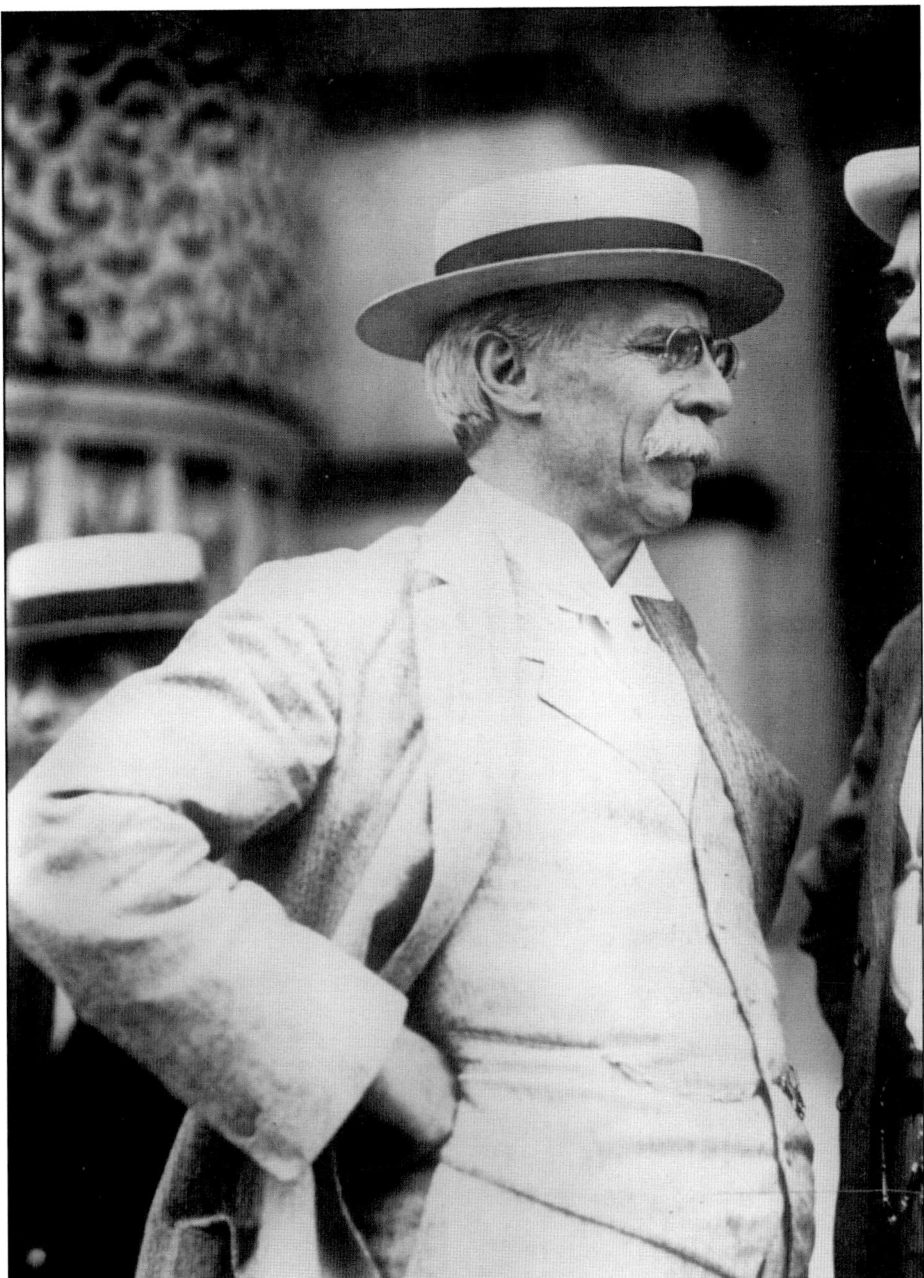

George W. Guthrie (1848–1917; Section 20, Lot 1). Guthrie's service as mayor from 1906 to 1909 was marked by two major improvements for the city of Pittsburgh. He assisted in the annexation of Allegheny City (now the North Side) in 1906, and in 1908, his implementation of a sand filtration system for the city's water system resulted in significantly fewer cases of typhoid fever. As chairman of the Pennsylvania Democratic Committee, he was twice a delegate to the Democratic National Convention. Guthrie supported Woodrow Wilson's run for president, and in turn, Wilson made Guthrie the US ambassador to Japan from 1913 until his death in office in 1917. The Japanese government regarded Guthrie so highly, his remains were returned to the United States in an imperial naval cruiser. (LOC.)

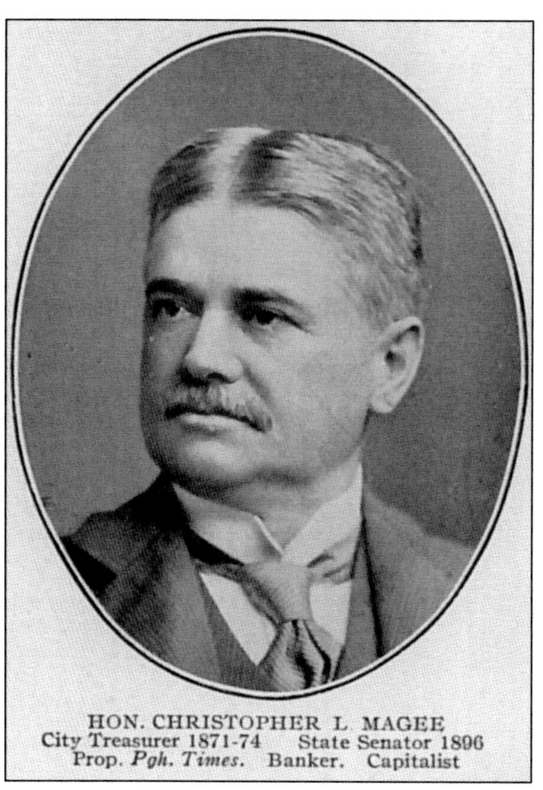

HON. CHRISTOPHER L. MAGEE
City Treasurer 1871-74 State Senator 1896
Prop. *Pgh. Times.* Banker. Capitalist

CHRISTOPHER LYMAN MAGEE (1848–1901; SECTION 8.5, LOT 2). Magee had a long and storied political career as a three-time delegate to the Republican National Convention and as state senator from 1897 until illness and death removed him from office at the young age of 52. He was a powerful political boss who partnered with a formal rival, William Flinn, and together dominated Republican politics in the city of Pittsburgh for years. Magee made a fortune from his Consolidated Traction Company and donated large personal sums to establish the Pittsburgh Zoo and Pittsburgh's first ice hockey arena, the Schenley Park Casino. Magee's lasting legacy lives on in the form of Magee Women's Hospital, established by an endowment set up in Magee's will for such a purpose and built out of his mansion, the Maples. (Left, AC; below, NF.)

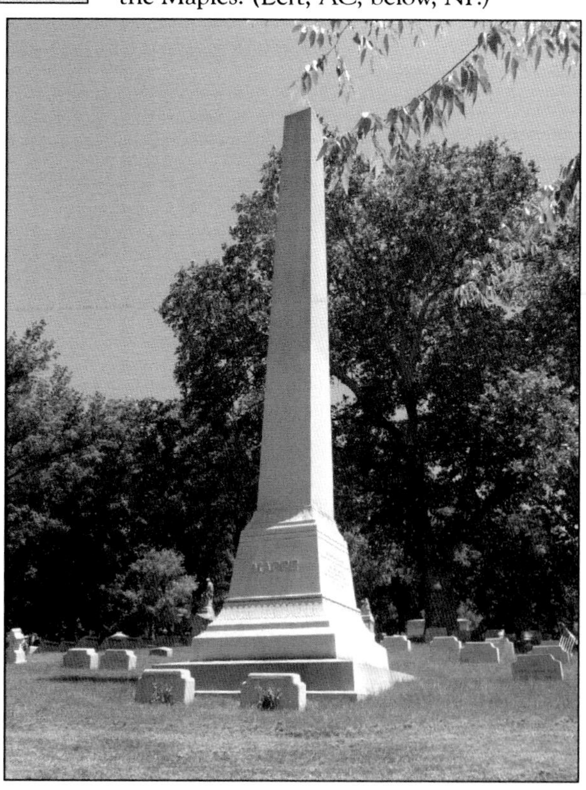

Seven

Artists and Entertainers

Artists and entertainers have always held a special place in the hearts of Americans. With varying forms of expression, these individuals provided a balance from laughter to tears, introspect to the superficial, satire to political agendas, and beauty where few could otherwise see it. It is often said that creative minds see the world a bit differently. Within this collection of painters, poets, writers, dreamers, sports legends, and musicians, this is certainly true. Something within them, a spark, an inkling, a devotion, caused them to pursue their passions, whatever those may have been. In doing so, their talents and tributes reached far beyond their individual abilities and were shared throughout societies around the world. Some graced the stage, others graced the field, and still others were known in opulent social and political circles. Throughout their careers, some intermingled with others who are highlighted throughout this chapter, crossing lines between influence, affluence, and the talents that encapsulated them all. Such passions for these artists, entertainers, and their talents are perhaps best summarized with lyrics from Lillian Russell's song "Come Down, Ma Evenin' Star:" "Search the sky from east to west / She's the brightest & the best/ But she's so far above me / I know she cannot love me / Still I love her more than all the rest."

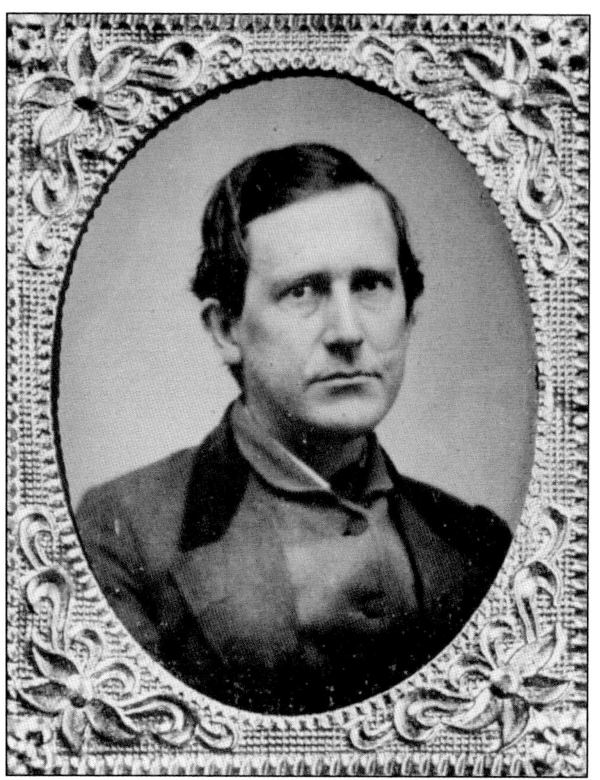

Stephen Foster (1826–1864; Section 21, Lots 30 and 31). Noted for being the "Father of American Music," Stephen Foster was best known for his parlor and minstrel compositions. Between 1850 and 1855, he wrote many of his best-known works, including "Camptown Races" (1850), "Nelly Bly" (1850), "Old Dog Tray" (1853), and "Jeanie with the Light Brown Hair" (1854), written for his wife, Jane Denny McDowell. He is perhaps best known for his song "Oh! Susanna," which was written between 1848 and 1849. Two of his songs, "Old Folks at Home" (known also as "Swanee River," 1851) and "My Old Kentucky Home" (1853) are the official state songs of Florida and Kentucky, respectively. In 1864, he died in New York under mysterious circumstances, subsequent to a fall. He was near penniless, and his wallet held a single scrap of paper, reading only, "Dear friends and gentle hearts." (Both, AC.)

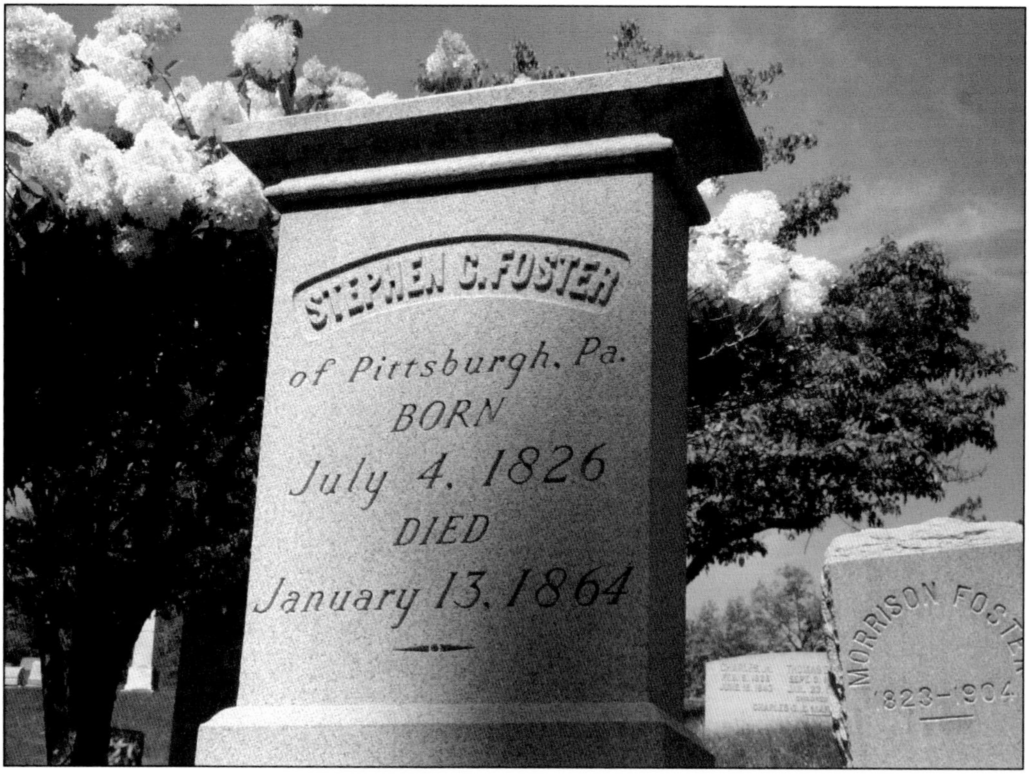

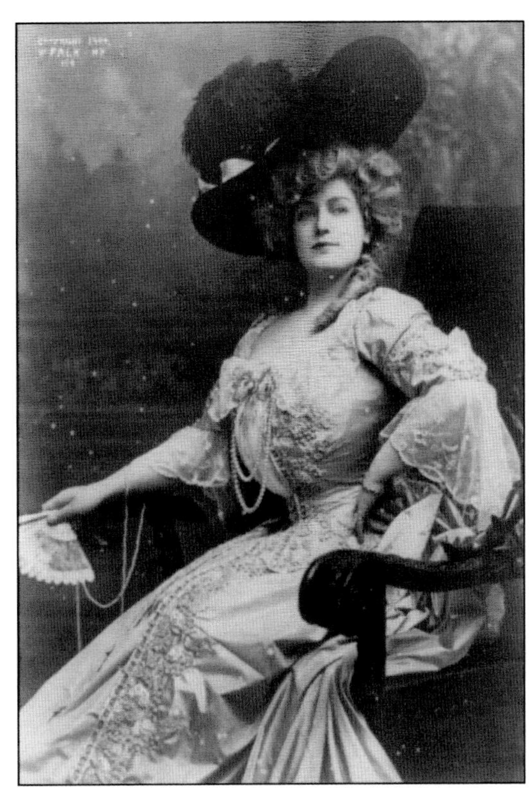

Lillian Russell (1860–1922; Section 40, Lot 5). Helen Louise Leonard was born in June 1860 on the outskirts of Chicago. Discovered by Tony Pastor around 1879, she changed her name to Lillian Russell. Her diverse career included stage work, vaudeville, musical theater, and opera. She was one of the most gifted sopranos ever to grace the stage, performing in numerous Gilbert & Sullivan productions. Although married four times, it was Diamond Jim Brady who was the love of her life. He gifted her with extravagance (such as a custom made Tiffany & Co. diamond encrusted bicycle) throughout the course of their four-decade love affair. In 1912, she married her fourth husband, Alexander Pollock Moore, of Pittsburgh. She is buried alongside him in a mausoleum that bears only her name and the inscription "The World Is Better for Her Having Lived." (Both, LOC.)

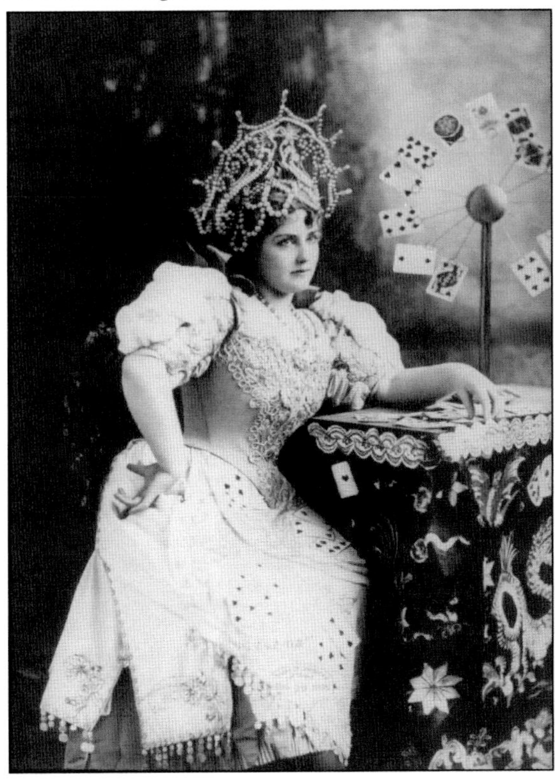

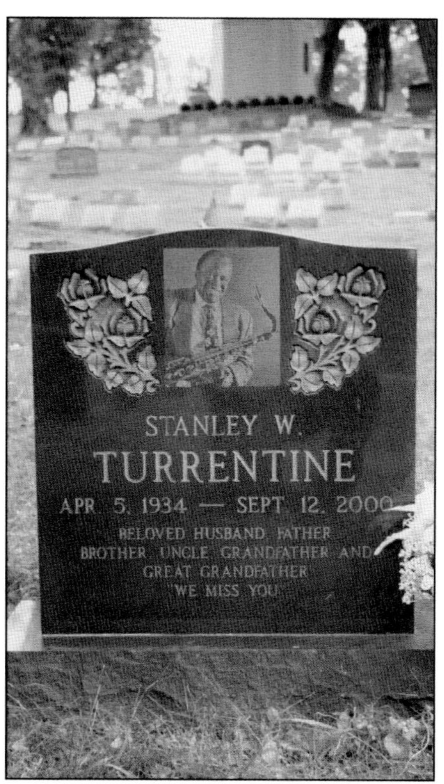

Stanley Turrentine (1934–2000; Section 26, Lot 722). "The Sugar Man" was born in Pittsburgh's Hill District at a time when the area was a hotbed for some of the greatest jazz performers of the era. While from a musical family, he never received a formal musical education. His career stretched through three decades, from the 1960s to the 1990s, and produced such well-known hits as "Sugar," "Sunny," "Pieces of Dreams," and "Don't Mess With Mr. T." Turrentine's beautifully engraved saxophone is now housed in the collection of Pittsburgh's Heinz History Center. (NF.)

William Augustus "Gus" Greenlee (1895–1952; Section 50, Lot 65). In 1933, Greenlee opened the Crawford Grill, drawing names such as John Coltrane, Miles Davis, Ella Fitzgerald, Louis Armstrong, Dizzy Gillespie, Martin Luther King Jr., and Roberto Clemente. Greenlee used his means (both legal and illegal) to provide scholarships and housing funds for his impoverished community. Greenlee also owned the Crawfords Negro League baseball team. The roster included future members of the Major League Baseball Hall of Fame—Josh Gibson, William Julius Johnson, Satchel Paige, and James Thomas "Cool Papa" Bell. (NF.)

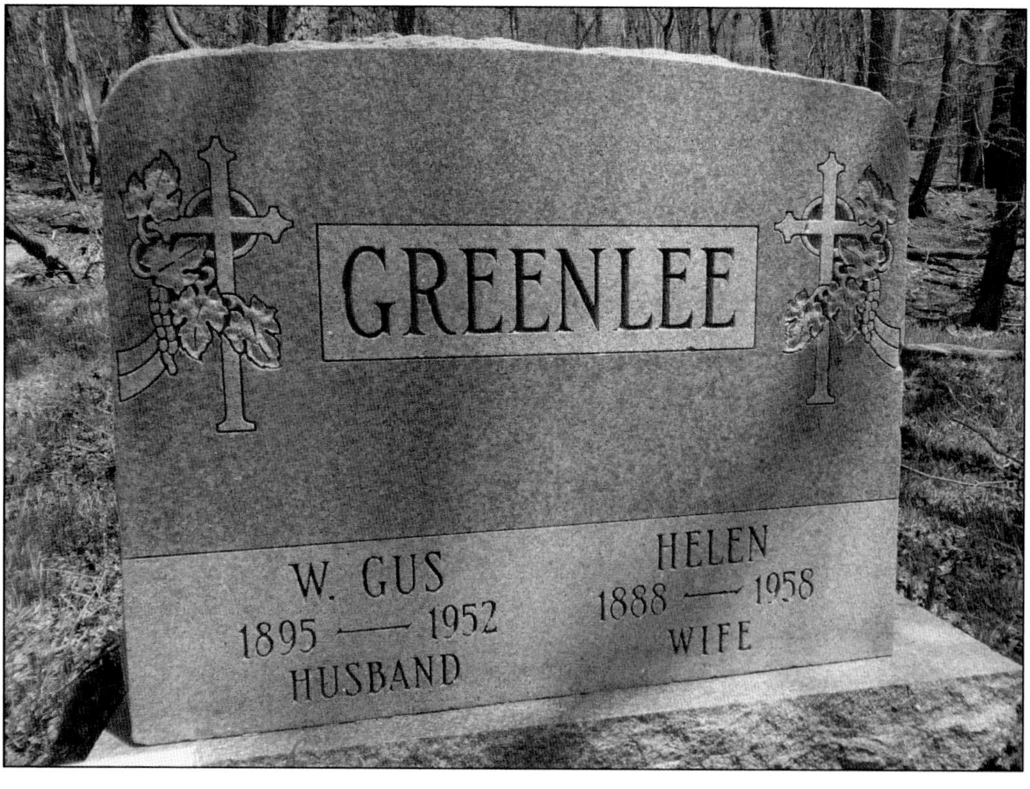

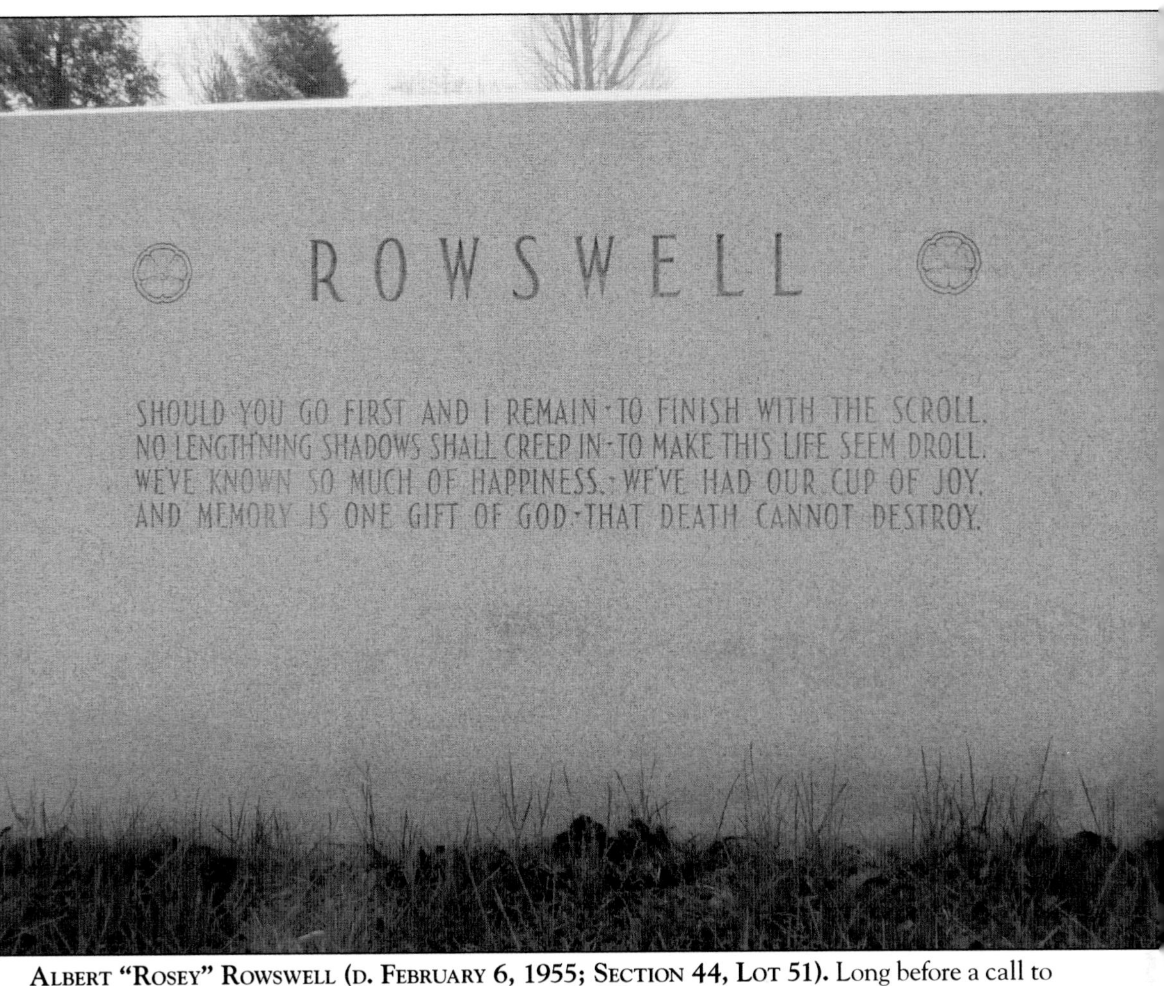

Albert "Rosey" Rowswell (d. February 6, 1955; Section 44, Lot 51). Long before a call to "Raise the Jolly Roger!" signaled a win for the Pittsburgh Pirates, the first official "Voice of the Pirates," Albert Kennedy "Rosey" Rowswell, was warning a fictitious dear old Aunt Minnie to raise her window. As a home run ball set sail above Forbes Field, Rosey would cry with abandon, "Raise the window, Aunt Minnie, here she comes!" before he let fall a tray of nuts and bolts in a theatrical interpretation of breaking glass. An extra base hit became a "dooziemaroonie," home runs were "round trippers," and the bases were never loaded, they were "F.O.B."—full of Bucs. Team owners originally feared his unprecedented style, but Rosey's untamable enthusiasm actually increased game attendance and widened the listening audience at home to include housewives and children. Rosey's infectious performances at the mic changed the character of sports broadcasting forever, and his allegiance to the home team became the identification badge all proud Pittsburghers would wear well into the next century. (NF.)

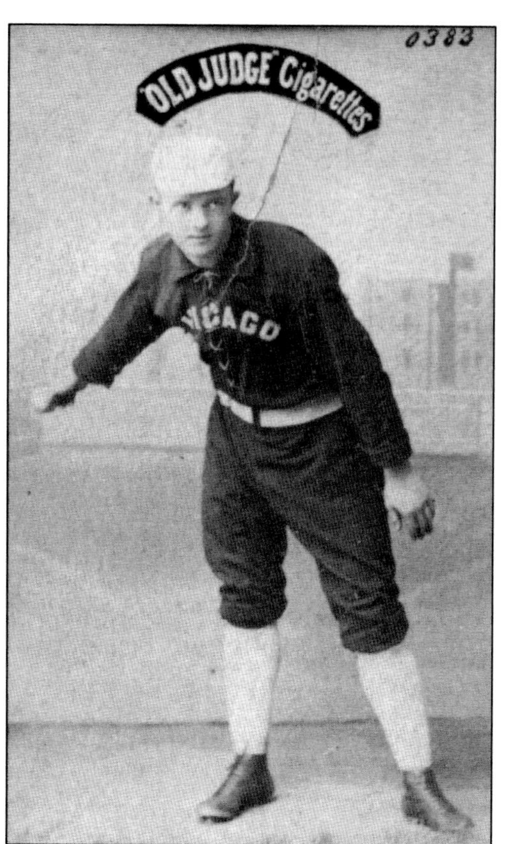

Marcus Elmore Baldwin (1863–1929; Section 22, Lot 409). "Baldy," or "Fido" as he was called, played seven seasons in Major League Baseball, notably as the pitcher for the Chicago White Stockings. Known as the "swiftest pitcher in the league," Baldwin's wild gesticulations preceded sudden, lightning-fast pitches, terrorizing opposing batters and catchers. No stranger to whiskey, his off-field antics were equally notorious, once being attacked by a monkey on the 1888–1889 World Tour after feeding it beer and pretzels. After baseball, Baldwin studied medicine and practiced as a physician and surgeon for 20 years. (LOC.)

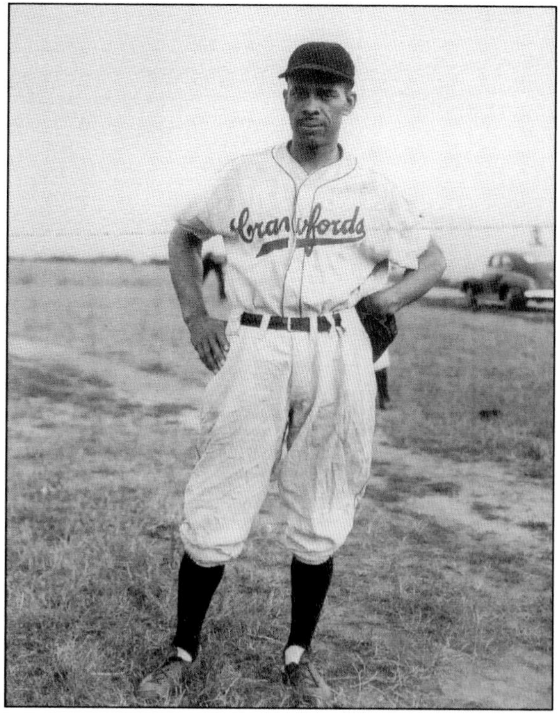

"Terrible" Ted Page (d. December 1, 1984; Section 54, Lot C 56). One of the fastest and fiercest to grace the plate, Negro Leagues star Ted Page played on the 1931 Homestead Grays and the 1932–1934 Pittsburgh Crawfords, becoming close friends with Josh Gibson. Page played rough and tough, often spiking opposing players while sliding into base, one time so hard and fast that a third basemen in Philadelphia died from injuries sustained by their collision. His own knee injury forced him to retire early in 1937 with a career batting average of .335. (AC.)

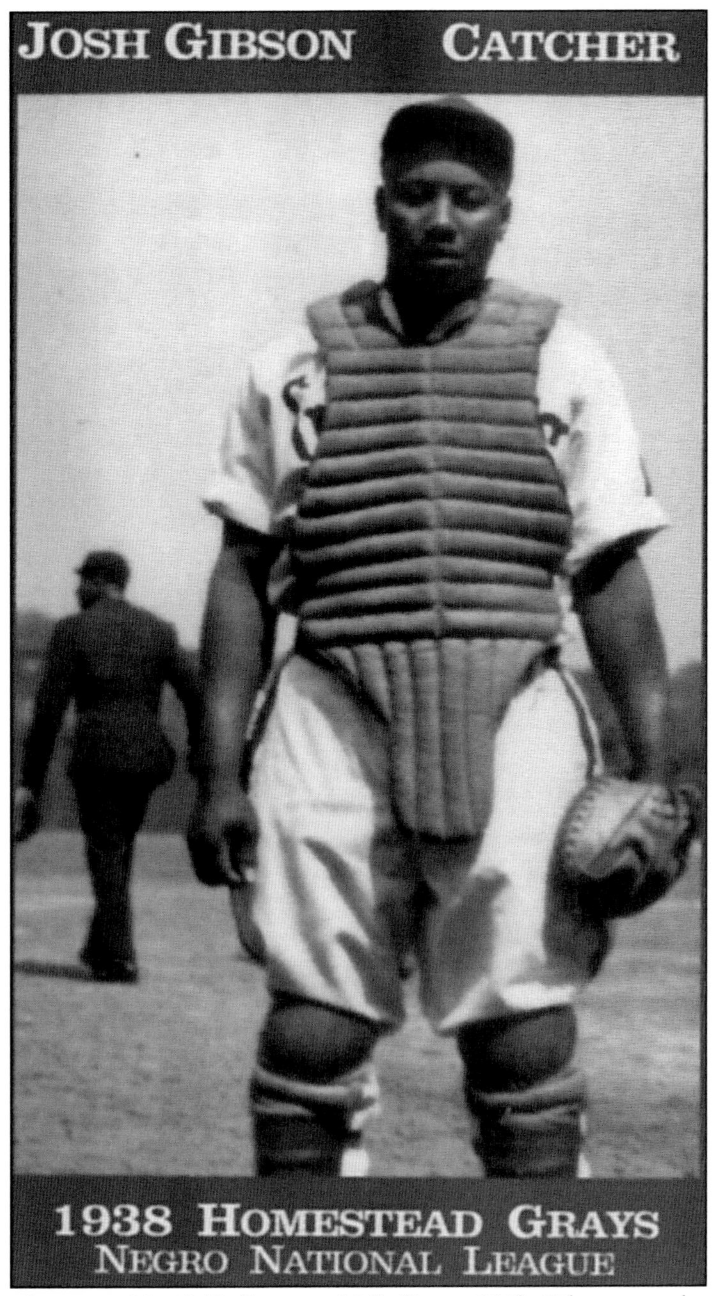

JOSH GIBSON (D. JANUARY 20, 1947; SECTION 50C, GRAVE 232). Gibson was already a legendary slugger when, at age 18, he hit a home run out of New York's Yankee Stadium—the only player in any league and of any color to ever be credited with the feat in regular play. Dubbed "The Black Babe Ruth," Gibson's talent as a catcher was matched at bat, with nearly 800 career home runs during his time with the Pittsburgh Crawfords and the Homestead Grays. Gibson was diagnosed with a brain tumor at age 32, but he refused to have it removed for fear it would cripple him. For the last four seasons before his death, he overcame constant headaches to play incredible games, earning another two batting crowns and three additional home run titles. He was posthumously inducted into the baseball hall of fame in 1972. (AC.)

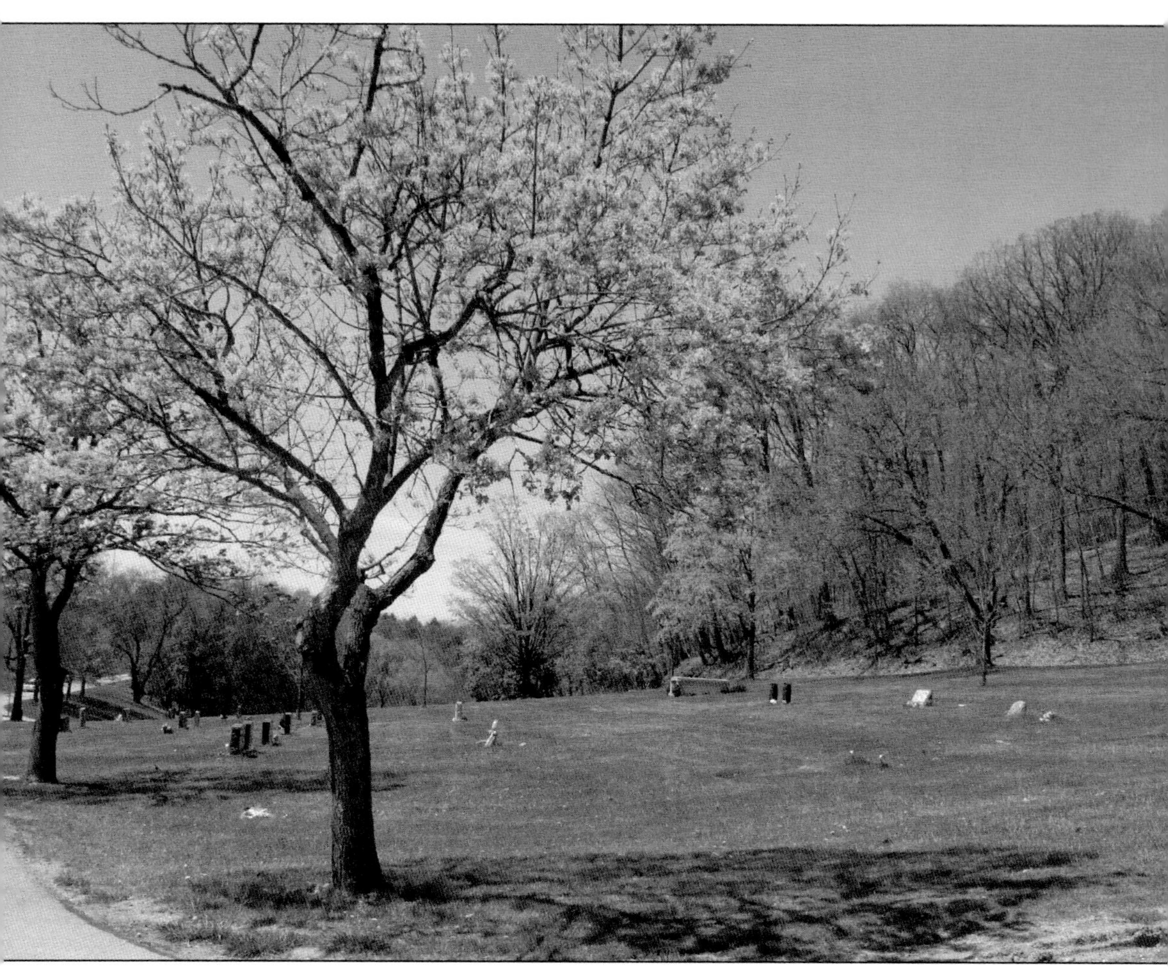

Carroll Hoff "Beano" Cook (1931–2012; Section 64, Lot 60). At age seven, Carroll Cook received the nickname "Beano" after he moved to Pittsburgh from Boston ("Beantown"). He graduated from the University of Pittsburgh in 1954 and spent two years in the Army. He worked for several years as a sports publicist, and in 1986, he joined ESPN as a studio commentator. During that time, he was continuously featured on Pittsburgh sports broadcasts for Fox Sports Radio and was a guest of Mark Madden. In 2010, he was selected as the recipient of the Bert McGrane Award for outstanding contribution to the Football Writers Association of America. (NF.)

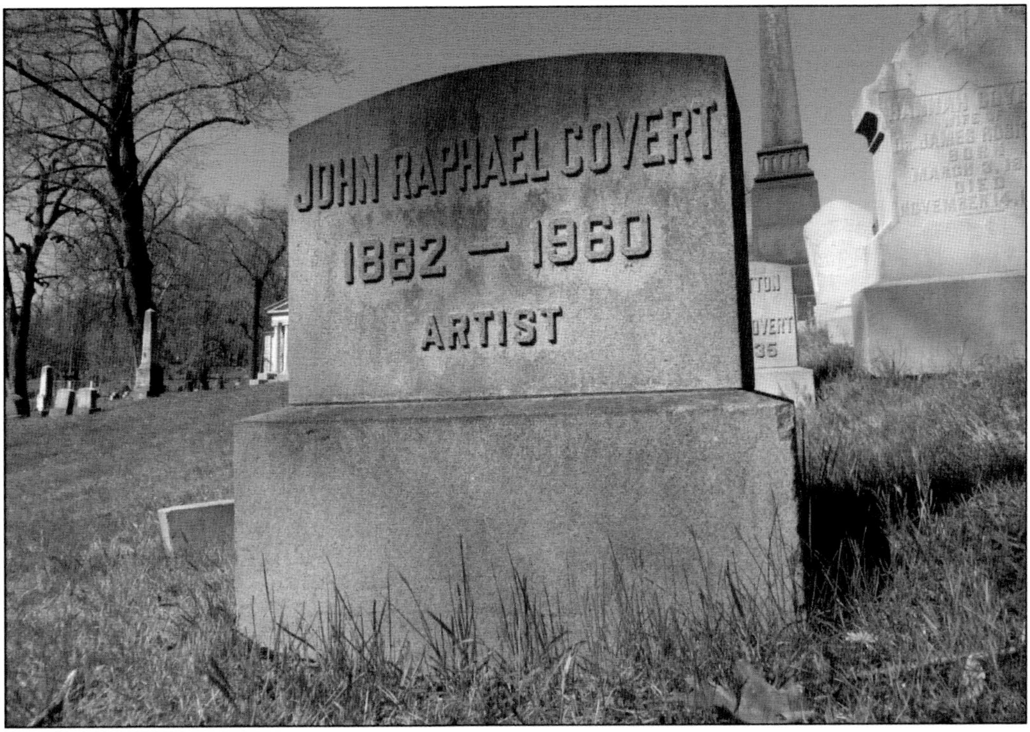

John Covert (1882–1960; Section 22, Lot 107). A Lawrenceville native, Covert studied in Munich and then Paris between 1909 and 1915, where he became lifelong friends with Marcel Duchamp. His years in New York City, from 1916 to 1923, were spent in the noted salon of his cousin Walter Arensberg exploring the realm of the avant-garde, dadaism, and cubism, and founding the Society of Independent Artists, whose inner circle included Man Ray. His most famous piece, *Time*, completed in 1919, is of mixed media and incorporates the artist's fascination with cryptography. By 1923, Covert returned to Pittsburgh, where he worked as a salesman in his family's Vesuvius Crucible Company until his death. (NF.)

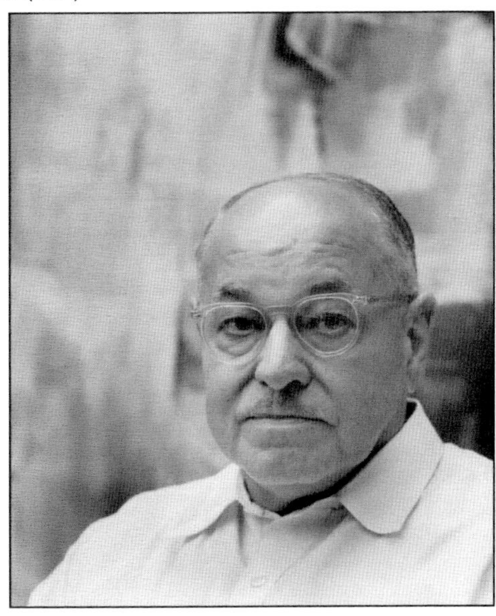

Samuel Rosenberg (1896–1972). Known as the "painter laureate of Pittsburgh," Samuel Rosenberg's styles included everything from portraits to landscapes and collages. For approximately 40 years, Rosenberg taught at the Irene Kaufmann Settlement, Carnegie Institute of Technology, the Young Men & Women's Hebrew Association, and the Pennsylvania College for Women. He made a point of inviting students into his studio for detailed lessons and skill workshops. Many will recognize the work of one of his best-known students—Andy Warhol. (Rauh Jewish History Program & Archives.)

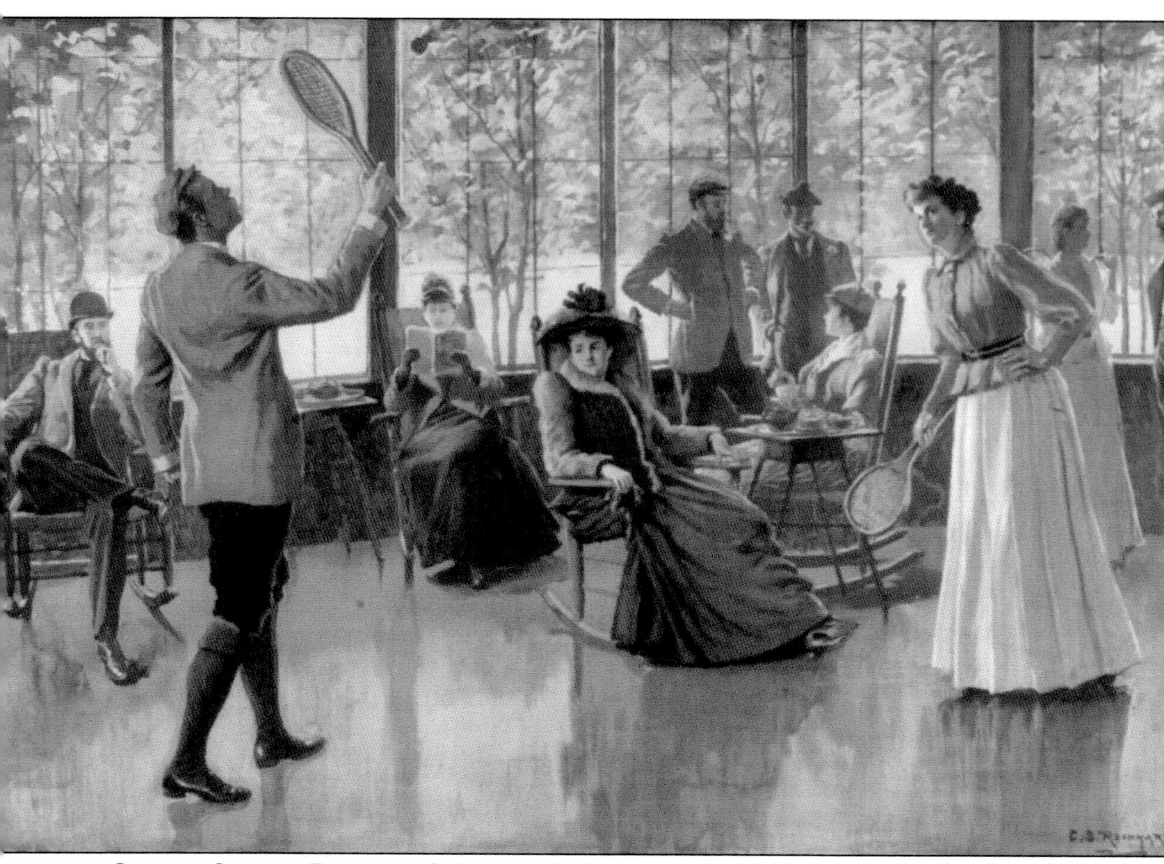

Charles Stanley Reinhart (1844–1896; Section 3, Lot 32). Born in Pittsburgh and having worked in both the steel and railway industries, Charles Stanley Reinhart was not truly content until he began to develop his talent as a painter and illustrator. In 1887, his work *Washed Ashore* (depicting observers of a drowned sailor along a beach) received an honorable mention at the 1887 Paris Salon and the 1888 Temple Gold Medal from the Pennsylvania Academy of the Fine Arts. Towards the end of his life, Reinhart would go on to win the prestigious First Gold Medal and the Second Silver Medal at the Paris Exposition in 1889. That same year, the Paris Exposition purchased his painting *Rising Tide*. Fans of his work included none other than Vincent van Gogh and Willa Cather, the latter of whom attended the erection of the monument in his name when he was buried in Allegheny Cemetery. (LOC.)

Seth V. Albee (1836–1924; Section 33, Lot 211.) Albee lived in Pittsburgh in 1877 during one of the most violent railroad disputes of the 19th century. Local law enforcement refused to fire on striking workers, but Philadelphia militiamen did. Twenty people were killed, 29 injured. Rioters razed dozens of buildings and destroyed hundreds of locomotives. The aftermath was frozen in time through Albee's photography. His documentation, often done with a heavy cart laden with glass plates, helped bring to the public eye a moment in time that once seemed unfathomable. (Pennsylvania State Archives.)

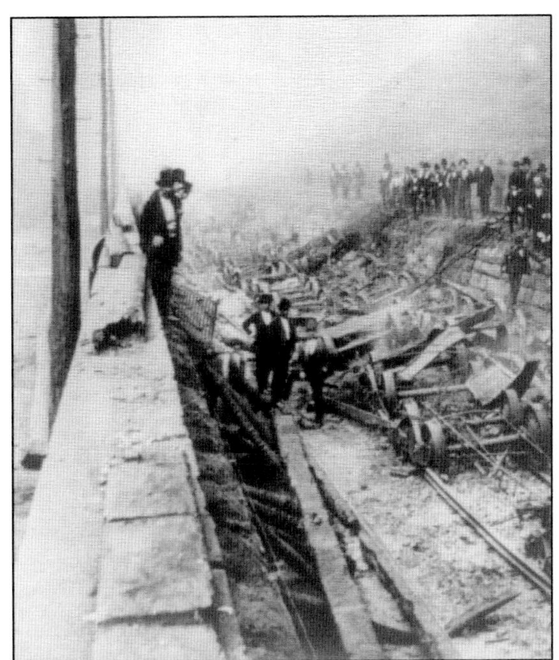

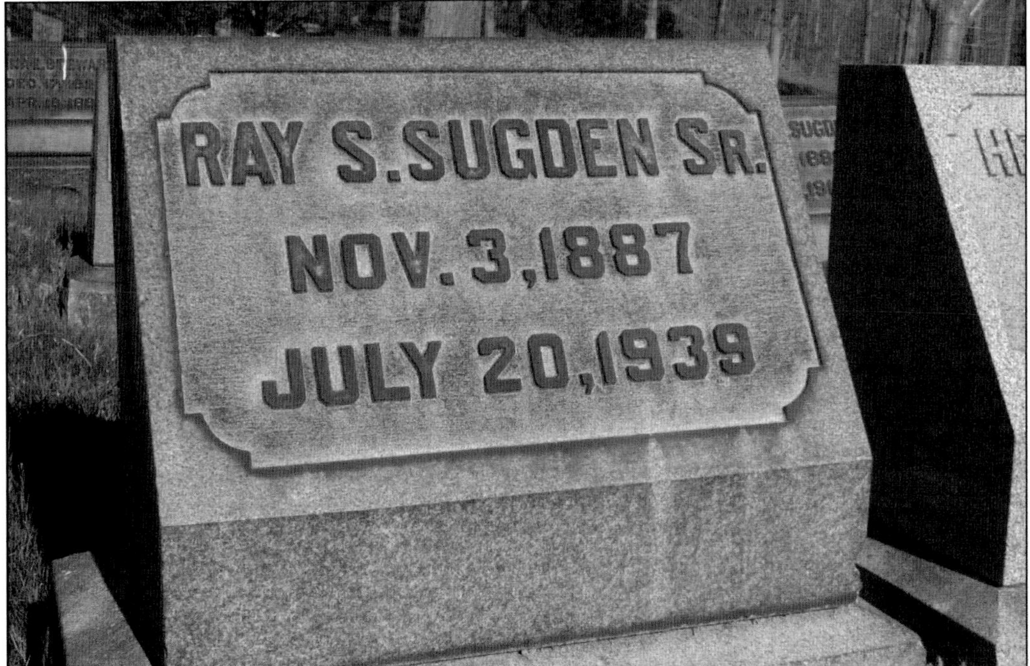

Raymond S. Sugden (1887–1939; Section 33, Lot 187). Born in Lawrenceville, Sugden was the son of a bank director who chose his own path in life, studying the mystifying arts of illusion and prestige and creating for himself the world-famous persona of "Tampa the Great." He performed for King George V in London and was also booked as "England's Court Magician." Both titles were household names in the 1920s and 1930s—posters and ephemera from his shows are still highly collectible. He pioneered the "spirit painting" act, a very difficult process that Houdini himself replicated. (NF.)

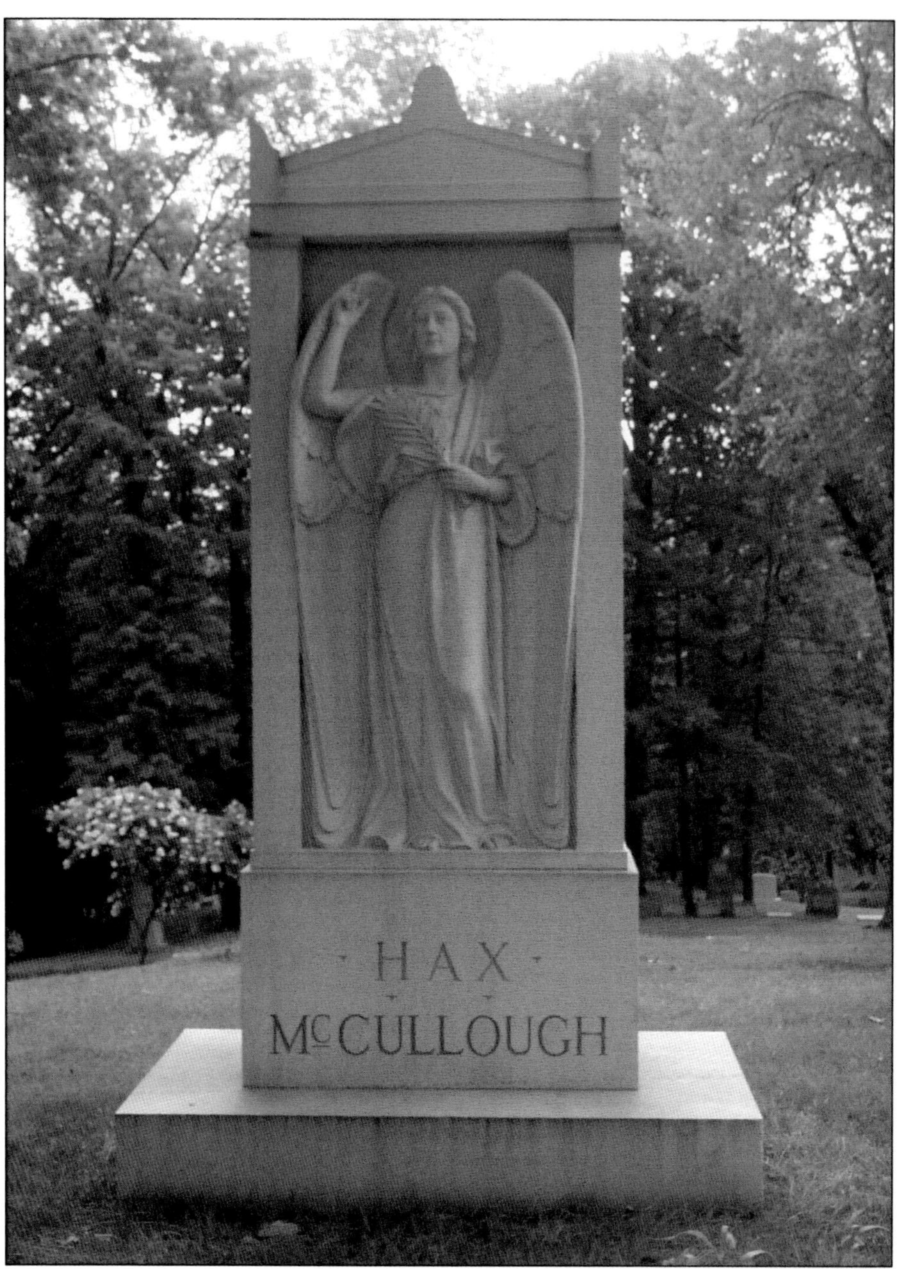

C. Hax McCullough Jr. (1926–2007; Section 20, Lot 14/15). Music and history are often intertwined to tell beloved tales. Fortunately for Pittsburgh, resident C. Hax McCullough Jr. was a patron of both. Known for his book *The Illustrated History of Opera in Pittsburgh*, "Hax" was in the process of writing another publication at the time of his death. A talented historian and writer, his work featured numerous companies throughout Pittsburgh, including Mellon Bank, Union Switch & Signal, and Pittsburgh Natural Gas. Beyond his literary contributions, he served as a corporator of Allegheny Cemetery and was much heralded by Pittsburgh's art community. His brother, acclaimed author David McCullough, noted in Hax's obituary: "The flame of his mind was blazing right up to the end. He was extremely bright and knew so much about opera, classical music, and was a real fount of knowledge about Pittsburgh. He loved that city." (Daniel Olesinski.)

Eight

Girl Power

It is impossible to write about the achievements of the women in this chapter without first considering the eras in which they lived. In a time before women were able to vote, hold influential political offices, or speak freely, these women shouted in the company of whispers. Fighting against societal norms, they utilized both their intellect and character to lay the foundations for great changes yet to come. Those like Gertrude Gordon and Carrie Reese, both pioneering female journalists, used the print medium to affect societal change. Several of these women used their copious wealth for great philanthropic efforts, and in doing so, changed not just society but the nature of the times in which they lived. Colorful characters like Cornelia Baldwin stand alongside those of quiet fortitude, such as Sylvia Coffin. Within this sisterhood of mothers, wives, and daughters, one thing is certain—at a time when a male-dominated society or profession could have stood in their way, each of these women stepped outside of themselves and their constraints in ways that ultimately bettered and benefitted every generation of women to follow. For that, they are owed not only a mention in this book, but gratitude, respect, and, perhaps, even a piece of oneself to continue the efforts they started.

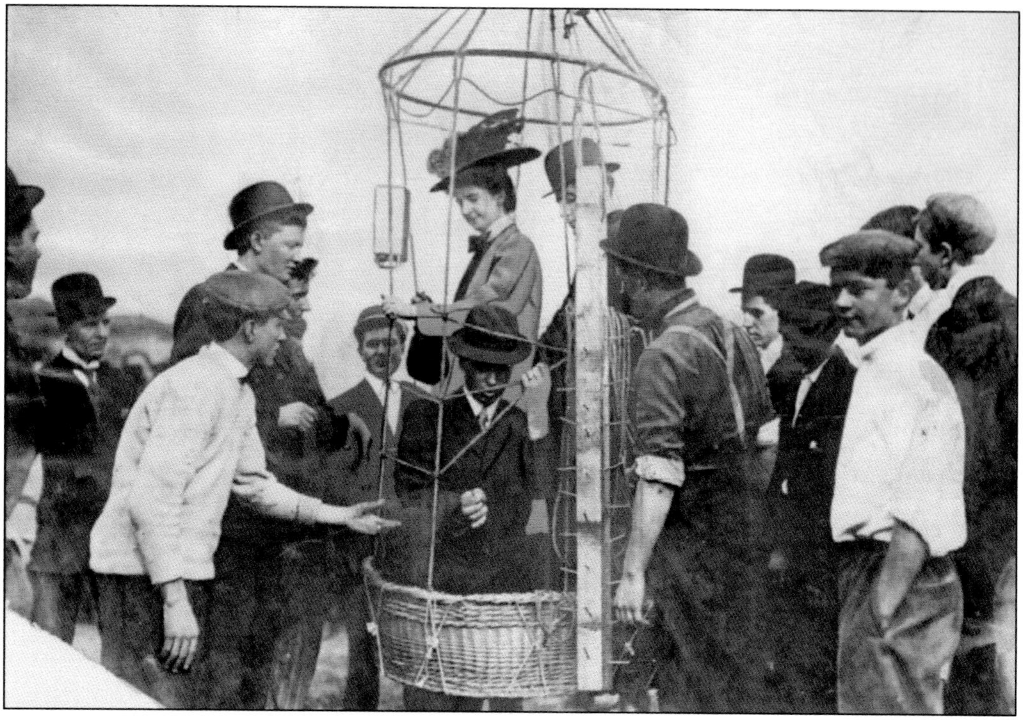

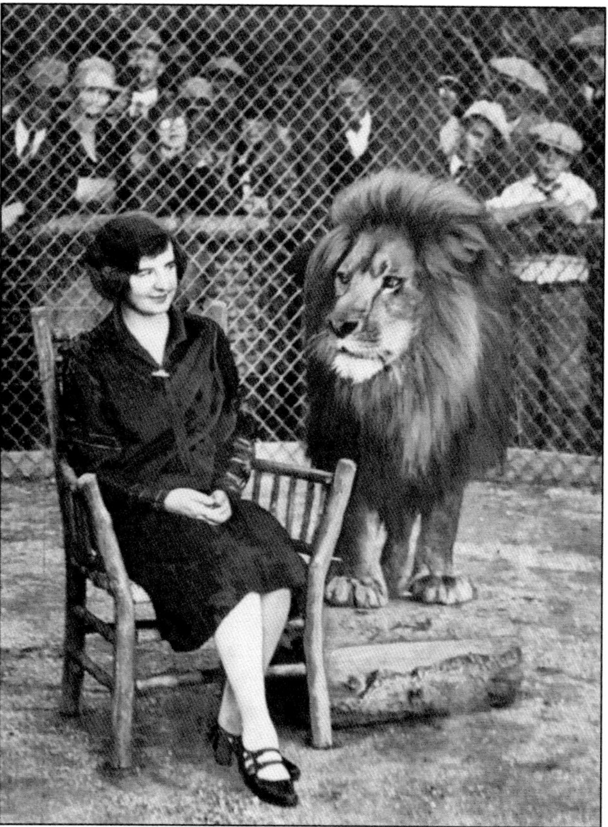

Gertrude Gordon (1883–1955; Section 31, Lot 612). A pioneer Pittsburgh journalist, Gertrude (Kelley) Gordon was one of the first women in Pittsburgh ever to receive a byline. Her fearless reputation was well-earned given the lengths she went for her stories. She once ascended 2,250 feet in a balloon (the first woman in Pittsburgh to do so) and in 1919 took a ride in an airplane in the early days of aviation. She literally stepped into the lion's den, climbing inside a cage with one while covering a story at the Hippodrome in 1909. According to Marylynne Pitz of The Digs, Gordon interviewed many notable people, including Amelia Earhart, Babe Ruth, Billy Sunday, Sarah Bernhardt, Mary Pickford, Theodore Roosevelt, George M. Cohan, Sir Arthur Conan Doyle, and Honus Wagner. She is remembered with a scholarship awarded by the Women's Press Club of Pittsburgh in her honor. (Both, *Pittsburgh Post-Gazette*/The Digs.)

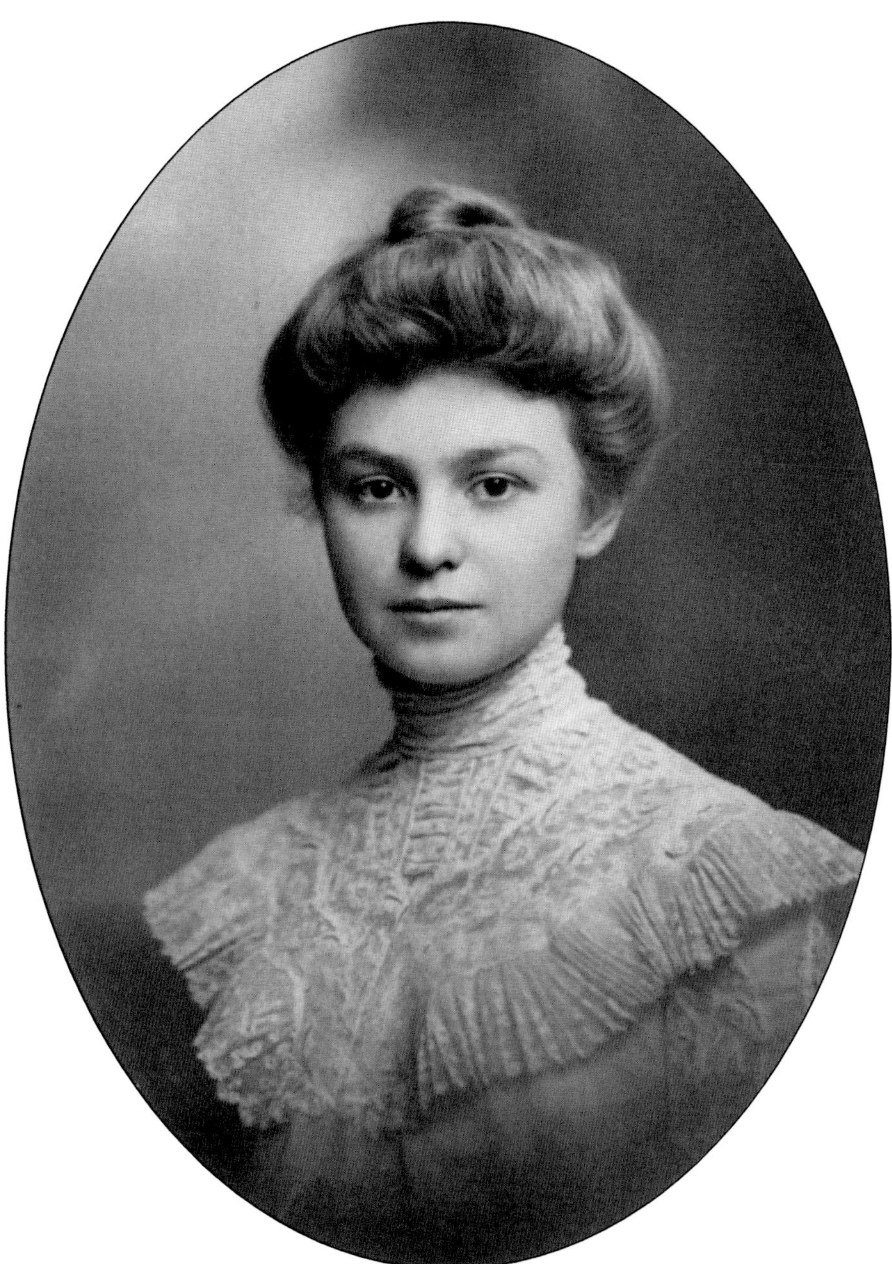

Rachel McMasters Miller Hunt (1882–1963; Section 44, Lot 5). Hunt had several great loves in her lifetime. Two of those—horticulture and books—emerged at a young age. At the age of 15, she purchased her first gardening book. She began to accumulate a definitive collection on the subject. This wealth of botanical knowledge encouraged her to indulge another interest—bookbinding—for which she was awarded an honorary degree by the Carnegie Institute of Technology. Her marriage to Roy A. Hunt in 1913 provided the environment in which all of her other loves flourished, and together, they would raise four sons. In 1961, the Hunt Institute for Botanical Documentation was established, which serves today as a valuable worldwide horticultural reference, including many of the original books Hunt once held so dear. (Roy A. Hunt Foundation.)

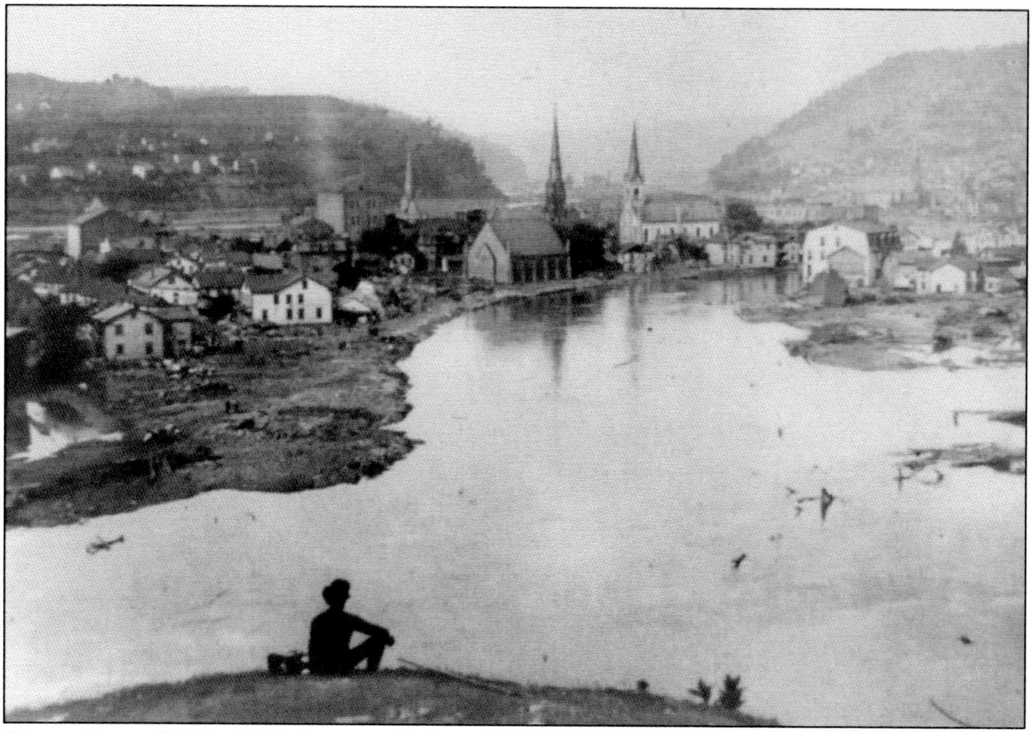

Carrie Reese (1856–1914; Section 18, Lot 81). Carrie Reese was a pioneering female journalist. "Cara's Column" was published in Pittsburgh's *Commercial Gazette* from 1884 to 1894. Following the Johnstown flood (shown here), she was one of the few women covering the event, with articles and her own illustrations for the *Pittsburg Dispatch*. She attended and presented at the 1893 World's Columbian Exposition in Chicago, focusing on women's interests. She concluded her speech there by saying, "Seek contentment. Crave not worldly rush. Better the pinch of occasional sacrifice than the loss of womanly dignity and reserve." (LOC.)

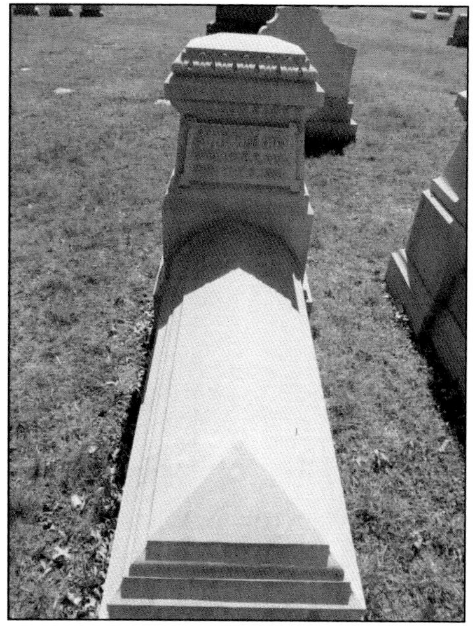

Jane Holmes (1805–1885; Section 11, Lot 2). Dubbed "Lady Bountiful," Holmes's charitable contributions displayed a liberality in giving theretofore unseen. She converted her family's Lawrenceville property into the Protestant Home for Incurables and established the Home for Aged Protestant Women, Home for Colored Children, and the Home for Aged Protestant Couples. These homes were so tenderly planned that no comfort was lacking, including beauty parlors, chapels, and immaculate gardens for walking. She named 17 bequests in her will, which established organizations still in operation, including the Western Pennsylvania School for the Blind and Pressley Ridge, among others. (NF.)

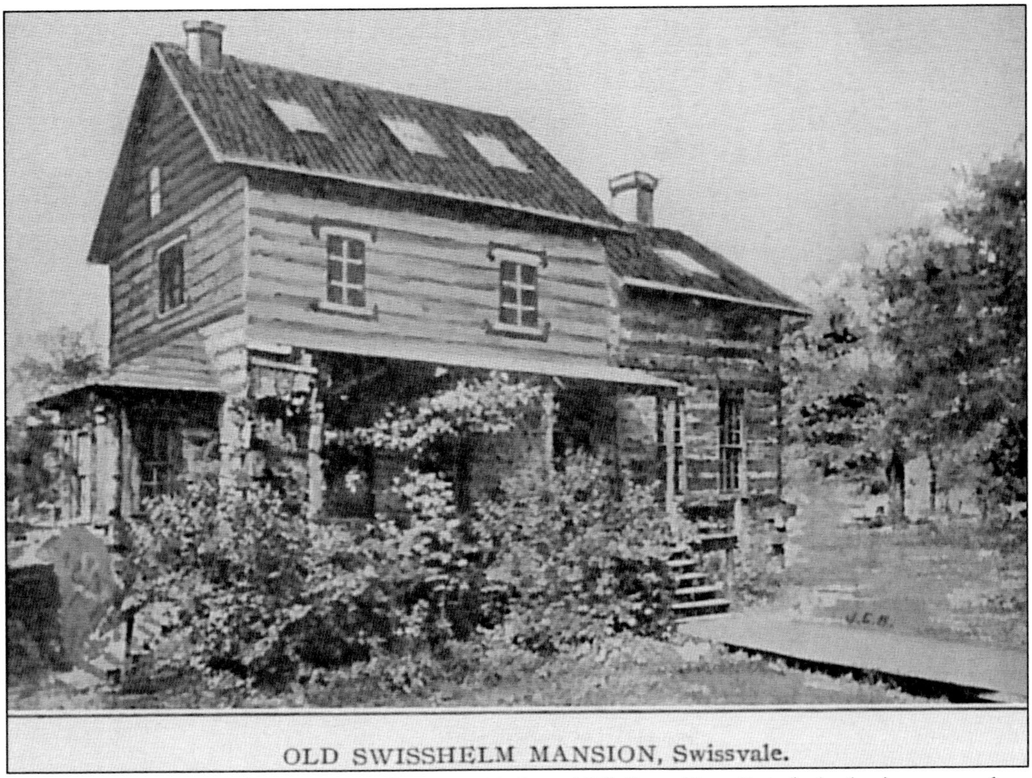

OLD SWISSHELM MANSION, Swissvale.

JANE GREY SWISSHELM (1815–1884; SECTION 10, LOT 485). Jane Grey Swisshelm had an outspoken career as a journalist and abolitionist in a time when women were seldom encouraged to speak their minds. Her printing press, typeface, and other writing materials were set afire in her office as a warning against her efforts. She continued to set the world on fire by replenishing her materials and continuing her assault against injustice. In her paper, the *St. Cloud Visiter,* she vehemently criticized a group of politicians who were still keeping slaves in free areas of the state. Returning to her roots in 1847, Swisshelm served as editor of the *Saturday Pittsburgh Visiter,* an abolitionist newspaper. For reasons unknown, towards the end of her life and career, Swisshelm set fire to her own words and works, leaving a hole in history that was impossible to repair. (AC.)

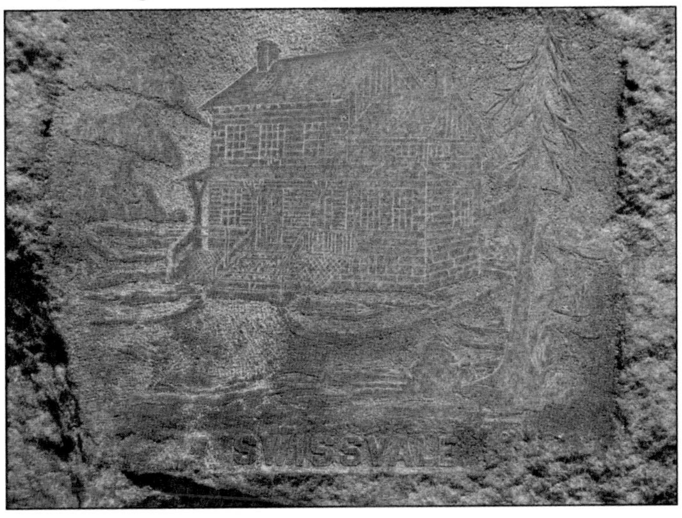

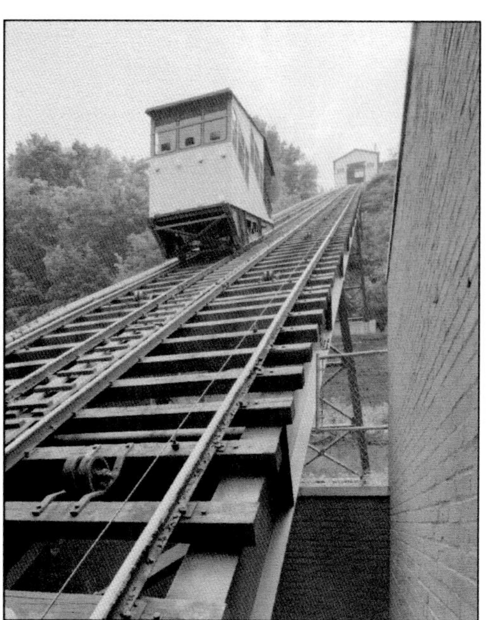

Caroline Endres Diescher (1846–1930; Section 28, Lot 183). A rarity in her time, Caroline Endres was educated in the predominately male field of engineering by her father, Prussian-born John Endres. She became one of the first female engineers in the United States. Alongside her father, they built the Monongahela and Mount Oliver Inclines. Caroline married her father's partner, Samuel Diescher, together responsible for the design and construction of Pittsburgh's famous Duquesne Incline. They formed one of Pittsburgh's power couples of the early 20th century, with a legacy that lives in the city to this day. (LOC.)

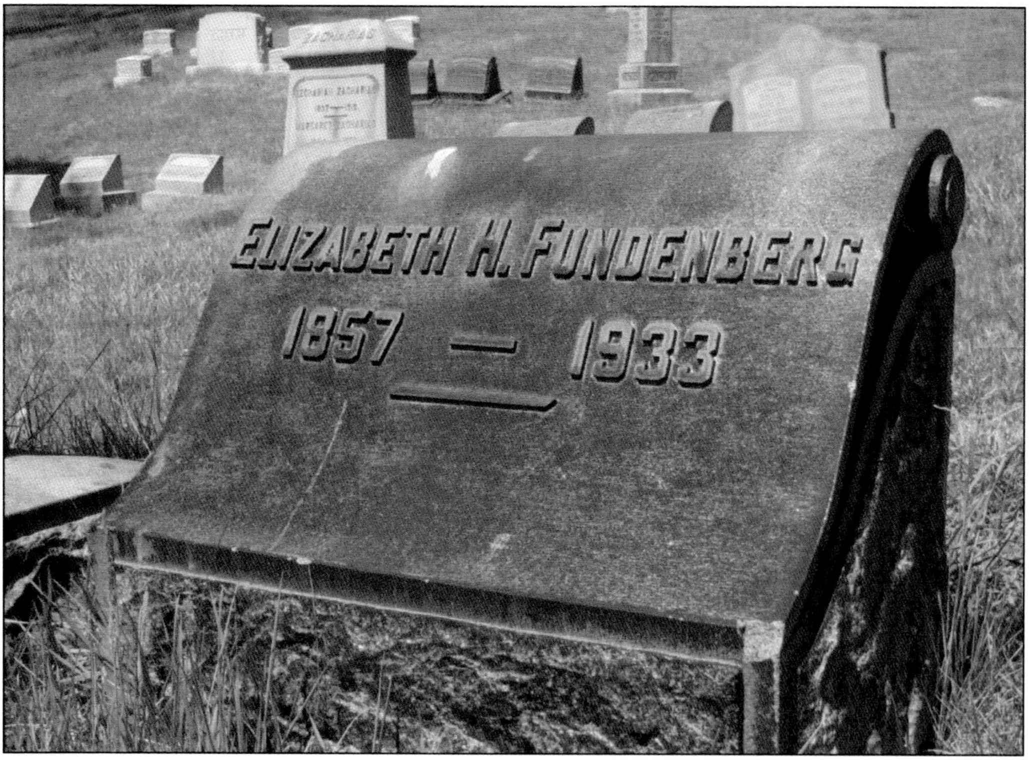

Elizabeth Horton Fundenberg (Section 31, Lot 718). In her 1933 obituary, the *Pittsburgh Press* lauded Elizabeth Horton Fundenberg as a "famous child educator and author" and a "pioneer in phonetics." She authored a textbook for students that was used throughout Pittsburgh and the state of Pennsylvania. With a focus on syllables rather than entire words, she created a method of literacy instruction that allowed many generations of children to embrace a love of learning. She eventually became a school principal and served as such up until World War I. (NF.)

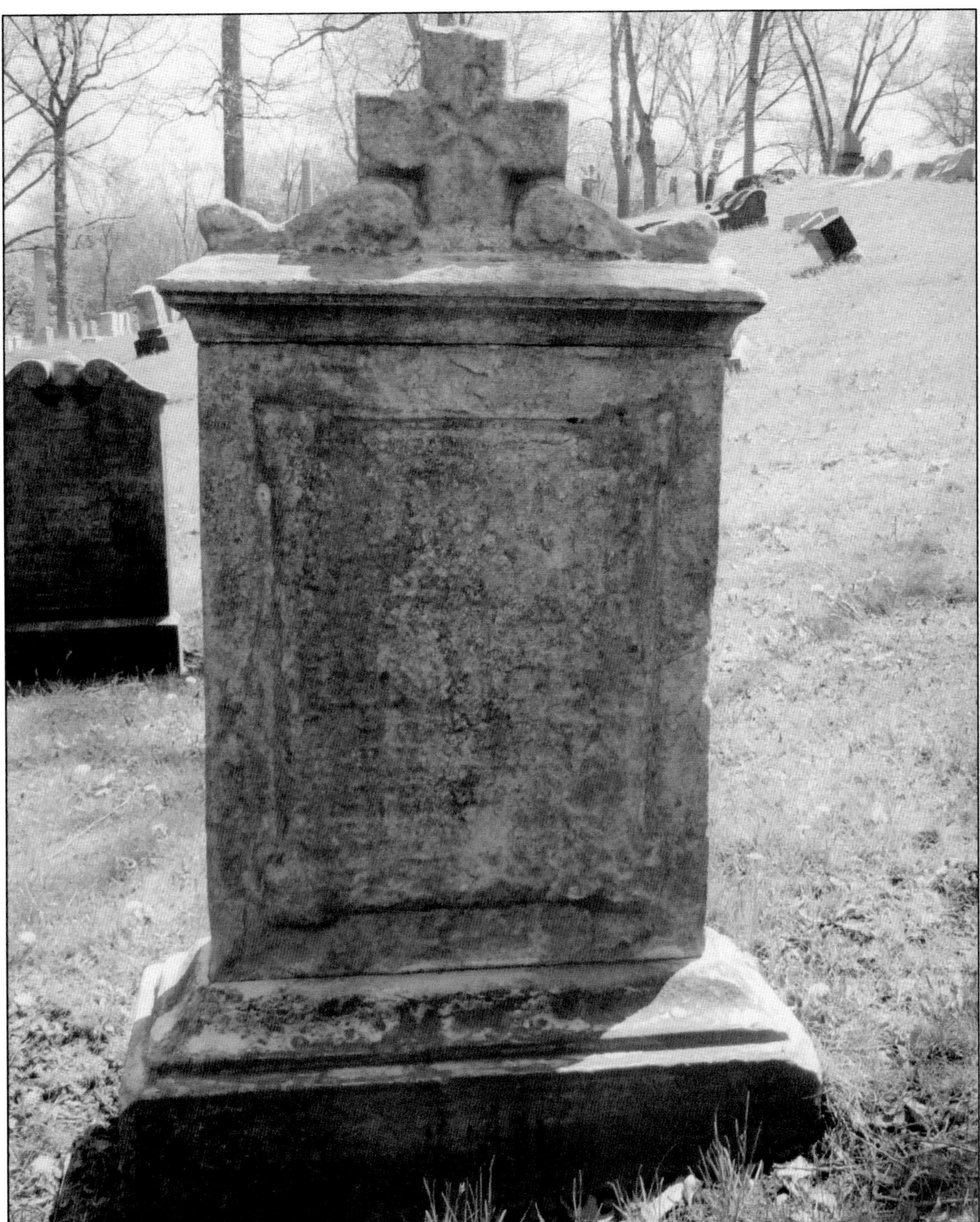

Sylvania Catherine Coffin (1846–1898; Section 2, Lot 104). One of the first nurses of the distinguished Red Cross, "Sylvia" Coffin was a veteran of the Spanish-American war and one of the first women to volunteer her services for the war in Cuba. Sworn in on the docks in New York, she arrived in Cuba and immediately began to assist those who were wounded and ill. In doing so, she contracted typhoid, but she was not aware of it and continued her service as long as she was physically capable. Her service was selfless and her illness brief. She died two months after contracting the disease but subsequent to helping those who desperately needed her most. She was an eighth-generation descendant of Tristram Coffin, founder of Nantucket, Massachusetts, and also related to Owen Coffin, of the infamous whale ship *Essex* disaster. (NF.)

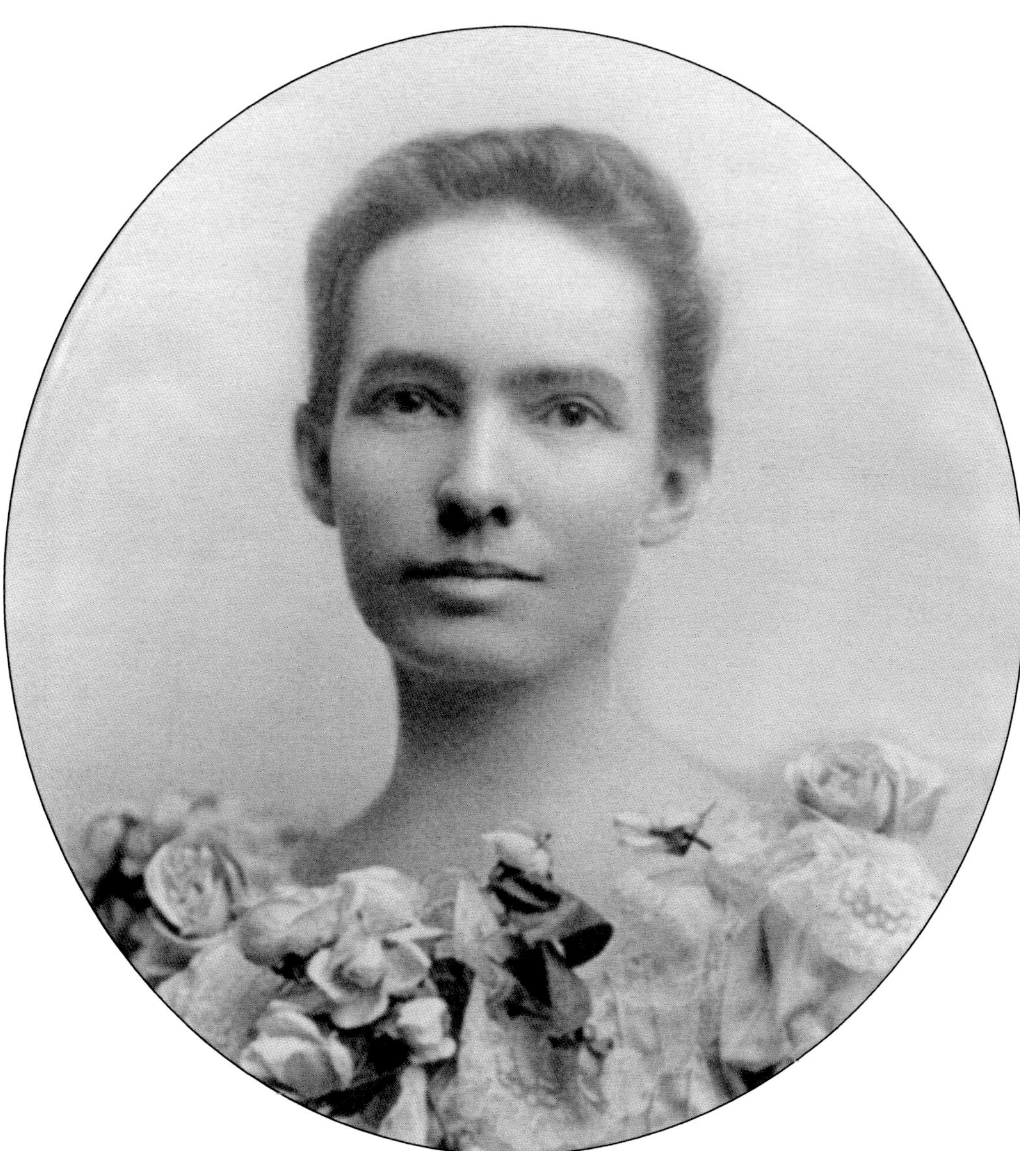

EDITH DENNISTON DARLINGTON AMMON (1862–1919; SECTION 11, LOT 31). With a passion for history instilled by her father, Ammon dedicated her life to the appreciation and preservation of western Pennsylvania's past. Descended from a Revolutionary War hero (James O'Hara), she joined the Daughters of the American Revolution in 1891. At that time, the Pittsburgh Chapter was working on efforts to save and restore the Fort Pitt Blockhouse, given to the city free of charge by Mary Schenley in 1894. Ammon fought tirelessly against the patriarchal city leadership, who wanted to demolish the blockhouse in order to advance the industrialism overtaking the city. Drafting a bill for the state legislature, Ammon lobbied to protect historical structures from demolition, asking "Have you no history? Have you no pride?" In 1907, the bill was passed and the blockhouse preserved for posterity. (ASC.)

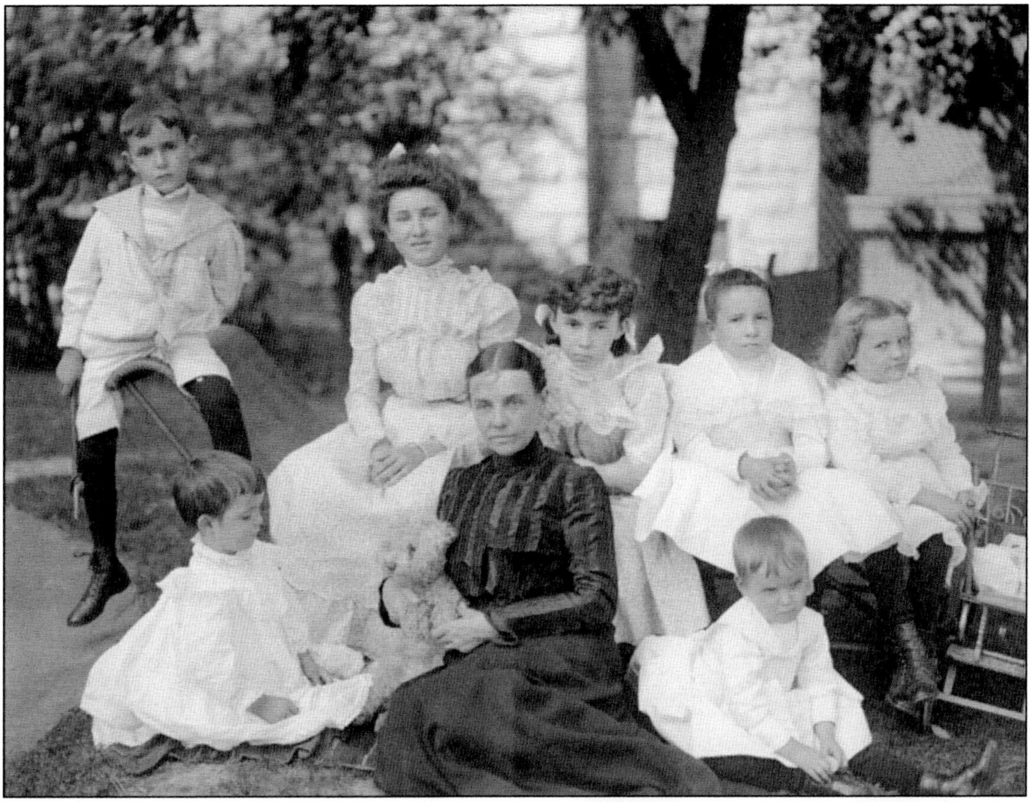

Mary Acheson Spencer (1863–1950; Section 14, Lot 99). Spencer was very beloved by her children and held a degree from the Pennsylvania College for Women. Her husband, Charles, was an amateur photographer, and Mary appears alongside their children in hundreds of well-documented images. Her devotion to her family was noted decades after her death when daughter Ethel wrote in her 1983 memoir *The Spencers of Amberson Avenue*: "When she went away we missed her more than tongue could tell." (ASC.)

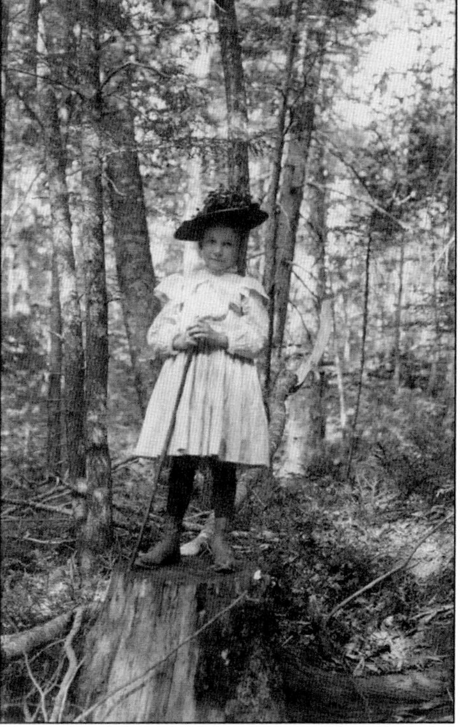

Ethel Spencer (1889–1966; Section 14, Lot 99–102). The third daughter of Charles and Mary Spencer, Ethel was an English professor and ran the Department of General Studies at Carnegie Tech, now Carnegie Mellon University. She wrote *The Spencers of Amberson Avenue* about being raised in an upper middle class suburb, and filled it with candid photographs taken by her late father (such as this one of Ethel vacationing in New York's Catskill Mountains in July 1898). The book provides a firsthand account of life for a moderately wealthy family during Victorian times. (ASC.)

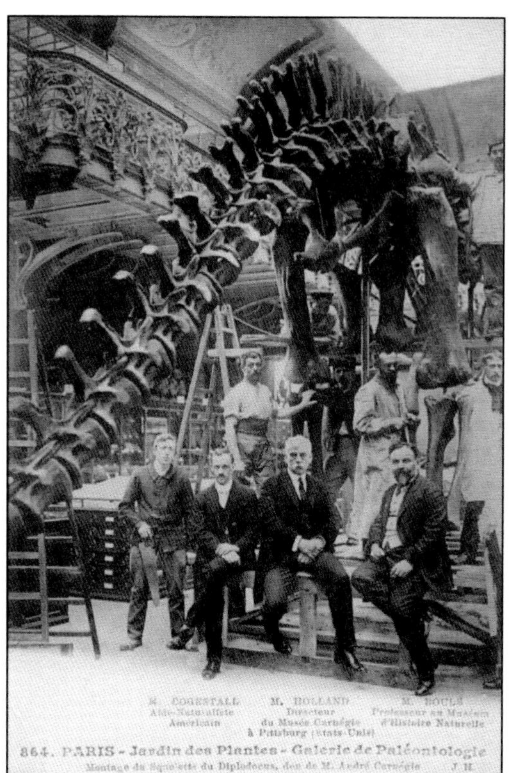

Rev. William Jacob Holland (1848–1932; Section 13, Lot 59). From 1891 to 1901, William Jacob Holland (seated second from right) served as chancellor for the Western University of Pennsylvania (now the University of Pittsburgh). Under his guardianship, the university was opened to women for the first time in its history. He continued to advance many aspects of education by adding programs of graduate studies. Under his tenure, the schools of law, medicine, mines, pharmacy, and dentistry were established. Throughout his lifetime, he advanced his own religious studies, settling in Pittsburgh in 1874 as the pastor of Bellefield Presbyterian Church. He became a trustee of the Pennsylvania College for Women, where he taught Latin, Greek, and ancient languages. In 1898, he was elected director of the Carnegie Museum and served in that capacity for the next three years. (AC.)

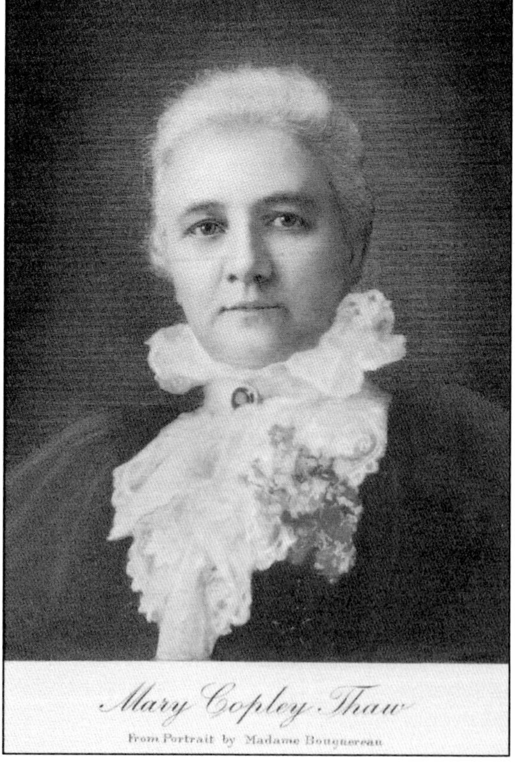

Mary Sibbet Copley Thaw (1843–1929; Section 16, Lot 119). Days before her 87th birthday, Thaw died of pneumonia, with son Harry Kendall Thaw by her side. During his trials, Mary used her great wealth in his defense. Her obituary noted: "Her loyalty to him during his trial for the murder of Stanford White has been pointed out as an example of motherly love seldom equalled." Conversely, she utilized her wealth for numerous philanthropic efforts throughout Pittsburgh. (AC.)

Nine

MAKING HEADLINES

Occasionally, there are singular moments in time that define a person, a place, or an experience. In this chapter, several of these momentous snapshots have been drawn together and brief homage paid here. For each experience, a lifetime of moments came before, but seldom after, and it was sadly sometimes the occasion of death that defined these lives. Within are touching expressions of fondness and tributes (Houdini), desperate attempts to prevent tragedy (Darragh), twisted elements of base depravity (Thaw), and heart-wrenching losses for which resolution was never found (Hogg). Amidst the tragedies, however, stand dazzling feats of achievement, including aviation marvels, trailblazing pioneers, and incredible displays of the power of nature, which sometimes take decades to overcome. For each of these moments, a story; for each of these stories, a memory. These are but a few of the tales to be told, long remembered after the time in which they once occurred has passed.

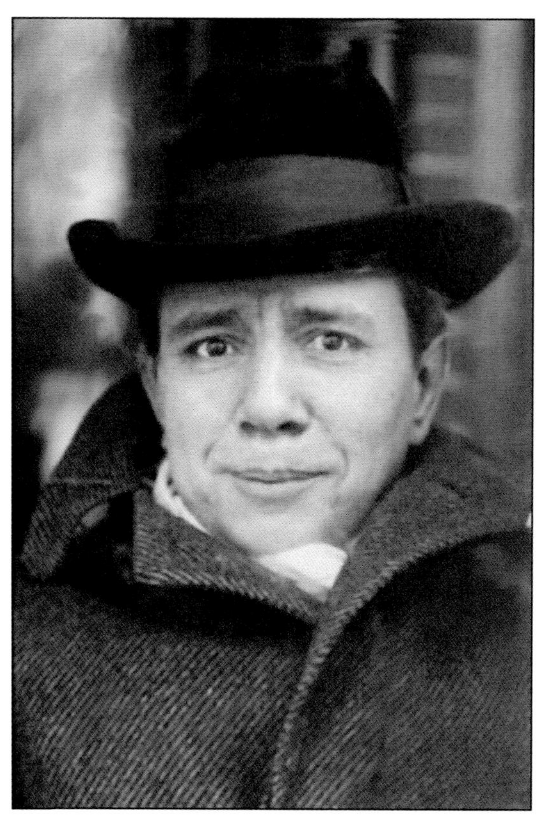

Harry Kendall Thaw (1871–1947; Section 16, Lot 119). Words cannot convey the depths of depravity within this man's mind. Infamous for murdering the architect Stanford White atop Madison Square Garden in 1906, Thaw exhibited sociopathic tendencies with an exceptional knack for cruelty. Evelyn Nesbitt attested to this while recounting the torments she suffered at Thaw's hands in an affidavit in 1903—two years before they were married. She wore a black bridal gown instead of the traditional white, at Thaw's choosing. If she was the beautiful light, he was the suffocating darkness, and in 1915, they divorced. Thaw lived the rest of his life in and out of asylums, as punishment for the murder of Stanford White and the kidnapping and torture of Frederick Gump of Kansas City. In his memoirs, Thaw denied having any remorse for his transgressions, taking a satiated but twisted conscience to his grave. (Both, LOC.)

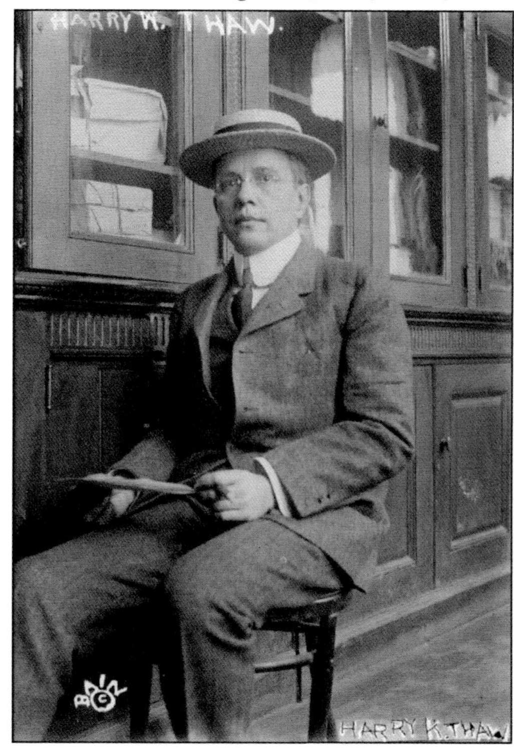

Joseph Barker (1806–1862; Section 29, Lot 196). Joseph Barker was easily the most colorful character to hold office in Pittsburgh. He was widely known as an anti-Catholic street preacher who was once arrested by Mayor John Herron for obstructing traffic and using lewd language. Barker was arrested at least eight times and won a write-in vote for mayor while incarcerated, at which time a crowd of citizens forced his release. He was struck by a train and killed while walking home from giving a speech in support of the Union cause during the Civil War. (AC.)

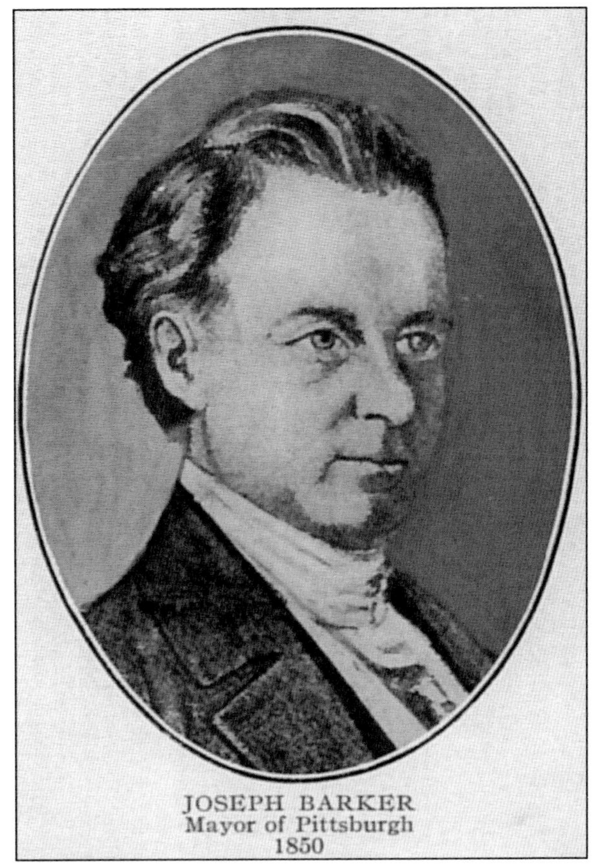

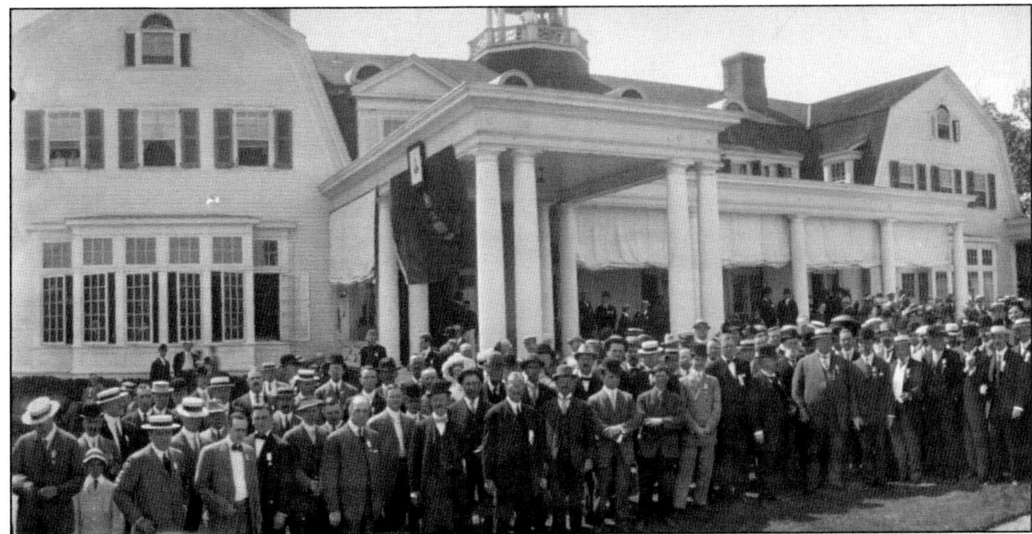

President Taft Visits. On March 13, 1910, the 27th president of the United States, William Howard Taft, traveled to Pittsburgh from Washington to attend the funeral of his wife's brother-in-law. Thomas Laughlin, director of J&L Steel, was married to a sister of Helen Herron Taft, who was unable to travel. The president brought with him their earnest sympathy and a memorial floral wreath from the White House conservatory. (LOC.)

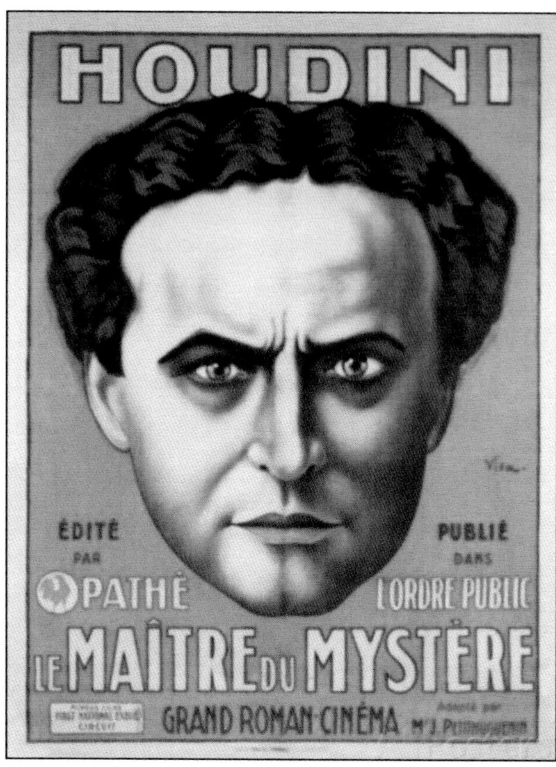

HARRY HOUDINI VISITS. Given Houdini's affinity for composer Stephen Foster, he felt it his responsibility to tend Foster's gravesite upon his death. Foster died near penniless, leaving his family with very little means. Houdini noted in *Magic, Unity, Might* that "until [Foster] wrote his melodies, we had nothing much in the way of real American songs." Correspondences document Houdini's upkeep of Foster's memorial and his visits to Allegheny Cemetery, honoring Foster's legacy and place in American pop culture long after his passing. (LOC.)

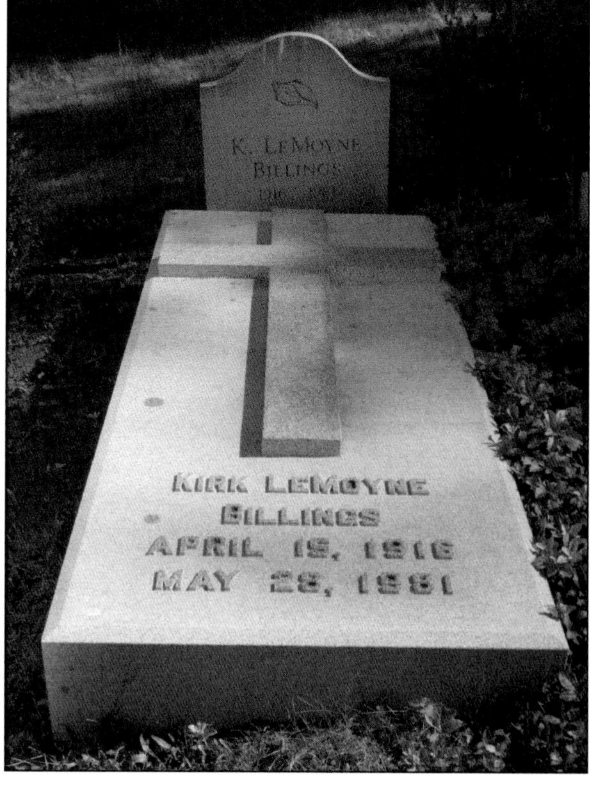

LEMOYNE BILLINGS (1916–1981; SECTION 12, LOT 92). The Kennedy clan (including Jaqueline, Caroline, and John) were graveside at Allegheny Cemetery to attend services for Kirk Lemoyne Billings. Overlooking the tranquil ponds, they honored the man who had been a roommate of John F. Kennedy while they were students at Choate, an elite prep school. Billings was a constant companion of the Kennedys, with father Joe referring to him as a "second son." Affectionately known as the "First Friend," he was a frequent guest at the White House and walked only steps behind Jackie at JFK's funeral. (NF.)

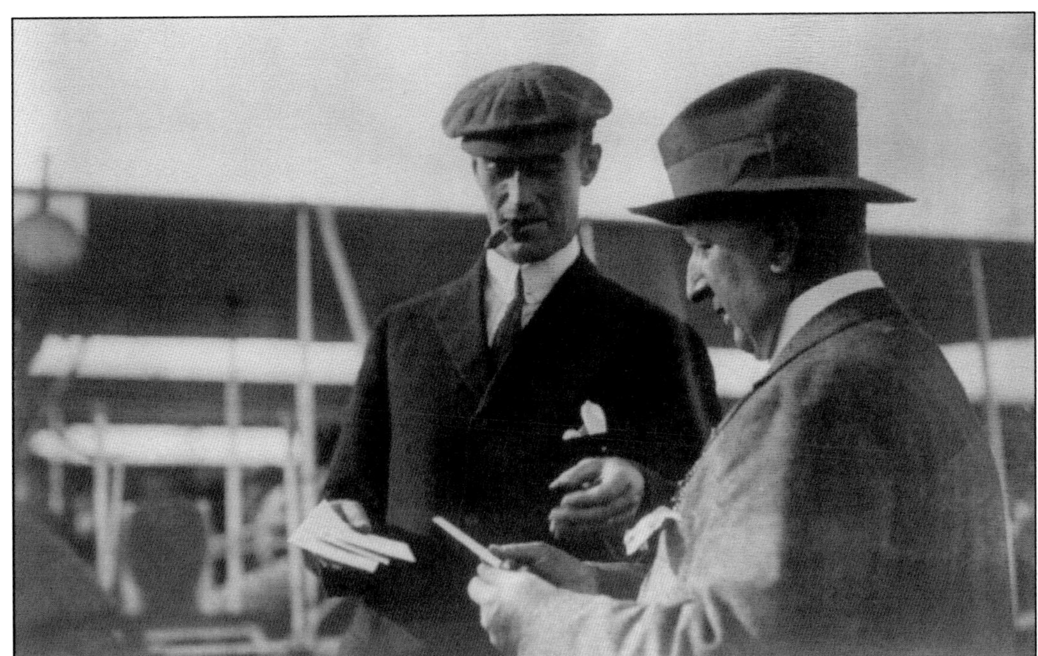

CALBRAITH PERRY RODGERS (1879–1912; SECTION 19, LOT 102). Cal Rodgers was related to Commodores Oliver Hazard Perry and Matthew Calbraith Perry. He made the first transcontinental US flight (in the *Vin Fiz*) from September 17 to November 5, 1911. On April 3, 1912, during a Long Beach, California, exhibition flight, he flew into a flock of birds, crashing into the ocean. He died instantly, a few hundred feet from where his original plane ended its first transcontinental flight. The *Vin Fiz* itself was later given to the Smithsonian Institution by his widow, Mabel Rodgers. (LOC.)

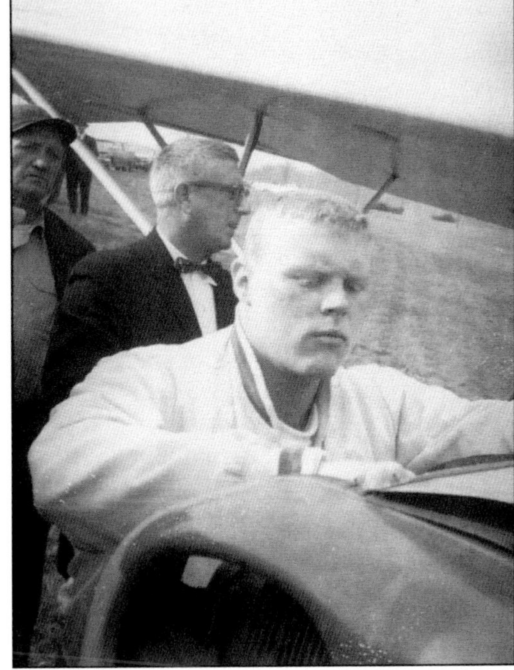

CRASH LANDING (JANUARY 5, 1962). Twenty-year-old student pilot Richard Rice circled the skies over Pittsburgh. The engine of his plane knocked, and oil blackened the windshield, filling the cabin with smoke. The closest landing area was an open clearing in the cemetery's Garden of Peace. Under construction, there were few graves and sparse trees. As the plane came down, it hit one of the trees, tearing off a wing at 120 miles per hour. Having survived the crash with only whiplash, Rice contacted authorities from a nearby house and was commended for his skillful handling of the accident. (AC.)

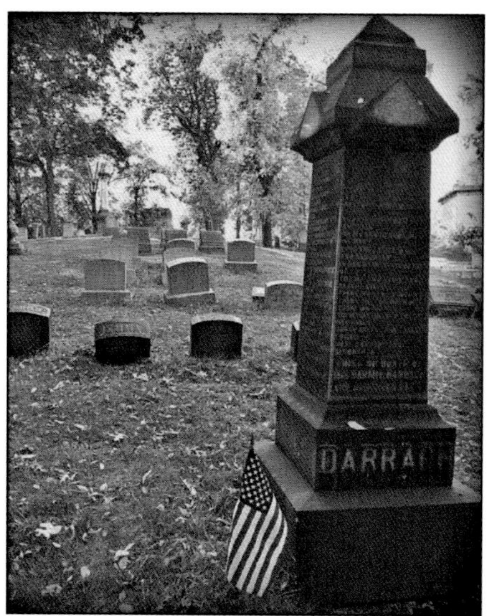

Darragh Monument (d. October 2, 1850, Section 23, Lot 66). On a shaded hillside, among aged trees, rests a small, cool, dark obelisk covered in words from a time gone by. It is easy enough to pass it by at first, but a moment's glance will make one stop. Inscribed upon it is the detailed account of Capt. John Darragh and the 1850 *Financier* steamship disaster. While tragic in any regard, the *Financier* disaster seems especially so as it tells the tale of how the captain's wife and daughter sailed with him on their first voyage upon his ship. At the time, such travel was fraught with dangers, including fires such as the one that overtook this vessel. As the captain ordered the gangplank lowered, he ushered his wife and child over the threshold to what he thought would be safety. In the chaos, the walkway overturned, and both his wife and daughter were lost to the depths of the rapidly moving waters. (LS.)

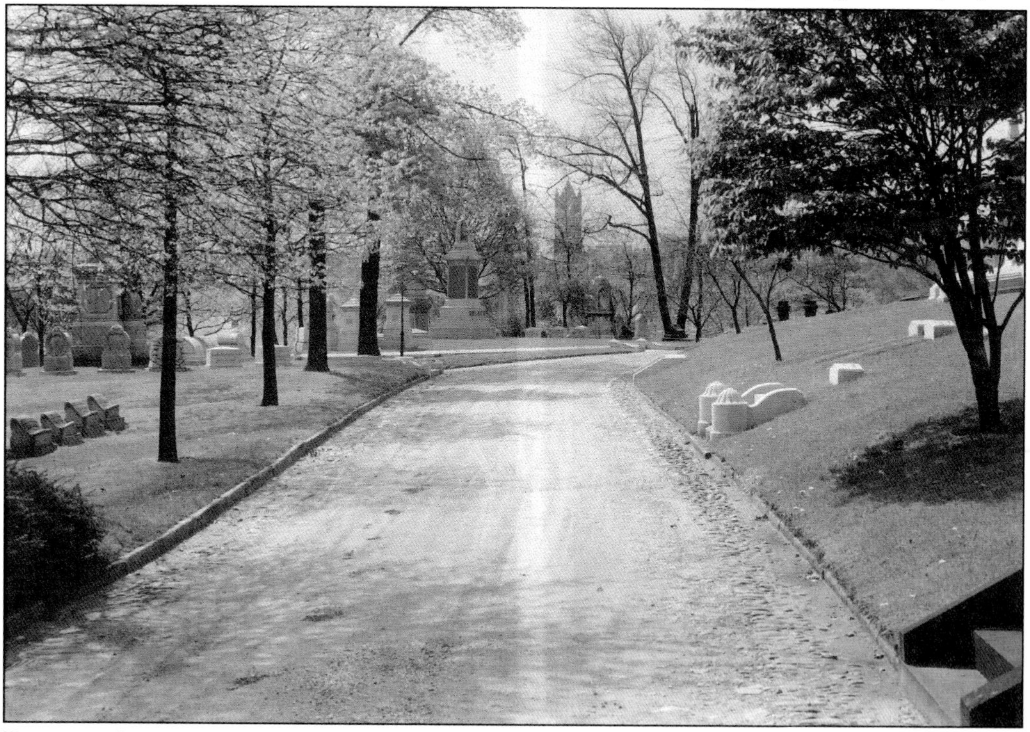

Benjamin Singerly's Bones. A curious thing happened in 1879, when Benjamin Singerly's family moved from Pittsburgh to Philadelphia. As was the custom at that time, the entire family was to be relocated, including the remains of Benjamin Singerly, who died several years prior in 1876. Upon attempting to remove Singerly from his grave at Allegheny Cemetery, it was determined that a process called petrification had taken place, and that Singerly and his coffin now weighed nearly 900 pounds. The *Pittsburgh Post* reported on April 19, 1879, that his body had turned as "impervious as stone." There was much talk about the town. Ultimately, the issue was resolved, and Benjamin Singerly's bones found their final resting place in Philadelphia's Laurel Hill Cemetery. (AC)

James B. Hogg (d. September 27, 1854; Section 13, Lot 42). James B. Hogg was lost on the infamous sinking of the Collins liner *Arctic* (below) due to a collision with the steamer *Vesta* off the coast of Cape Race on September 27, 1854. There were approximately 400 souls on board, 250 passengers and 150 crew. Of those, 24 male passengers and 61 crew members survived. Every last woman and child was lost. Prior to the sinking of the *Titanic*, it was one of the most notorious maritime disasters in history. Among the survivors was the captain of the ship, who was never called to account. Hogg's body was never recovered, but his cenotaph depicts the sinking that cost so many lives. The James B. Hogg cenotaph was designed by Piatti and quite graphically illustrates the sinking. (Right, LS; below, LOC.)

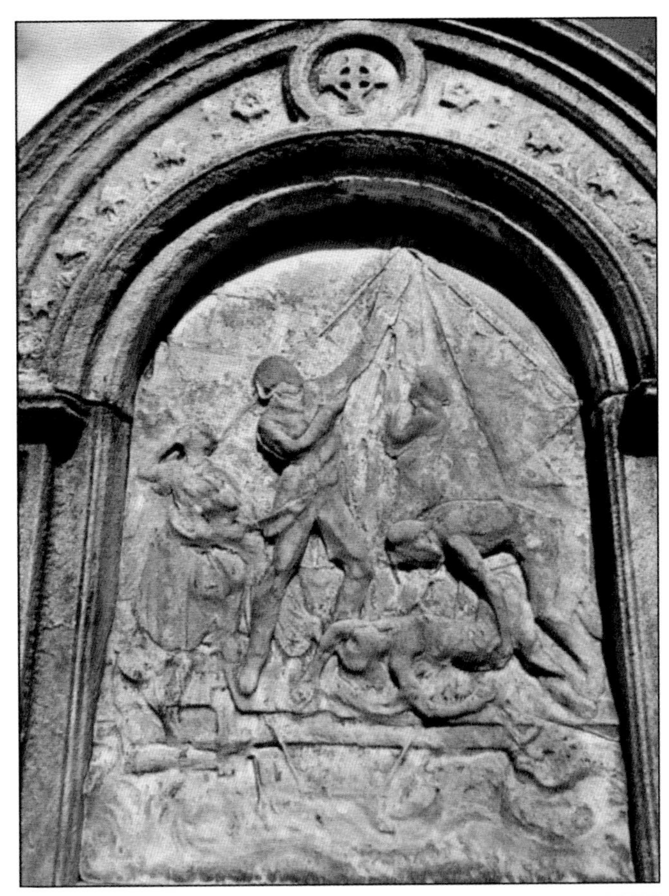

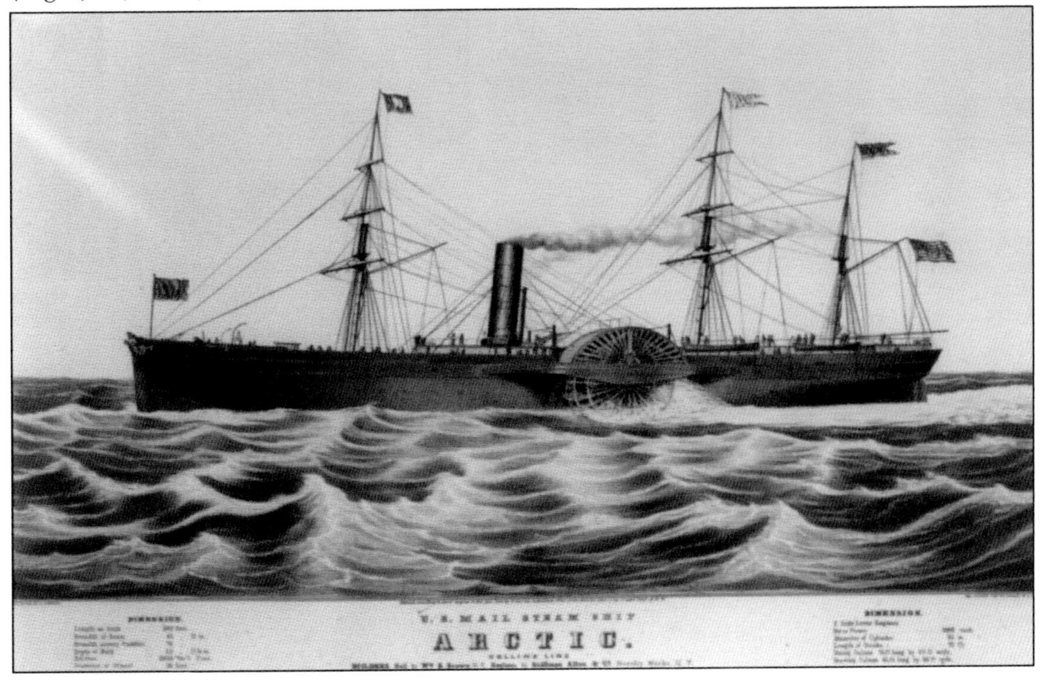

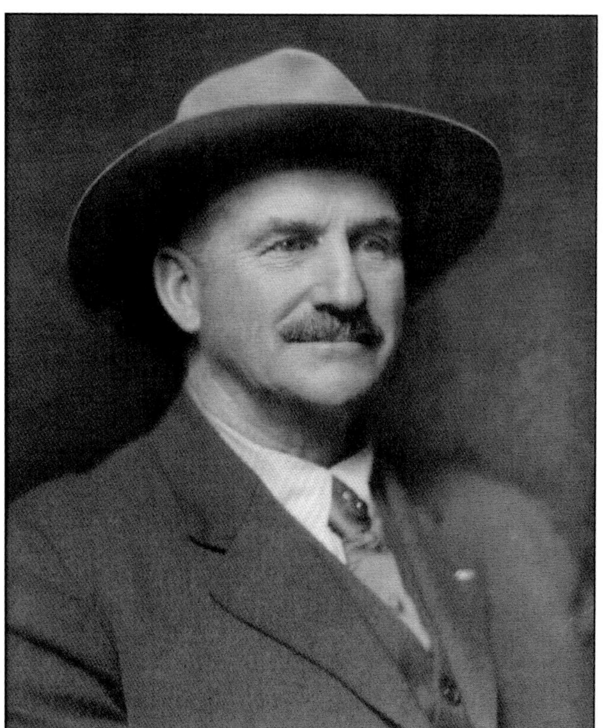

Howard Eaton (1851–1922; Section 7, Lot 54). As a young man, Howard Eaton set out for the Dakota Territory and established what became the first ever "dude ranch" in 1879. Stories of Eaton's time in the Wild West lured his two brothers and hordes of wealthy city folk, including a young Teddy Roosevelt, to visit. By 1882, the brothers Eaton needed to charge $10 per week to cover the cost of room and board, plus guided tours of the Badlands by horse, hunting, fishing, shooting, and cattle tying. In 1904, the Eatons relocated to Wolf Creek, Wyoming, an expanse of 7,000 acres that still operates today. (Frank and Kathy Eaton.)

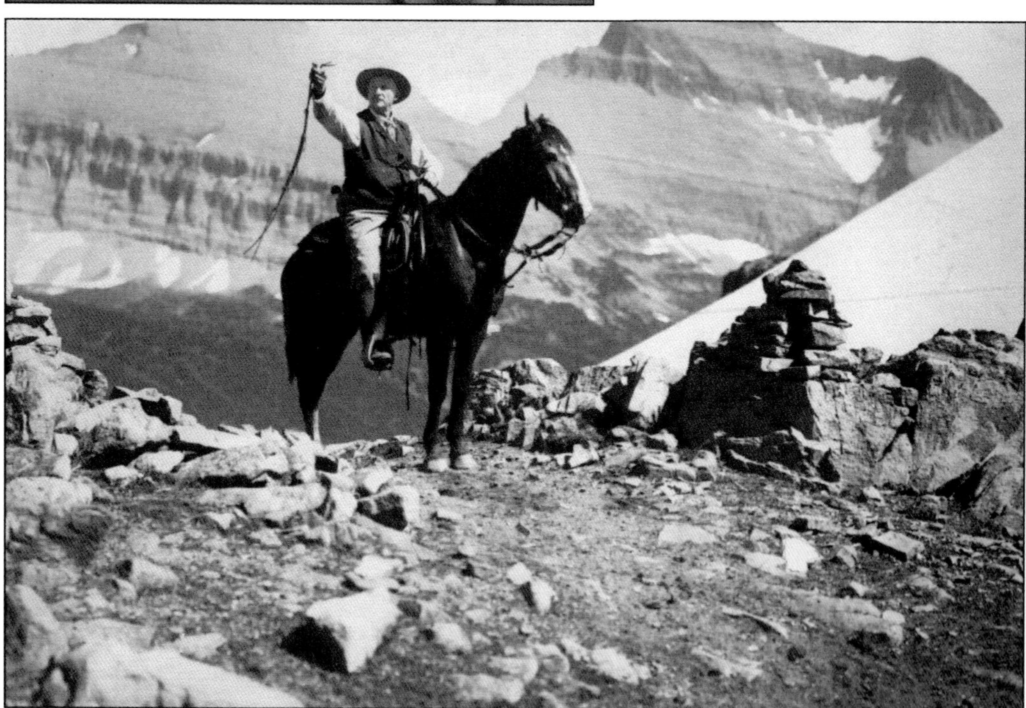

Eaton, Immortalized. Eaton's lifestyle was the subject of Mary Roberts Rinehart's 1916 work *Through Glacier Park; Seeing America First with Howard Eaton*, which recalls the author's exhilarating experience traveling 300 miles through the Rocky Mountains with Eaton as her personal guide. The Howard Eaton Trailhead at Yellowstone is named in his honor. (Frank and Kathy Eaton.)

Eben Byers (1880–1932; Section 13, Lot 67). Eben Byers was a socialite and award-winning golfer. In 1927, he fell from a berth on a train after the Harvard-Yale football game, suffering an arm injury. William Bailey, falsely claiming to be a doctor, prescribed a radium-laced cure called Radithor. Over time, Byers ingested nearly 1,400 bottles, inundating his body with radium. By 1930, Byers stopped taking the medicine, but the damage was done. MIT studies conducted in the 1960s found that his body was still radioactive enough to create an X-ray without the use of a machine. Byers is in a lead-lined coffin in the family's private mausoleum. The headline at right was published in the *Pittsburgh Post-Gazette* on April 2, 1932, shortly after Byers's death. (Right, *Pittsburgh Post-Gazette* Archives; below, NF.)

BYERS' DEATH STARTS RADIUM CURES INQUIRY

One Federal Agency Finds "Radithor" Sales Legal.

FUNERAL PLANS MADE

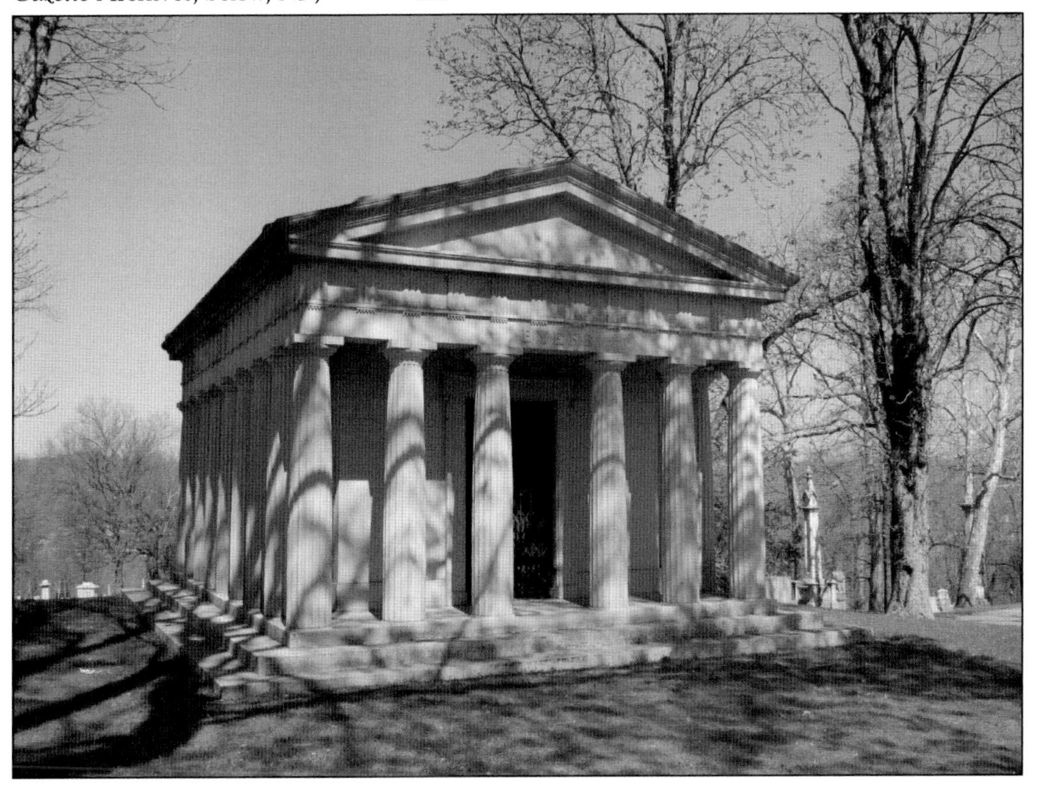

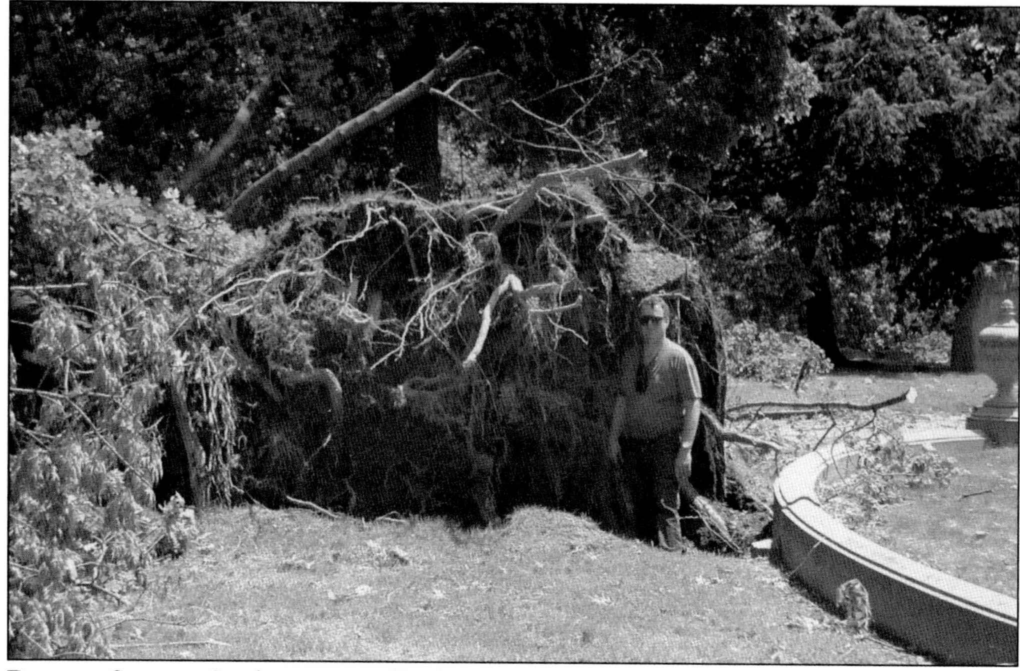

Disaster Strikes. On the evening of Friday, May 31, 2002, Allegheny Cemetery was suddenly and violently struck by a macroburst storm, the damaging effects of which would take over a decade and $2 million to repair. Century-old mature trees were snapped in half at the trunk or entirely uplifted by their roots, leaving gaping trenches in the earth and exposing root balls some 15 feet in diameter. Wind gusts up to 105 mph shot tree limbs like arrows into neighboring lots, toppling solid granite obelisks and leaving smaller memorials cracked or permanently scarred. (AC.)

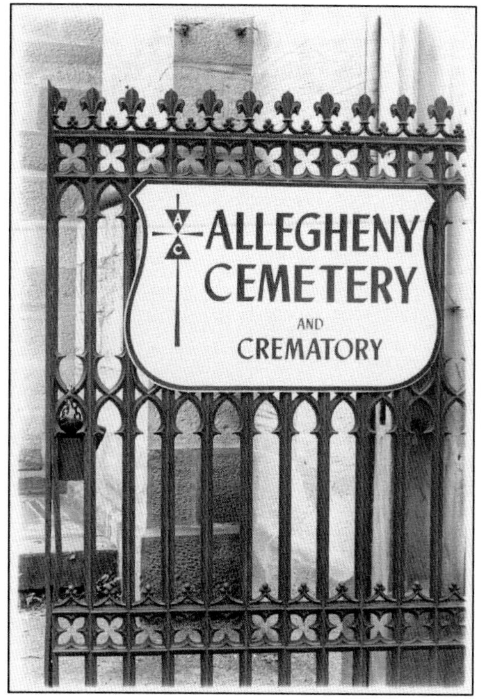

A Landmark Loss. This ornamental gate was custom made by the firm of W.W. Wallace at a cost of $4,000 in 1848 and commissioned by the cemetery for installation in the Butler Street entranceway that same year. The cast-iron structure, measuring 8.5 feet tall and 12 feet wide with bars 2 feet thick throughout, was utterly destroyed by a head-on collision in the early morning hours of January 1, 2015. The cemetery has constructed an exact replica, though permanent imprints of this explosive historic event will forever mar the administration building's sandstone facade. (AC.)

Ten

The Little Guy

None of these people are famous. The stories briefly captured in this chapter likely would not show up on a Google search or appear in newspaper archives. They may not even have been recorded on a census, their names seeming to have been written in invisible ink upon the pages of time. They did not build skyscrapers, cure diseases, or even take much to the grave aside from the respect and admiration of the few who knew them. Some were immigrants finding their way in a new world that may or may not have had the "streets paved in gold" as they had imagined in the Old Country. Some toiled on the railroad, opened small shops, or labored in the mills. All contributed in their small way to the great legacy of industrial modern America, though most, if not all, did not live to see the grandiose fruits of their labor. For many, their life's biggest accomplishment was simply being loved or raising a family, and that alone is more than worthy enough of remembrance for generations to come.

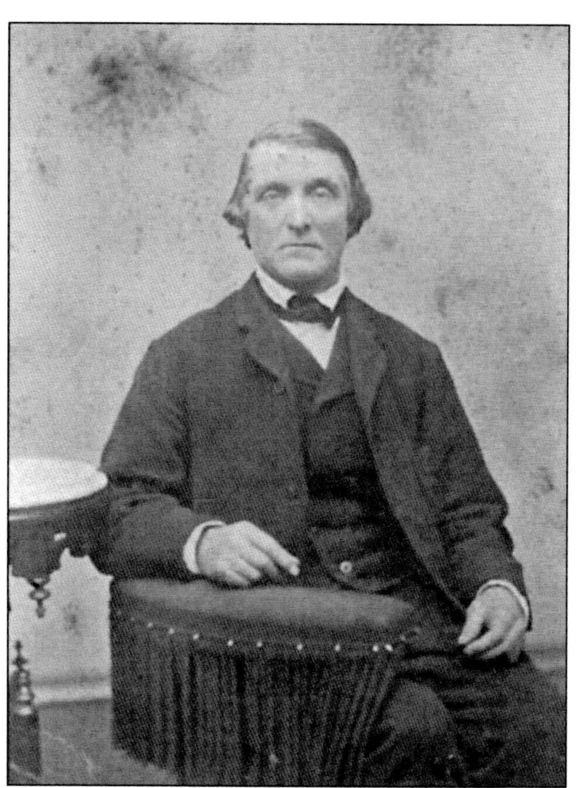

EMANUEL ECKER (D. 1884, SECTION 29). As Pittsburgh bloomed from a frontier town into a metropolis, Emanuel Ecker held brick in hand and helped shape the history of the city. He was a bricklaying contractor during the mid- to late 19th century. His work was noted on both private residences throughout the city, as well as larger buildings like the well-known Monongahela House (1845–1847) in downtown Pittsburgh and Pittsburgh's city hall (1872), shown below. As noted in the *Pittsburgh Post-Gazette* on August 16, 2012, Ecker's Monongahela House hosted such guests as Stephen Foster, Charles Dickens, the Prince of Wales (later to become King Edward VII), P.T. Barnum, Teddy Roosevelt, Ulysses S. Grant, and, on February 14, 1861, president-elect Abraham Lincoln. Generations of families have lived (and still do) in the structures that Ecker helped build, which serves as a formidable testament to the quality of the work and the man who helped build it. (Left, Ecker family; below, ASC.)

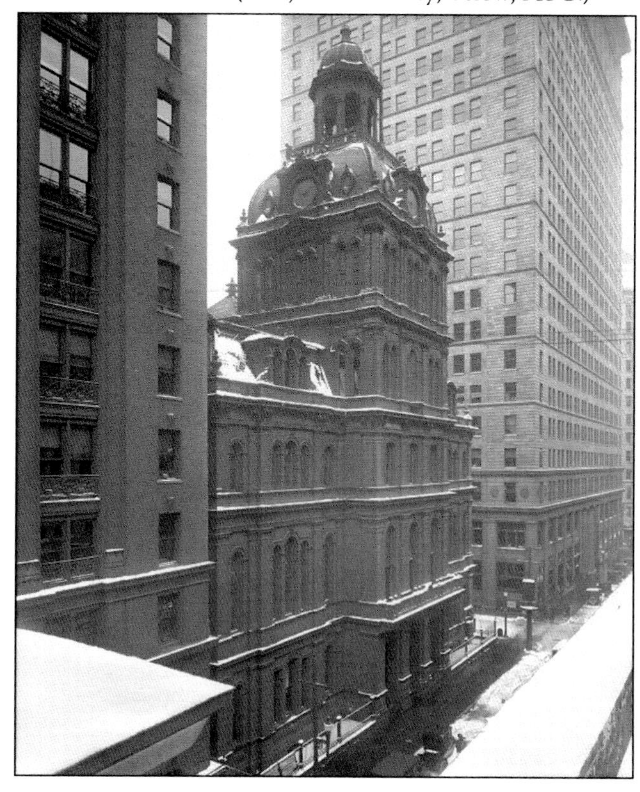

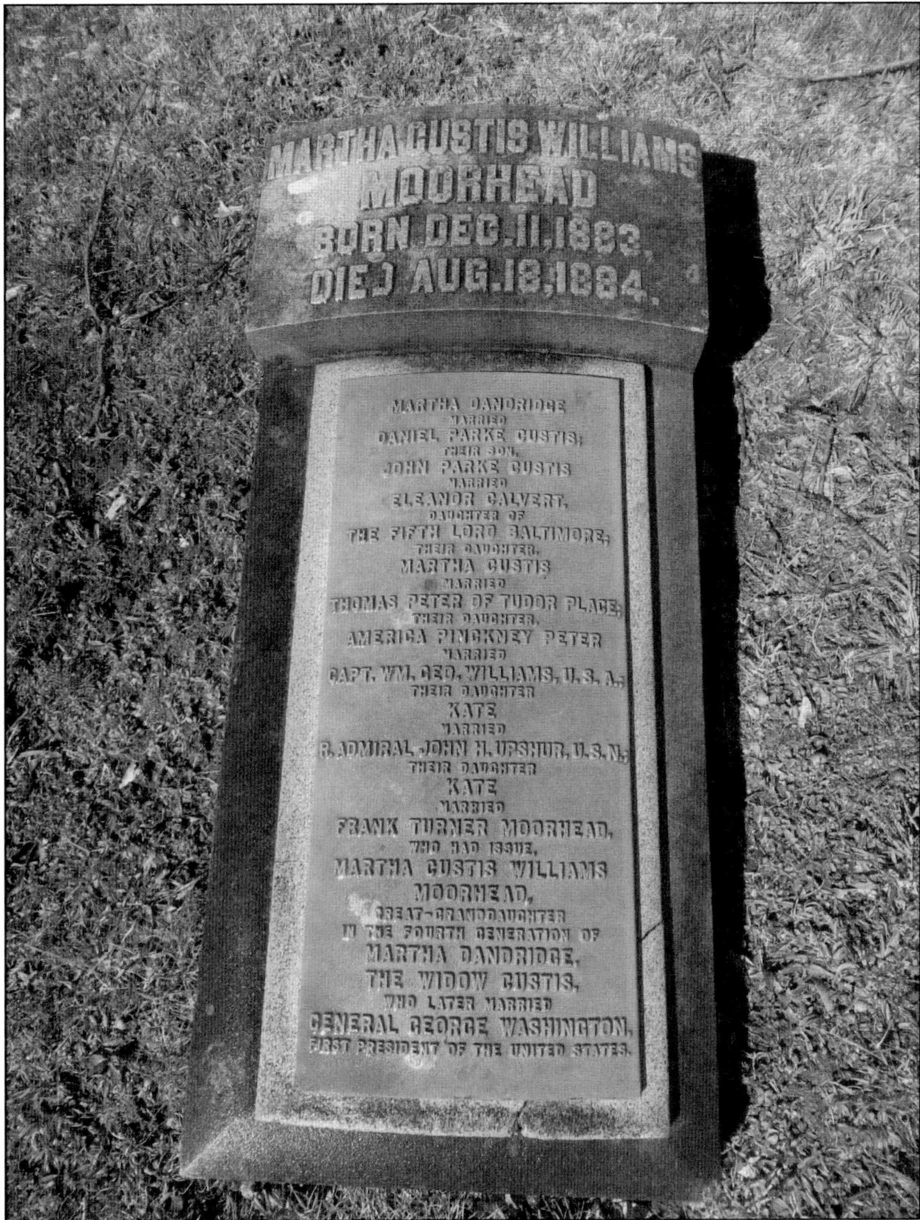

Martha Custis Williams Moorhead (1883–1884; Section 13, Lot 59). Many know Martha Washington as the country's first first lady. Prior to marrying George Washington, Martha was married to Daniel Parke Custis. He died approximately seven years after they were married. Together, they had four children, only two of whom would live into adulthood. Martha Dandridge Custis's son John ("Jacky") Parke Custis bore a line that would, generations later, lead to Martha Custis Williams Moorhead, the great-great-great-great-granddaughter of Martha Washington. Martha Custis Williams Moorhead was but a baby when she died from whooping cough, having lived only from December 11, 1883, to August 18, 1884. Her inscription, however, encapsulates a genealogical lineage that researchers can only dream of. Generations of Martha's lineage are spelled out, including marriages and relationships that one might spend years searching for. Beside little Martha's stone rest her parents, Frank Turner Moorhead and Kate Upshur Moorhead. (NF.)

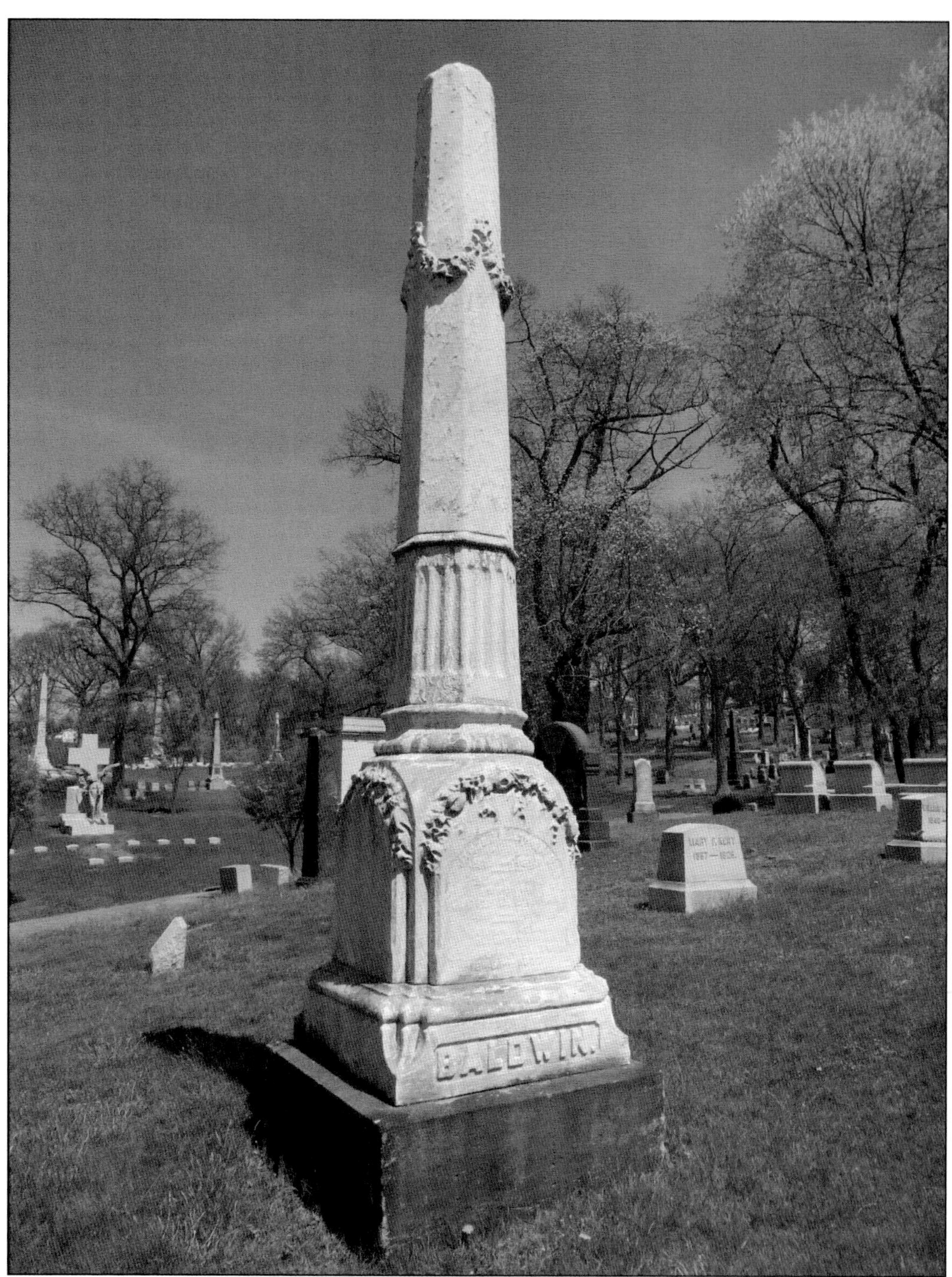

Cornelia Baldwin (d. 1882; Section 8, Lot 81). Cornelia Baldwin was an entrepreneur—as a madam of a house of ill-repute in Cincinnati. Financially savvy, she eventually owned multiple establishments, taking excellent care of the women in her employ. She was known for copious lawsuits against those acting inappropriately in her houses, including a suit against a man who carved up her piano. Sadly, a tumor ravaged her, and she died with her son (and another man, unnamed, who had been her constant companion) by her side. (NF.)

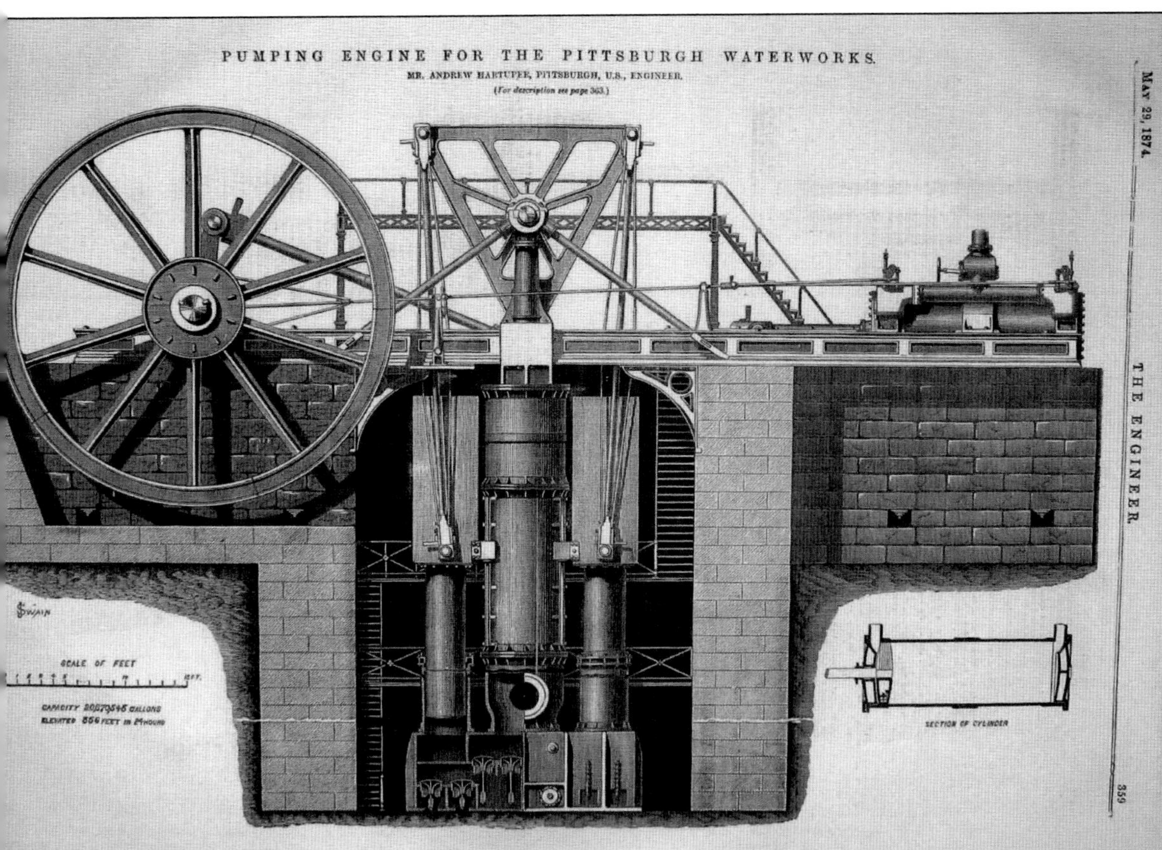

Andrew Hartupee (d. 1891; Section 11, Lot 58). Pittsburgh is a town that was built on her rivers. As industry strengthened, this once nestled village became a leading hub, with its rivers making it possible. Throughout the late 19th century, steamships ferried both passengers and cargo along these waterways. Andrew Hartupee sought to improve this method of transportation by developing and engineering a steam-flow cutoff valve, allowing (from his patent, pictured here) for the "steam [to be] cut off at any portion of the stroke . . . and yet capable of speedy adjustment and variation, at the will of the engineer, while the engine is in full operation." This image of Hartupee's patent appeared in an 1876 issue of the journal *The Engineer.* (AC.)

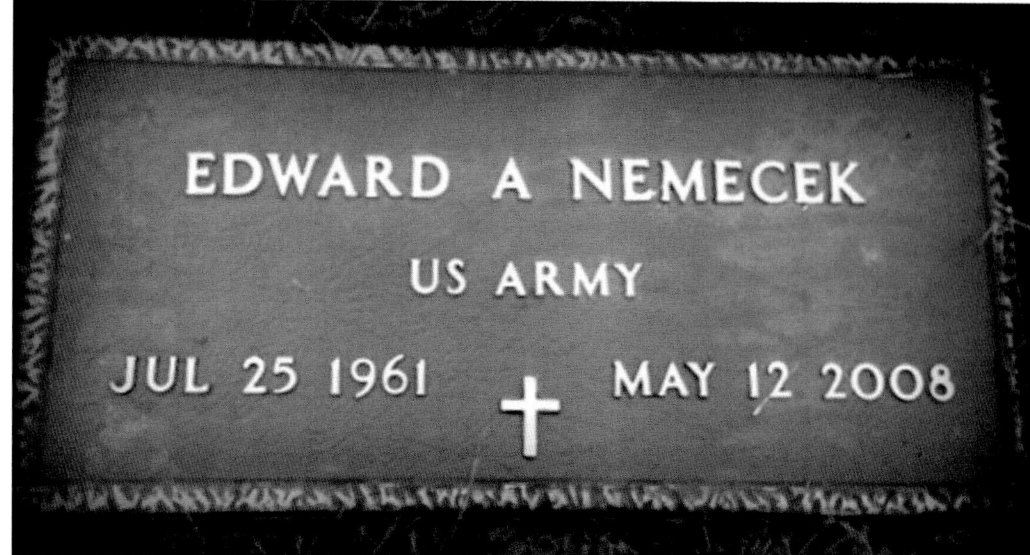

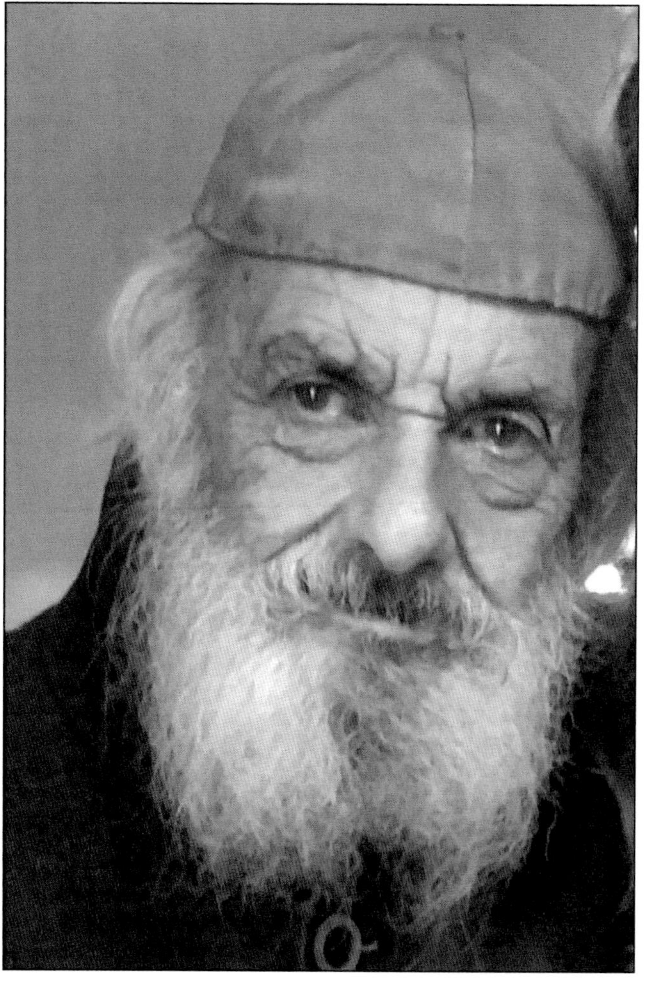

Eternal Bonds of Friendship. Every year, 76-year-old Leonard Aronowicz travels a great distance to attend the annual holiday service in honor of his dear friend. He boards a bus in Atlantic City, New Jersey, and spends hours on the road. Once, he found no public transportation available, and feared he would be unable to attend the service. Kind souls ensured his safe arrival to the cemetery, where he was able to take part in the event he had traveled so far to reach. Before departing, cemetery staff made sure he received a small token of their appreciation for his heartfelt dedication in memory of his friend. When he boarded the bus for Atlantic City, he carried with him a small photo of his friend's headstone, along with a note from Allegheny Cemetery. (Above, Roger Galbraith; left, LS.)

ALBERT GUSTAVE WALTER (1812–1876; SECTION 13, LOT 51). Noted in his obituary as "one of the most eminent surgeons in the United States," Walter came from humble beginnings. A Prussian immigrant, he put himself through medical school at Berlin University, specializing in orthopedic surgery. Arriving with recommendations in New York City, he was shunned in surgical circles for being a Dutchman. Rejected, he pursued manual labor in Philadelphia. Arriving in Pittsburgh in 1836, he was met by the same prejudice he had faced in New York. Street speeches were made in front of his office in an attempt to dissuade him from practicing. As a result, he sought out patients on his own, often offering to pay them to allow him to operate rather than the other way around. In doing so, he was able to cure cases of deformities deemed incurable, and his successes soon conquered previous prejudices. His obituary concludes that "his heart overflowed with the milk of human kindness." (NF.)

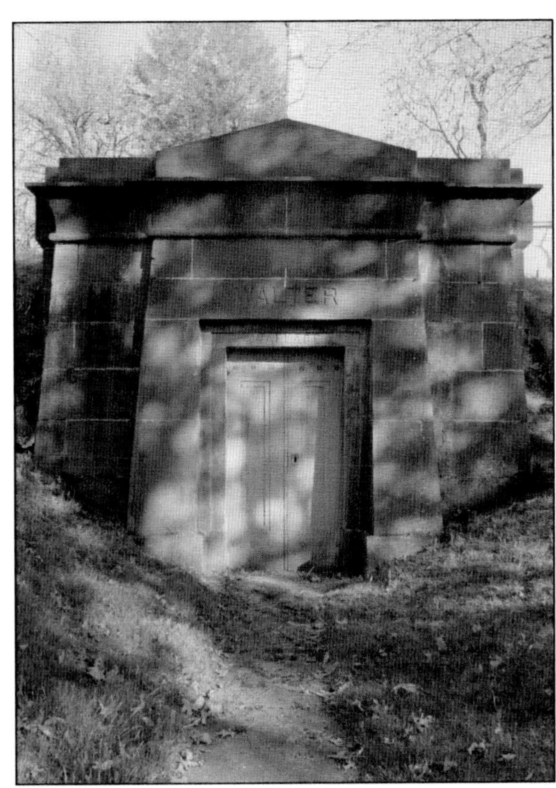

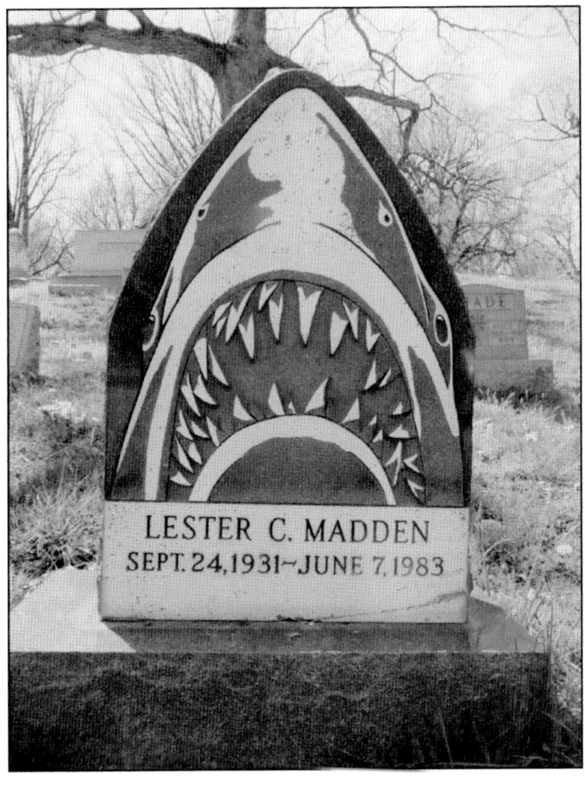

LESTER MADDEN (1931–1983; SECTION 26, LOT 65). It is perhaps one of the most unexpected and yet commonly sought out memorials in all of Allegheny Cemetery. Many have seen it, and the stories are whispered far and wide. Of all the fish tales, surprisingly, none are quite right. Lester Madden, it seems, was an avid fan of the movie *Jaws*. So much so that his final instructions to his family were that his headstone should resemble the movie poster. It is both a striking memorial and tribute and certainly an unexpected surprise while traversing these grounds. (NF.)

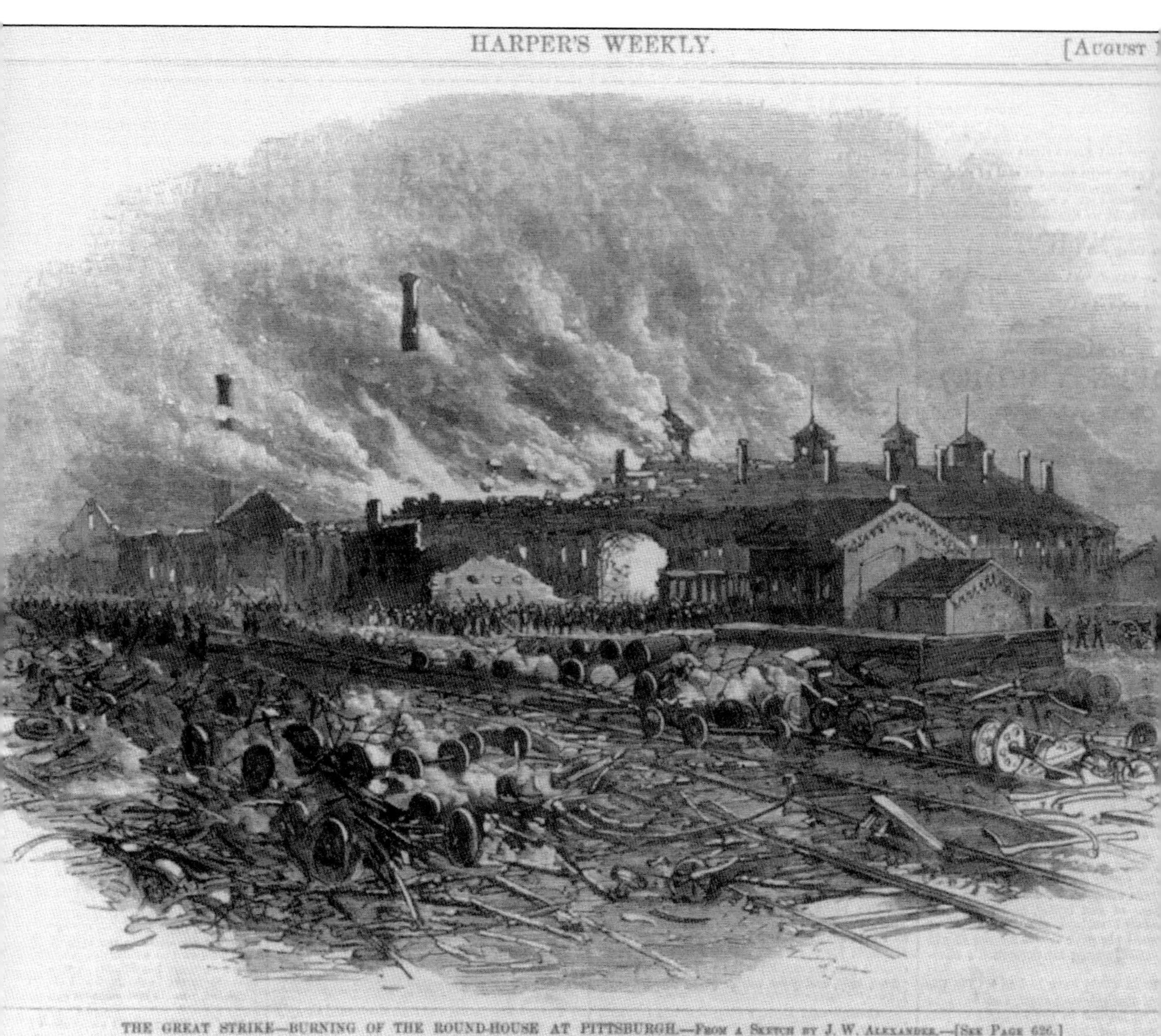

JAMES SIMS (D. JULY 22, 1877; SECTION 8, LOT 136). In 1877, Pittsburgh was embroiled in a railroad riot due to workers' wages having been severely cut. On a searing hot July day, the Philadelphia militia that had been called out to quell the riot turned their weapons against the striking workers. Brother stood against brother, and then someone opened fire. Melee and panic overtook the stunned parties on both sides, and a volley of gunfire was exchanged. Workers fell alongside soldiers, their blood indistinguishable as it choked the city streets. Rioters destroyed buildings, properties, and even locomotives in some of the worst damage the city had ever seen. James Sims, a fireman for the city, went above and beyond while pulling a wounded man from the chaos. In doing so, he lost his own life but gained a dignity and courage that still echoes today. (LOC.)

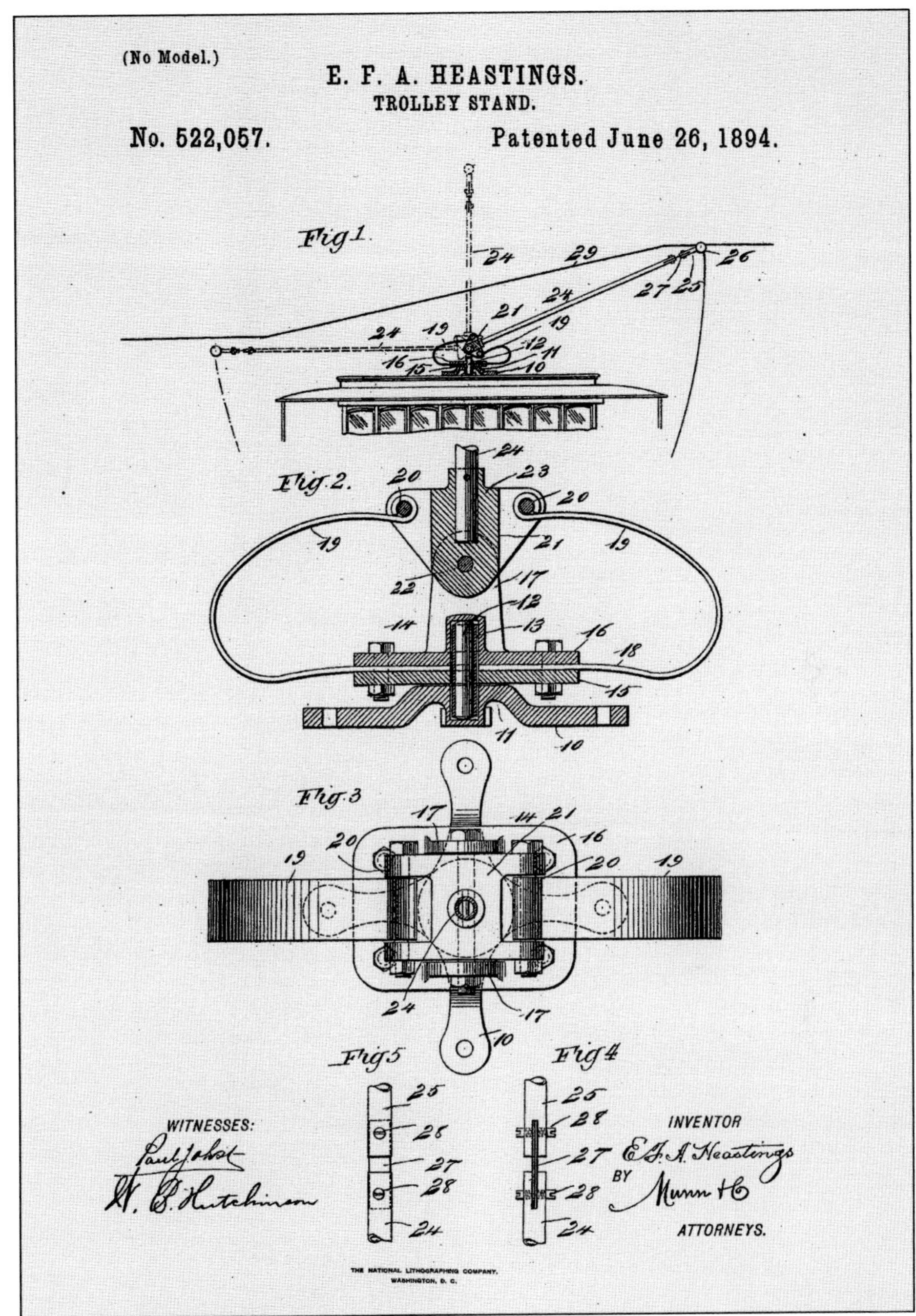

Eleazer F.A. Heastings (d. 1901; Section 33, Lot 16). At the turn of the 20th century, Pittsburgh was a bustling metropolis and major industrial hub of the East Coast. This necessitated a strong infrastructure of public transportation, which Eleazer Heastings sought to improve. In 1894, he submitted a patent to improve the connectivity of the trolley itself with the electrical power lines that ran overhead. His mechanism, per the patent, was designed to "hold the pole in such a way that the trolley wheel always presses firmly against the trolley wire so as to make a good contact." (Martina Scheuring Martucci.)

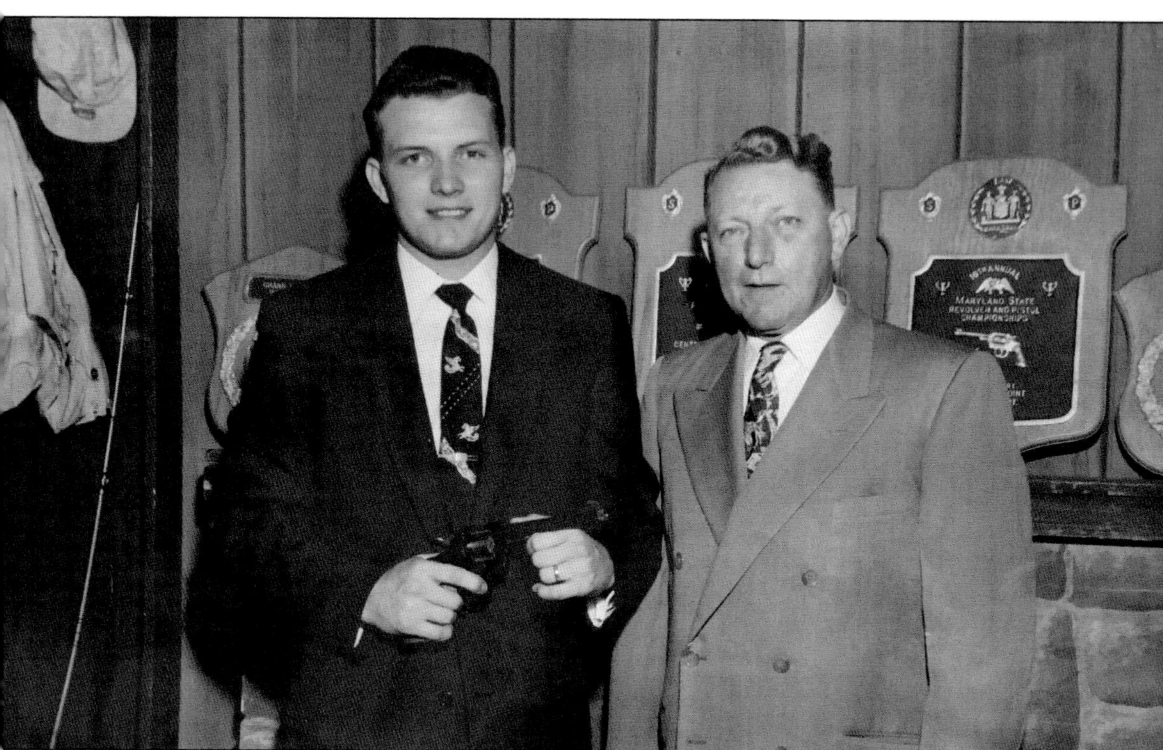

ROBERT FADZEN (1931–1986; SECTION 4, LOT 121). Robert Fadzen was a lifelong resident of Pittsburgh and one of the most decorated members of its police force. In 1952, he began his early career as a patrol officer. His skill as a marksman quickly became evident, and he achieved numerous awards for shooting competitions throughout Pennsylvania and Maryland. In 1966, due to his marksmanship, he was selected to join the manhunt during Pennsylvania's notorious Shade Gap kidnapping incident. Months later, he was one of the few officers nationwide who were invited to participate in the FBI academy's firearms course. He was one of few to ever complete the course with a perfect score. For his efforts, he was personally awarded the Possible Club medal by FBI director J. Edgar Hoover. His 30-year career with the Pittsburgh Police Department included serving as both a homicide detective and firearms instructor. Upon retirement from the Pittsburgh police force, he became the chief of security for Carnegie Mellon University, a position he held until his death in 1986. He is shown here at left in 1955 with his father, Sam, and several of his awards (LS.)

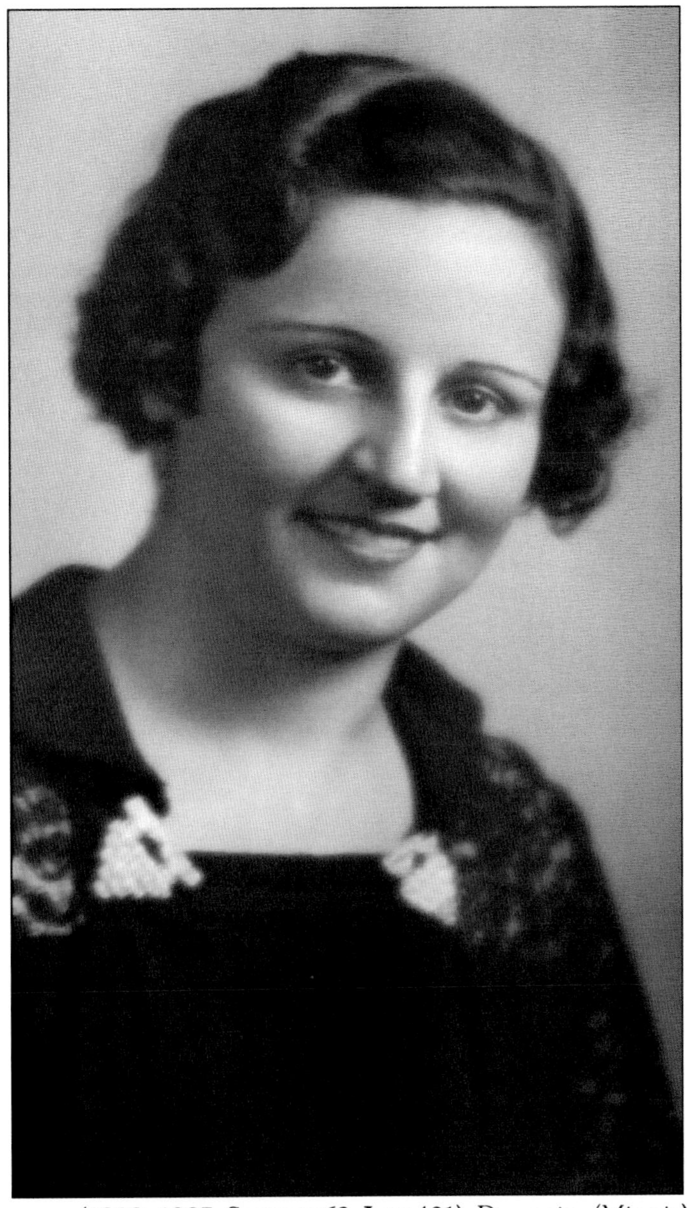

MINNE V. LIBERATORE (1908–1987; SECTION 62, LOT 401). Domenica (Minnie) Scotti was born in 1908 in Uniontown, Pennsylvania, the youngest daughter of Italian immigrant parents. While her siblings Mary and Laura would eventually settle near Detroit and Chicago, Minnie stayed close to Pittsburgh. In 1925, she married Pasquale Liberatore (from Castel di Sangro, Italy), and the family settled in Bloomfield, alongside many other Italian immigrants. Pasquale only formally completed second grade and Minnie, sixth. As they raised their children (Giacamo, Dante, and Teresa), Pasquale worked for US Steel, and Minnie baked bread for the trucking company near their home. She also worked in the cafeteria of the local school and church. As the country entered World War II, Minnie began a job with the Miller Printing Machine Company on Reesdale Street in the North Side of Pittsburgh. Minnie and Pasquale later moved to Palo Alto, California, where their grown children had settled. There, they raised several generations born as Americans but deeply rooted in the Italian traditions they both always treasured. (LS.)

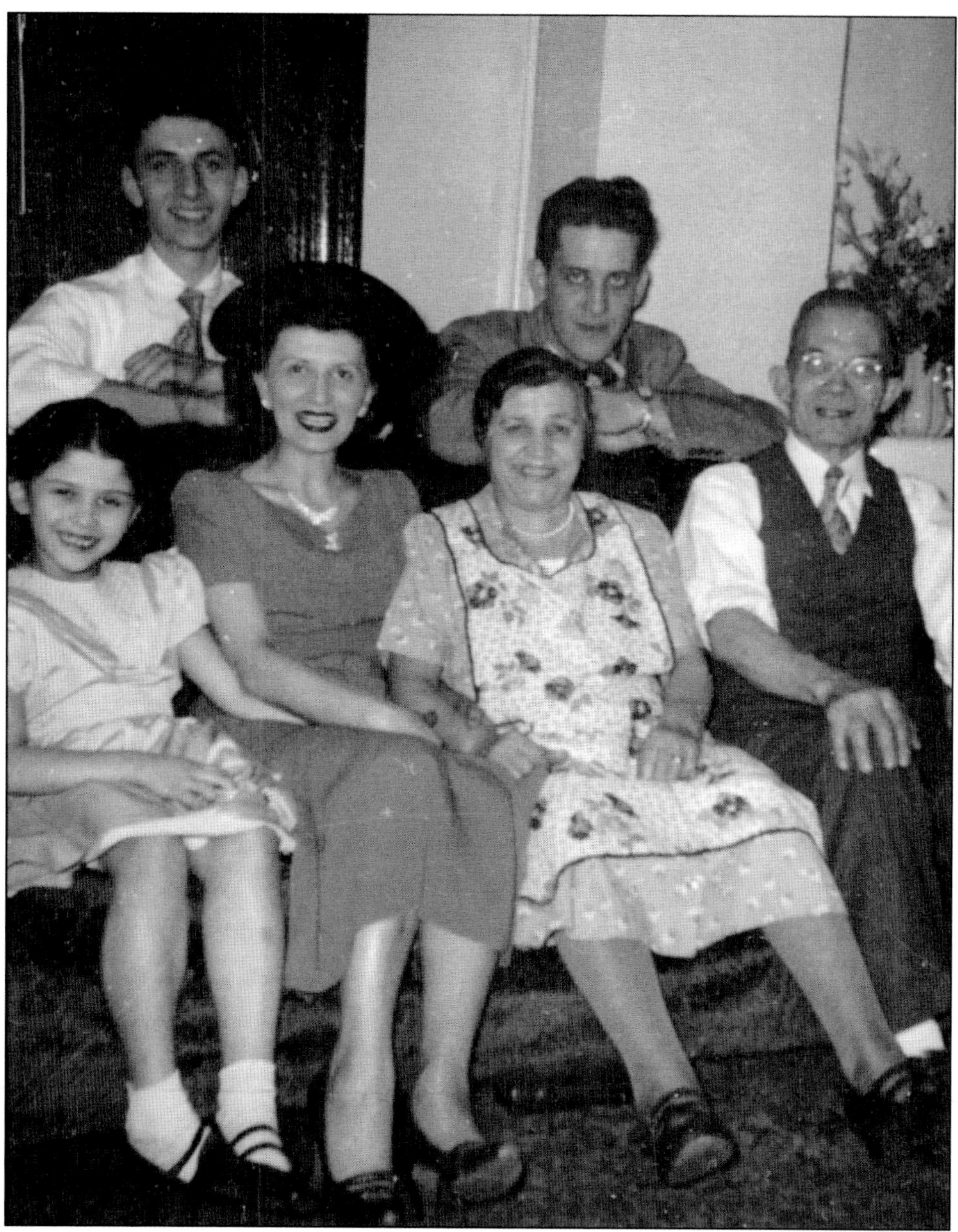

Leonard(o) and Maria Tiso (Temple of Memories, 102b). Leonard(o) Tiso was born in the hillside village of Orsara di Puglia, Italy, in 1888. The political climate was unstable, illnesses were often fatal, educational opportunities were scarce, and legends of prosperity in America were yarns well spun. In 1912, he left his wife, Maria, at home and sailed to the New World, enlisting in the US Army, where he learned English and sewed leather saddles for the cavalry. By 1918, he was a naturalized citizen, and it was time for Maria to join him in Pittsburgh, where they settled first in Bloomfield. It was a golden time to live in Pittsburgh's "Little Italy," where friends were numerous and Italians became Italian Americans who loved baseball as much as bocce and adopted Americanized names. The Tisos later moved to 5239 Butler Street, where they opened a hat shop and raised a family of four. Their granddaughter Barbara Held worked for 45 years at Allegheny Cemetery, and her sister Deborah Craigo still serves as its office manager. (Deborah Craigo.)

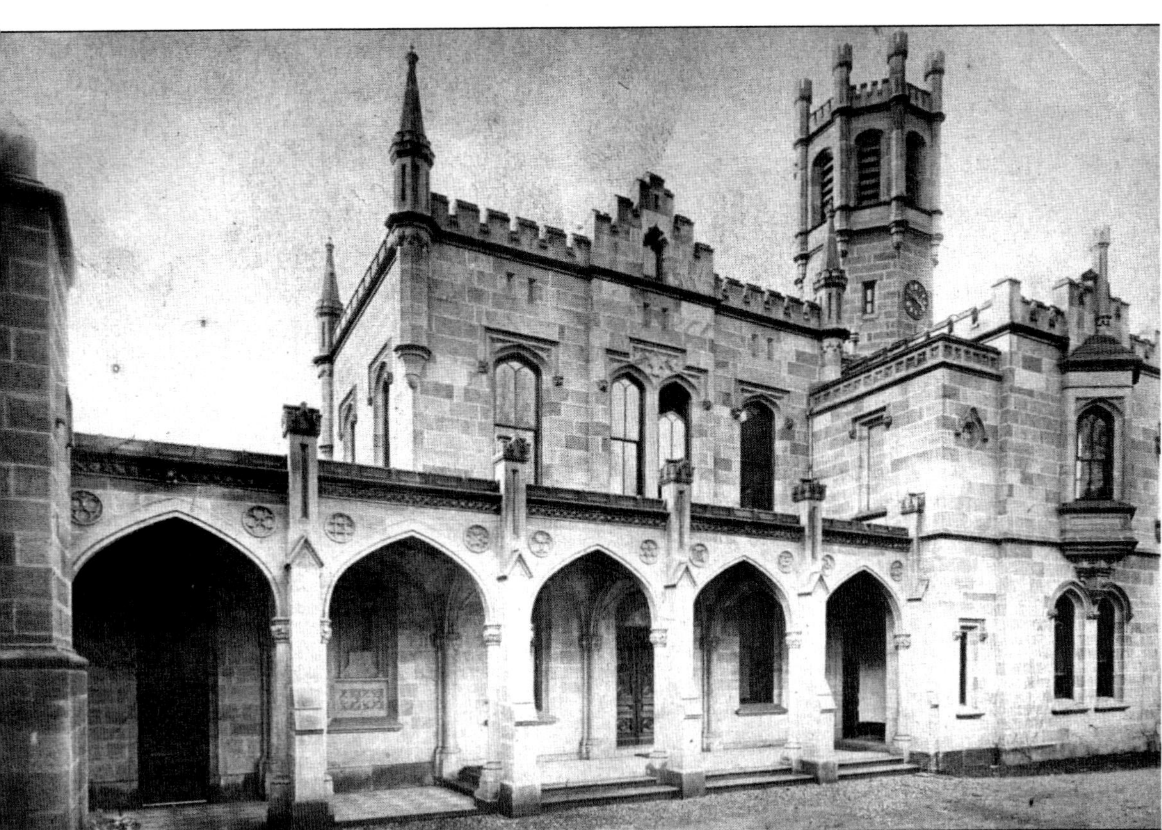

STEPPING THROUGH THE STONES. Allegheny Cemetery is so much more than a place to visit, or a place to reflect. The bucolic grounds are a place in history, of a town, her people, and those who continue to revere the value of each of those things. Each person interred here, each stone set, each flower, note, and photograph left behind—these are all woven into the fabric of a place intended for the dead, but treasured by the living. As we step between the stones, we leave our footprints on those stories and legacies, like words written on the pages of so many lives. In doing so, we share in those memories, while building new ones in the process. As long as we pause to remember, these lives are perpetual, never-ending, and will continue to be appreciated by generations long after we, too, are gone. (AC)

Discover Thousands of Local History Books Featuring Millions of Vintage Images

Arcadia Publishing, the leading local history publisher in the United States, is committed to making history accessible and meaningful through publishing books that celebrate and preserve the heritage of America's people and places.

Find more books like this at
www.arcadiapublishing.com

Search for your hometown history, your old stomping grounds, and even your favorite sports team.

Consistent with our mission to preserve history on a local level, this book was printed in South Carolina on American-made paper and manufactured entirely in the United States. Products carrying the accredited Forest Stewardship Council (FSC) label are printed on 100 percent FSC-certified paper.

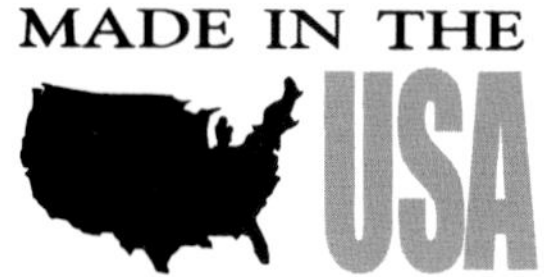